THE DYN...

READE...
WR'TING.
THE M...

FIN...
IN
BF

The Dynamics of Irish Politics

Paul Bew
Ellen Hazelkorn
Henry Patterson

LAWRENCE AND WISHART
LONDON

Lawrence & Wishart Limited
144a Old South Lambeth Road
London SW8 1XX

First published 1989

Photoset in North Wales by
Derek Doyle & Associates, Mold, Clwyd
Printed and bound in Great Britain by
Billings & Sons Ltd, Worcester.

Contents

· The Republic of Ireland ·

Donegal

NORTHERN IRELAND

ULSTER

Sligo

Leitrim

Monaghan

Cavan

Louth

Mayo

CONNAUGHT

Roscommon

Longford

Meath

Westmeath

Dublin

Dublin

Galway

Galway

Offaly

LEINSTER

Kildare

Clare

Laois

Wicklow

Tipperary

Carlow

Kilkenny

Wexford

Limerick

Limerick

Waterford

Waterford

MUNSTER

Kerry

Cork

Cork

- – – – Province boundaries
- .... County boundaries
- •...... Northern Ireland border

Acknowledgements

We would particularly like to thank John Heatley for permission to quote from his thesis on the Blueshirt movement. We owe much to the friendship and advice of Una Claffey, Richard Dunphy, Peter Mair and Paul Sweeney. They are, of course, in no way responsible for any errors or failures of analysis which may follow. We were also helped by interviews with Francie Donnelly, Cathal Goulding and Dick Walsh. In the early days of the project, Professor A.J.A. Morris provided us with much support. Stephen Hayward has been a sympathetic friend to the book from start to finish.

Introduction

Well into the 1960s the predominant image of the Irish Republic, even amongst those in Britain who might have been expected to be more sympathetic to the heirs of the 1916 rising, was strongly negative. Asked by the *New Statesman* to report on the state of the Irish nation on the fiftieth anniversary of the Easter Rising, Mervyn Jones gave the reaction of a friend, a left-wing academic,

> 'You're going to Ireland? That must be a dreadful country.' He meant, it developed, a country in which the economy is stagnant, emigration is the only road to betterment, the radical impulse associated with the name of James Connnolly is extinct, the government is subservient to bigoted priests and all worthwhile literature is censored.[1]

Jones would discover that such an image of Ireland was increasingly out of touch with crucial new developments in the economy and society of the Republic. For although the left in Ireland was indeed feeble, there were signs of new life and possibilites of expansion, unthinkable in the drab, depressed decades of the 1940s and 50s. Even the Catholic Church's formidable grip on much of the moral and social life of the country was facing new international and domestic challenges. As Jones recognised, the crucial material precondition for ending Irish backwardness in so many spheres of social and political life was the break with economic autarky initiated at the end of the 1950s. The gradual reintegration of the Republic's economy into the international economic order would produce a radical transformation in its economic and social structure. Most starkly it would put an end to over a century of emigration and population decline. Thus in 1966, after over forty years of independence, the population of the Republic at 2.88 million was less than it had been in 1926 (2.97 million) whilst that of the part of Ireland still 'unfree' was larger (1.25 in 1926 and 1.48 in 1966).[2] Economic growth, new forms of industrial employment and an accelerated development of urbanisation created conditions for new demographic patterns; by 1970 population in the Republic had risen to just under 3 million and by the the mid-1980s to 3.5 million.

A very different society began to emerge, a sometimes baffling mixture of modernity and backwardness. Its ultra-nationalist critics in Sinn Fein see it as a 'neo-colony' with a ruling class abjectly subservient to Britain, its very being as a nation retarded and corrupted by the 'incompletion' of the 1916-21 national revolution – its failure to include the six counties of Northern Ireland. There is certainly much that any self-respecting liberal, let alone socialist, critic could find to complain about in contemporary Ireland. The rapid economic and social change that has occurred since the 1950s has done little to mellow the long-term effects of what was a profoundly conservative national revolution against Britain. The Republic remains an extremely unequal society in which over one third of the population was estimated to be living below the poverty line at the end of the 1980s and where, despite the official ideology's continued commitment to a united Ireland, all serious commentators acknowledge the Republic's fundamental economic incapacity to absorb Northern Ireland.[3] Modernisation and the breaking down of the Catholic moral protectionism of de Valera's period (1932-59) has produced the beginnings of a serious indigenous critical intelligentsia, not by any means solely of the left. It has also produced more negative results – a major urban crime and drugs problem, particularly in Dublin where a heroin culture has put down deep roots amongst the most deprived sectors of the inner city working class. One stark and tragic index of the distance the contemporary Republic has travelled from the rural, Rousseauesque idylls of de Valera is its having the highest incidence of HIV-positive babies per capita in Europe.[4]

The inevitable focus of much of outside attention on what

has happened in Northern Ireland since 1968 has tended to obscure the very important and substantial changes that have occurred in the Republic. For many on the left in Britain, Europe and America the 'Irish Question' continues to be discussed as if the majority of the people of Ireland still lived under colonial rule. Yet if it began to be realised that in fact they live in a what has been for over sixty years an essentially independent and sovereign state, which has learnt, not without a large dose of official piety and hypocrisy, to live without the six county area, the implications for existing soft-headed identification with the 'anti-imperialist struggle' or for the equally problematical reformist support for the peaceful nationalist agenda of the SDLP are immense.

This book is written with the conviction that people who want to think seriously about contemporary Ireland need a knowledge of more than what goes on in West Belfast. It was commissioned to inform and educate the British, European and American left on the history of the state in which the majority of the people of Ireland live and the development of which holds the key to any progressive resolution of the murderous conflict within Northern Ireland. We also hope that it will be of value to those in Ireland looking for a serious and radical analysis of the history and contemporary reality of the state in the Republic. Such people, and those outside Ireland who have taken an interest in the 'Irish Question', have not been well served by existing analyses from a left perspective.

The paradigm of socialist thought about Ireland remained, at least until the 1960s, mired in the concepts and concerns of the 1920s and 30s. What this meant was what we can term an 'anti-imperialist' perspective which was in esssence very similar to the thinking of that section of the Irish republican movement which had rejected the Treaty settlement of 1921, fought and lost a civil war and regarded the new Free State as a puppet regime collaborating in the continued British imperialist domination of Ireland. All domestic contradictions were treated as forms of expression of the fundamental contradictions between the 'Irish People' and 'British Imperialism'. There was a consequent lack of interest in analysing how the social and economic order developed over the next four or five decades. Of course certain developments – like the weakening of the remaining constitutional links with Britain by Fianna Fail in the 1930s, the development through protectionism of a new bourgeoisie, the decision in 1948 to declare a Republic and leave the Commonwealth – could not be completely ignored, but the essentialist Irish socialist tradition treated these developments as superficial, superstructural floss on the unchanging realities of imperialist domination.

Like other forms of nationalist Marxist analysis found in countries that have been colonised, the sole focus on the colonising country as a source of all evil leads to an incapacity to grasp the complex and changing *internal* balance of economic and political forces. These forces are not understood on the basis of a serious investigation of their actuality but rather by speculative attempts to define them by their supposed relationship to 'imperialism'. That Ireland, north and south, is and has been affected by imperialism is clear to us. However here, as in earlier work, we see imperialism as a structured international system and not in the way it is characteristically used in Ireland – as a series of bad things done to 'Ireland' by 'England'; the moralistic and anthropomorphic tones of the approach are just the most obvious signs of its primitivism.

Imperialism, conceived as a structured and constantly transformed system of capitalist relations of production, takes the form of a hierarchical chain into which the Irish Republic is inserted. This chain creates a set of material limitations on what any Irish government can achieve. However, it also creates possibilities for development.[5] How these limitations and possiblities are dealt with is largely dependent not on 'imperialism' but rather on the internal configuration of class forces in the Republic as expressed in the state itself. Our approach will stress the relative autonomy and central importance of such internal factors and of the state in particular.

We will be particularly concerned with what has seemed to many commentators a defining characteristic of Irish politics – the absence for much of its history of a serious class alignment in ideology and politics. In the 1987 general election the two parties of the left, the Irish Labour Party and the Workers' Party got just 10 per cent of the vote between them. Many factors have been suggested to explain this – the role of an ultra-conservative Catholic Church, the long-standing historical weight of a conservative peasantry and the 'national question' to mention three of the most prominent. While the first and the second must figure in any explanation, we consider that a crucial weakness in previous attempts to deal with the question has been the failure to focus on the role of the state and of the main bourgeois party, Fianna Fail. This has become all the more evident over the last two decades during which the Republic has undergone a period of economic and social transformation of an unprecedented sort. But an economic and social revolution appears to have left the political superstructure largely untouched. New movements like feminism have appeared, there has been a substantial liberalisation of the dominant Catholic ethos, there have been massive popular protests over the inequities of the taxation system, yet in the main the traditional parties still dominate the political stage.

We will argue that the comprehension of these contradictory realities needs little recourse to notions of the peculiarities of the Irish and no plumbing of the depths of '800 years of Oppression'. Instead our focus will be on the substantive strategies elaborated by the Irish state and its predominant party, Fianna Fail. These strategies have undergone three periods of development – in the early 1930s, the late 1950s and since 1979. In the first two the Irish left was reduced to a pale imitation or reactionary caricature of Fianna Fail politics. The end of the 1970s saw the opening of a new period in the history of the Irish state and the dominant forms of rule, a period which while it has already shown the potential for a right-wing assault on social issues, has opened up for the first time since independence the possiblity of a serious breach in Fianna Fail's hitherto unshakeable hegemony over the working class.

Notes

1. Mervyn Jones, 'Ireland's Unfinished Revolution', *New Statesman*, 1 July 1966.
2. Basil Chubb, *The Government and Politics of Ireland*, London 1982, (2nd edition), p.341.
3. The report of economic consultants commissioned by the New Ireland Forum commented that 'Unity, a federal or confederal Irish state would be increasingly difficult to achieve without enormous economic sacrifices on the part of both south and north.' *Irish Times*, 21 May 1982. Figures on poverty are from an Economic and Social Research Institute report quoted in *Irish Times*, 28 September 1988.
4. *Irish Times*, 28 September 1988.
5. We are influenced here by the work of Nicos Poulantzas – *Classes in Contemporary Capitalism*, London 1975, and *The Crisis of the Dictatorships*, London 1976,

1   The Social Foundations of the Irish Free State, 1916-1932

There is no doubt that the Dublin Easter Rising of 1916, or perhaps more particularly the execution by the British of its leaders, including the romantic intellectual Padraig Pearse and the socialist leader James Connolly, unleashed a tide of emotional Irish nationalism which in the next five years effectively destroyed British rule in Ireland. Before the rising Catholic and nationalist Ireland had not fallen too far behind Protestant and unionist Ireland in the matter of supporting the British effort in the First World War – by December 1915, out of 75,795 Irish recruits to the UK forces, 36,775 were Catholics as against 38,121 Protestants – of these 18,200 were politicised National Volunteers and 24,628 Ulster Volunteers.[1] Even when allowance is made for the fact that Catholics and nationalists were in a substantial majority in Ireland, these were respectable figures. They do show, however, that radical nationalism's hostility towards Britain had probably had some impact in reducing recruiting figures prior to the rising.

When the First World War began, John Redmond, the leader of Irish nationalism, had committed his followers to the support of the British war effort 'wherever the firing line'. Redmond's obituary in the sympathetic *Freeman's Journal* concluded:

> He [Redmond] came to the conclusion that there had to be a break with the Irish tradition and that a new meaning should be given to O'Connell's saying, 'England's difficulty is Ireland's opportunity.'

Redmond felt that the passing of the Home Rule Bill (in an

15

admittedly suspended form) constituted an offer of a measure of justice by the 'British democracy' towards Ireland which required some reciprocal response. But the possibility of some form of partition clearly remained on the agenda. Redmond's lieutenant John Dillon tended to argue – for example in a Belfast speech of 25 October 1914 – that Ulster opposition might still be overcome by force applied by the 'forty thousand true Irish nationalists in the new army'. Redmond hit the same note at Wexford on 4 October: 'If it ever came to force which God forbid – and we all know it never will – but if it ever came to force two can play at that game.' But Redmond's heart was not really in such rhetoric and in a speech in Connaught on 6 December 1914 he adopted his preferred conciliatory tone. He made a reference to the Ulster Volunteers at the front and was greeted with groans. He replied angrily, 'No, no, believe me, that is the wrong spirit!' He added, 'These men will be fighting shoulder to shoulder with nationalists in the trenches in France and in God's name let us try to grasp from the situation a real unity of our own people in Ireland.' Following his trips to the front Redmond always chose to dwell on the unity between different sections (unionist and nationalist) of the Irish soldiers. Redmond was initially able to retain the support of nationalist Ireland for his position.

The formation of the new British coalition government in May 1915 was to be a key moment in the development of Irish disenchantment. The Ulster Unionist leader Sir Edward Carson was appointed Attorney-General while Redmond, perhaps unwisely according to nationalist critic D.P. Moran, took the traditional Home Rule position and refused the offer of a balancing place in the UK Cabinet. Perceptions of the British state and its war effort became increasingly negative ones. Father Michael O'Flanagan, an influential Roscommon priest soon to become Vice-President of Sinn Fein, had already made himself famous by declaring that the Belgians did not want liberation and were happy with German rule.[2] A relatively nuanced police analysis of 1916 for western Galway – a traditionally turbulent region – argues that even before the rising the fear of conscription had enabled Sinn Fein to obtain plenty of recruits, so that by Easter 1916 a 'large percentage of the labourers, farmers' sons and shop assistants were active Sinn Feiners or in favour of its policy'. The rural areas of the county, which had traditionally been a stronghold of agrarian secret societies, found it was 'second nature' to obey the dictates of Sinn Fein. Outside these areas, however, most of local people were neutral or opposed to the rebellion; it was the execution of the leaders which changed their feelings.[3]

The leaders of the rising had known that they had little hope of conventional military success, and instead in a mood of passionate exhilaration forced themselves to act out the drama of a 'blood sacrifice'. Constance Markievicz has recalled this moment in a description of James Connolly:

> I never saw him happier than on Easter Monday morning when he came downstairs with the other members of the Provisional Government of the Republic. We parted on the steps of Liberty Hall for the last time. He was absolutely radiant, like a man who had seen a vision. The comrade of Tone and Emmet, he stood on the heights with them, his spirit one with theirs. The rapture that comes only when the supreme sacrifice is made intentionally and willingly in a man's heart was his. The life of the flesh was over for him: the spirit life had begun.[4]

Joseph Lee has offered us a more clinical interpretation of the meaning of these events:

> In one respect it was shrewd tactics to ally with the republicans, the only nationalists who might conceivably pry Ireland loose from the grip of the obesely bourgeois home rule party. But by allowing himself to become involved in the blood sacrifice of Easter week Connolly buried Irish socialism for several decades. Blood sacrifice made some sense in Pearse's eschatology, but none at all in Connolly's. Nationalists are as useful to their cause dead as alive, but there was only one Connolly. The prospects for socialism were slender in any event, but Connolly's death ensured that whatever phoenix rose from the embers of Easter would unfurl no red flag.[5]

In the same work Lee also argues that Connolly lacked a good grasp of the land question which so concerned the majority of his fellow countrymen – 'Connolly's fatal tactical error was his reluctance to acknowledge the existence of rural Ireland.'[6]

The result was that Connolly in effect excluded himself from the principal concerns of mainstream nationalism in his own lifetime. Certainly there is nothing in Connolly's work to compare, even relatively speaking, with the effort devoted by Lenin or Kautsky to the analysis of tendencies of development within Russian and German agriculture, or indeed the political debates linked to the land issue in these countries. The Home Rule movement of Connolly's day, for all its 'obese' and 'bourgeois nature', was committed to 'Ireland for the Irish' and the 'land for the people', but what did these phrases mean?

The Irish farming society from which the nationalists drew their support was socially divided. There was on the one side a large peasant class undertaking small- or medium-scale farming; on the other, a growing stratum of rich graziers. To be considered a grazier, a man had usually to hold over 200 acres; more usually a grazing holding was probably between 400 and 600 acres, though there was also an elite grouping which held much more. It was not difficult to find these so-called 'ranchers' in every region of Ireland but they were particularly notable in three regions; the lowlands of North Leinster, including the counties of Meath, Westmeath, Dublin, Kildare and Offaly; the plains of east Connaught and north Munster including the counties of Sligo, Roscommon, east Galway, Clare and Tipperary; the mountain pasture and boglands of west Connaught including west Galway, Mayo and north-west Sligo and even parts of Donegal.

The Irish Parliamentary Party of the 1890s and 1900s was, in theory, committed to the breaking up of large grazing farms and their redistribution among the poor and landless. Between 1898 and 1903 and again between 1906 and 1910 the party leadership sanctioned a so-called ranch war in rural Ireland. Some have been tempted to see in this conflict between highly capitalised ranchers and a land-hungry rural poor the true location of Ireland's potential social revolution. In reality, despite much verbal hostility to the allegedly evil grazing system, the Irish nationalist leadership was forced to recognise at all the key points that the cattle trade was crucial to the livelihood of the great majority of Irish farmers; it is, therefore, hardly surprising that many leaders of the ranch war were themselves shown to have grazing interests. Ranch wars always fizzled out in the end.[7]

It now seems clear from the jaded and cynical comments which appear in the *Workers' Republic* journal with which Connolly was associated that he was probably aware of the flawed and ambiguous nature of Irish rural class conflict. He linked this with another oddity of rhetoric – the way in which the Irish Parliamentary Party, which would quite happily talk about expropriaton of the landlord's interests, would prove itself to be highly sensitive to property rights in all other contexts. With the publication of *Labour in Irish History*, Connolly argued that the Land League and subsequent land legislation had helped Ireland move into the epoch of capitalist farming. But this had happened at precisely the moment when agriculture was becoming an international industry – with an increase of 50 per cent in the area of the world under cultivation in the years betwen 1840 and 1870. Irish farmers thus found themselves in competition with the large-scale, more mechanised farming of North America. In Connolly's view only social ownership of all the resources of Ireland and a protected economy could save the rural population from impoverishment.

Yet this response hardly answers the question. It is a retreat into an abstract 'purist' solution of a type which has bedevilled Irish socialism throughout the twentieth century, and was neatly parallelled when the left-wing Republican leader Peadar O'Donnell argued that Fianna Fail's economic programme of the 1930s might be progressive in some respects but it failed to ensure that production was carried out on the basis of need rather than profit.

It ignores, as Marx did earlier and with rather more excuse, the social and political weight of the Irish rural bourgeoisie. At this point it is worth looking at an article published by Connolly in the *Harp* in August 1908, called 'Michael Davitt: A Text for a Revolutionary Lecture'. In this essay, Connolly attempted to come to terms with the meaning of the Land League crisis of 1879 to 1882: 'We believe,' he writes, 'that a close study of the events of that time would immensely benefit the militant socialists of all countries.' Connolly's view of the Land League was essentially positive: its leaders had transformed Irish nationalism from a 'sterile parliamentarism' into a 'virile force'. According to Connolly:

> The Land League made adhesion to the cause of the tenants synonymous with the call of Irish patriotism, and thus emphasised the point we have so often laboured viz., – that the Irish question is a social question.

Yet, as Connolly admitted, the 'Land League did not entirely succeed in its mission'. To what was its element of failure due? For Connolly, the answer lies in the divisions amongst its leadership as to ultimate objectives:

> The promoters were not in agreement as to their ultimate ideal and were unable to educate their followers against the fallacy of accepting concessions which divided and disorganised their forces when at the flood tide of success.

Such an interpretation lays too much stress on the leadership and too little on the nature of the Land League as a mass movement. Even more revealingly, when describing the working of this movement, Connolly lays exclusive stress on the tactics which expressed the communal solidarity of the poor peasantry. He neglected to note the equally important tactics which revealed the existence of significant class division within the Irish peasantry as the wealthier farmers imposed their price for participation in the struggle against the landlords. In short, by 1881 a substantial rural bourgeoisie had shown its hand in the Irish countryside and this class was prepared to accept limits on the pace of agrarian change in order to protect its own interests against challenge from below.[8] The nationalist leadership of Connolly's generation in the 1900s, was, therefore, always caught uneasily between pressure from the rural 'haves' on the one side and the rural 'have-nots' on the other.

By 1914 roughly two-thirds of Irish peasants had got what they wanted – their land. They no longer needed a party at

Westminster to wring further reforms; indeed, they were sometimes irritated by the Irish Party's concessions to the rural poor. Moreover, the Westminster parliament was beginning to talk worryingly about taxes on property to finance social reform. A bottom one-third of discontented Irish farmers still existed – they resented the old Irish Party's failure to do anything much for them. In the emotional circumstances created by the Easter Rising and the execution of patriots like Pearse and Connolly, both sections of the Irish farming community found they had no material reason not to ditch the Irish Parliamentary Party and embrace Sinn Fein; indeed, the balance of material (as well as ideological) reason favoured such a ditching. In some places the land-hungry men gave Sinn Fein its radical tinge; much more often the satisfied conservative majority imposed its vision on the new movement and later on the new Irish parliament.

Class or Nationality? 1918-1923

Following Sinn Fein's electoral landslide in 1918, guerrilla warfare designed to break Britain's hold in Ireland was probably inevitable. As the IRA newspaper *An-t-Oglach* put it, even before hostilities began:

> The Irish Volunteers are the key to the situation. They are the reality, the grim reality that England cannot get rid of. They represent the concrete form, the original determination of the Irish nation to be free. They are the facts that cannot be got rid of by the most cunning of politicians and the most ingenious of statesmen. Besides them and their magnificent courage, all resort to political expediency sinks into insignificance.[9]

And so it proved to be – but inevitably the successful war of independence (1919-21) was accompanied like all the great popular revolts in Ireland since the 1870s by activity in the west of Ireland designed to force a radical redistribution of land. Since 1880 it had been clear that this threatened the interests not only of the unionist and landed interests but also of sections of the nationalist wealthy farming classes. On 26 April 1920 the unionist *Irish Times* spoke of 'agrarian bolshevism' in the west of Ireland: land was being seized at the 'pistol's mouth'. On 8 May the *Connaught Telegraph*, which sympathised with this local activism, reported: 'The agrarian struggle in the west has developed to the extent that no government can ignore it.' The *Mayo News* argued on 5 June that the 'war in Ireland' presents 'three distinct phases marked by many dissimilar features'. It noted:

> We have in the first place the war on police and police stations by a section of the population who cannot be defined and whose methods are characterised by a secrecy and effectiveness hitherto unknown in any phase of the Irish struggle.[10]

The second phase of the war was the 'struggle to secure the land for the people'. The English government, it was said, supported the ranching system which kept the people off the land. The third phase of the Irish war was between Irish labour and the British government over the question of the transport of munitions.[11] The failure of English railwaymen to support their striking Irish brothers was, however, seen as evidence of the need to strengthen the 'Sinn Fein principle [i.e. separate organisation along Irish national lines] in Irish trades unionism'.

In response to these threats, particularly those in rural Ireland, the authorities reacted by sending in reinforcements of troops. Significantly, though, the Sinn Fein leadership also acted to cool down the passions of the land-hungry. At an extraordinary Sinn Fein-sponsored Galway meeting of 21 May the dominant tone was set by the local nationalist clergy who called for a more equitable distribution of land, but admitted that in 'the recent movement towards this laudable object, great abuses have arisen'. New measures were proposed – including arbitration courts – to bring the land war under control.[12] Whilst it is difficult to be precise about the exact weighting to be accorded to the two factors,[13] it seems clear that the combination of Sinn Fein hostility to direct action with state repression significantly curbed agrarian activism. Between 1 January and 8 June 1920 the RIC recorded 864 agrarian 'outrages' (including five murders) as compared with 144 for the same period in 1919.[14] Yet by the end of 1920 the figure rose only to 1,114 outrages and the rate of agrarian crime slackened further in the new year. From 1 January to 8 June 1921 there were a mere 143 outrages, 721 less than in the same period of 1920 and one less than the same period in 1919.[15]

This helps to throw some light on one of the most surprising facts about the war of independence. The relatively poor western province of Connaught – where, in fact, Sinn Fein was most densely organised – was actually less to the fore in terms of acts of violent resistance to British rule than Munster. Traditionally, during the Land League (1879-82) and United Irish League (1898-1900) agrarian mobilisations, Connaught had been the most aggressively violent province. *An-t-Oglach* acknowledged this development with a brutal frankness:

In the West, the guerrilla warfare was not sufficiently energetic to greatly relax the grip of the old 'RIC' in the countryside; and they are now striving desperately to regain their hold, with the aid of the foreign reinforcements, by wholesale terrorism. They actually hope to succeed by Christmas, as is shown by a secret order intercepted by us. The Volunteers of those parts of the West where this campaign of terrorism is being carried on have themselves to thank for it. For a year we have been preaching the necessity of a vigorous and sustained offensive everywhere against the enemy's front line, the 'RIC', and pointed out that the slackness of certain parts of the country made the problem unnecessarily simple for the enemy. In the South, the guerrilla offensive has been carried out for so long and so vigorously that any attempt by the 'RIC' to regain control of areas is out of the question and the enemy can only rely on a big military concentration. Months ago we warned those Brigades that if they were slack and inefficient and failed to take their full part in the guerrilla warfare that they would get it.[16]

Erhard Rumpf has asked the obvious question posed by these developments: 'What then was the relationship between the land question and the war of independence?'[17] He notes that, 'The districts where the most violent agrarian unrest occurred during the period were not the centres of the national struggle.' Rumpf argues that the conservatism of the IRA's leadership was partially responsible for a failure to mobilise the full potential of the west behind the 'national struggle'. It is possible to give further illustrations of the operation of class conflict within the national revolution.

The police reports reveal that Bartlemy, County Cork, was one of the most potent sources of IRA activity during the war of independence. Again and again the local County Cork police bitterly report a 'state of terror'[18] or a 'perfect orgy of crime'[19] angrily admitting – at a time when other counties were claiming a mild improvement – that the county 'could not be in a much worse state than it is at present'.[20] A particularly unpleasant feature of this activity was the murder of isolated Protestant farmers – four in one month – on the grounds that they had given evidence to the security forces, thus giving issue to very real fears that the 'small Protestant community would be wiped out'.[21]

At the core of this activity was the IRA unit based in Bartlemy; this unit included some seventy agricultural labourers who were also members of the expanding Irish Transport and General Workers' Union, the branch chairman of which (Maurice O'Regan) was on full-time active service with the flying column. It was an epoch of rising expectations for the labourers. The British corn production Act of 1917 had set a minimum wage and with the further assistance of the ITGWU the labourers won 'fairly decent wages': in particular they had gained a £4 harvest bonus.[22]

Immediately following the truce agreed with the British in July 1921 the labourers found these gains threatened. The farmers – arguing that they had borne much of the cost of the IRA campaign by supporting the Dail loan but also by sheltering men on the run and by accepting absences or tired work from labourers exhausted by their nocturnal activities – demanded the withdrawal of the harvest bonus. The labourers (supported by the farm women) immediately went on strike. The IRA was then called upon by the local employers to terrorise the workers: the entire working-class membership of the IRA (with the exception of 'two scabs') immediately resigned. IRA units from outside the district were sent in to impose order; they attempted to inflict terms suggested by a Sinn Fein court dominated by local employers involved in the strike. The labourers – less than

18 per cent of the agricultural workforce – found themselves isolated, as so often before, and with little public support.[23] 'One type of Black and Tan had gone out and another had come in, and thus began a new phase of the struggle for freedom,' recalled Maurice O'Regan. At this point IRA headquarters intervened and imposed a compromise more favourable to the local labourers, and in the period from the truce to the treaty of 1922 a degree of expectant nationalist unity was established: indeed IRA ranks were swollen by new recruits.[24]

The British were prepared in the treaty negotiations of 1921 to offer dominion status to Ireland but insisted upon an oath of fidelity to the crown; the scene was set for the bitter civil war between the pro-treaty 'Free State' forces (who lost over 800 dead) and the anti-treaty 'Republican' forces (who lost many more).[25] Some western areas which had been relatively quiet during the war of independence became more active in the civil war – though even in the heartlands of western agrarian radicalism there were those who dismissed the civil war as the factionalism of the strong-willed. The *Mayo News*, which had an impeccable record of nationalist and agrarian purism, declared coldly,

In Ireland every county and, in some counties, each parish is a law unto itself, and every parish leader has his own following, who follow blindly, thoughtlessly, nay ruthlessly, whatever road along which the hero they adore may lead them.[26]

In May 1923 the defeated Republican forces dumped their arms. Although the occasion of the split in the nationalist leadership was purely political ('the oath') there was clear evidence too that certain forms of agrarian radicalism were simultaneously defeated: in Meath, Clare and Waterford pro-treaty forces physically repressed small farmers' and labourers' militancy. In Bartlemy the local employers took the opportunity of the treaty split within Sinn Fein to reject the compromise agreed with the IRA headquarters, and this time 'the employing elements in the IRA' made sure that they had a superiority of armaments to break any resistance. The leadership of the local labourers was absorbed within the anti-treaty forces and subsequently interned. Roy Foster has concluded:

> The unwritten history of the events from 1916 to 1923 must include the post-war challenge of Irish labour – defused not only by the effects of recession and emigration but also by the polarisation of nationalist politics. In this arena, exalted leaders first fought out a brutal duel over a form of words, and then constructed a new state around preoccupations that resolutely ignored even the vague social and economic desiderata once outlined for Pearse's visionary Republic.[27]

Symbolically, the new Free State government led by W.T. Cosgrave cut the old age pension by a shilling a week in 1924. One minister, Patrick McGilligan, icily declared, 'People may have to die in this country and die through starvation.'[28] And starve they did in some cases – a fact which is the starting point for Peadar O'Donnell's 1929 novel *Adrigoole*. Patrick Hogan, the Minister of Agriculture, was such a solid supporter of the ranching stratum that he became known as the 'Minister for Grass'.

The Revival of Politics

To the surprise of his pro-government critics, Eamon de Valera, leader of the defeated Republican forces, proved to be flexible enough to respond to the opportunity posed by this rightist government. He broke in 1926 with the rump of Sinn Fein/IRA irreconcilables and founded a new party, Fianna Fail, with the intention of entering the Dail – though the issue of the oath still appeared to stand in the way. This shift towards acceptance of the Free State institutions, fraught with ambiguity as it was, surprised some of his opponents; as the Dublin weekly the *Leader* sourly observed, 'The move was inconsistent with all he had said and done for the previous four years.'[29]

The themes of Fianna Fail in this period were those of an apparently radical, populist nationalism. There was a constant harping on the 'anti-national' nature of the Free State government. A key theme was the Dail admission by Minister for Foreign Affairs, Desmond FitzGerald, that in the event of a foreign attack on Ireland, 'It is perfectly obvious that our army must co-operate with the British army.'[30] FitzGerald had added that it was 'practically inconceivable that our army would be opposed to the British army'.[31] This speech provoked rage and indignation within Fianna Fail ranks and was linked with a general denunciation of Free State economic policy as a 'surrender to the rich'.[32] R. Walsh, soon to be elected as Fianna Fail TD, caught this tone perfectly in a speech at Brackloon in the west:

> They appealed today to that section – the people of no property or of very little property. They appealed today to the men with four or five acres, to the worker with the pick or shovel in his hand, and on the strength of the nationality and patriotism of those people they relied.[33]

The current Fianna Fail leadership still likes to recall the party's radical roots. Charles Haughey in 1974 reminded Dublin members:

> At that time, Fianna Fail was looked upon by certain sectors as a troublesome, even dangerous arrival on the scene. It represented a threat to the established order of things. That the established order included slums, chronic unemployment, subsistence level farming and primitive health services, did not deter them from condemning Fianna Fail for wanting to upset it.[34]

Haughey was here reiterating a view of the party's history which had been established by Eamon de Valera. Peter Mair quotes an interview given by de Valera in 1976 in which he claimed that in the early years of the party he was worried that it was being perceived as too oriented towards the working class: 'In those days I believe we could be called socialists, but not communists.'[35] Indeed de Valera was not above calling up the ghost of James Connolly at crucial junctures at this time. The left in Ireland may well have underestimated the party's continuing ability, down to Haughey's denunciation of the 1982-87 coalition government's 'Thatcherism' as inspired by a reactionary clique of monetarist economists and declaration of his own affiliation to Keynes – 'the last economist worth his salt' – to maintain a populist, radical appeal.[36]

But it would be seriously wrong to underestimate de Valera's own shrewd evaluation of the balance of political forces in the Free State, to take him at his word on these issues. A better insight into his real calculations is given in a letter to Joseph McGarrity, a leading émigré nationalist figure in the USA. It was written after the extraordinary Sinn Fein Ard Fheis in 1926 and the subsequent decision to create the new party. Justifying this decision de Valera provided an interesting evaluation of the political situation in the Free State:

> You will perhaps wonder why I did not wait any longer. It is vital that the Free State be shaken at the next general election for if an opportunity be given it to consolidate itself further as an institution – if the present Free State members are replaced by farmers and labourers and other class interests, the national interest as a whole will be submerged in the clashing of rival economic groups.[37]

The failure of abstentionism as a tactic after the civil war has been ably documented by Pyne.[38] But clearly de Valera was not simply concerned with Sinn Fein's inability to hold on to its constituency. The letter demonstrates a real fear that despite the limitations on, and truncated nature of, the independence of the Free State, an early prediction of Connolly's about the progressive effects of self-government might be materialising:

> An Irish Republic would be ... the natural repository of popular power; the weapon of popular emancipation, the only power which would show in the full light of day all those class antagonisms and lines of economic demarcation now obscured by the mists of patriotism.[39]

The end of 'civil war politics' is something which has been often proclaimed since the 1960s, with the Progressive Democrats being simply the latest in a long line of would-be realigners, more usually from the left. Ironically it was de

Valera, too often portrayed as a man of illusions and dreams, who clear-headedly perceived that the civil war fissure, though a deep and bitter one, would not inevitably reproduce itself as the fundamental alignment in Irish politics.

Although the division in the leadership of Sinn Fein over the treaty had little social or economic dimension to it, despite the clear reliance of the anti-treatyites on the small farmers of the west, the rather ramshackle lumber room of Sinn Fein policies in these areas would be visited increasingly by de Valera and his main lieutenants in the post-civil war years. This was in part a response to the conservative evolution of the party of government, now calling itself Cumann na nGhaedheal, an evolution which in itself helped to 'socialise' the civil war division. The unsuccessful army mutiny of 1924 and the secession from the party of a group which constituted itself as Clann Eireann in 1925 visibly distanced it from important elements of the nationalist legacy and made it relatively easy to portray it as a rump of pro-British reaction. Thus when J.J. Walsh, Minister of Posts and Telegraphs, resigned in 1927 over the government's lack of commitment to protectionism, he wrote an open letter to Cosgrave alleging, amongst other things,

> The party itself has gone bodily over to the most reactionary elements of the state ... A government cannot depend on the votes of ranchers and importers and at the same time develop industry and agriculture.[40]

To allow such a government to continue in power when the main opponent was the Labour Party would have been precisely to risk the institutionalisation of class divisions in the Free State: the Labour Party's relatively strong performance – 12.6 per cent as against Fianna Fail's 26.1 per cent and the Cumann na nGaedheal's 27.4 per cent – in the first election of 1927 demonstrated the danger. The June election was more marked by the decline in support for the government than a substantial increase in 'Republican sentiment' (see Tables 1 and 2).

Table 1: Cumann na nGaedheal Electoral Support, 1923-27: Percentage of Popular Vote

Constituency	1923	1927	Gains/losses
Dublin City North	48.4	29.2	−19.2
Dublin City South	55.5	30.4	−25.1
Cork City	35.4	28.3	−7.1
Dublin County	48.2	32.8	−15.4
Wicklow	34.6	16.4	−18.2
Kildare	27.0	19.2	−8.8
Meath	42.6	24.9	−17.7
Louth	46.9	33.6	−13.3
Monaghan	55.5	25.8	−29.7
Cavan	28.7	16.6	−21.1
Longford-Westmeath	26.7	25.7	−1.0
Laois-Offaly	26.6	22.5	−4.1
Kilkenny-Carlow	47.4	35.4	−12.0
Wexford	17.6	12.0	−5.6
Waterford	14.7	16.1	+1.4
Tipperary	39.4	26.6	−12.8
Roscommon	41.6	29.1	−12.5
Sligo-Leitrim	47.9	42.4	−5.5
Donegal	36.9	29.8	−7.1
Mayo North	53.8	42.5	−11.3
Mayo South	53.7	35.5	−18.2
Galway	43.6	35.0	−8.6
Clare	29.8	18.9	−14.8
Limerick	41.5	26.7	−14.8
Kerry	32.6	33.3	+0.6
Cork West	38.7	20.4	−18.3
Cork North	13.6	9.0	−4.6
Cork East	31.8	16.7	−15.1
University (National)	68.9	61.3	−7.6
Averages	39.1	27.3	−11.8

(*Source: Nation*, 25 June 1927)

It is perhaps worth pointing out that the issue of partition had nothing to do with Fianna Fail's revival. The propaganda of the anti-treaty forces had had less to say about the north than those of the pro-treaty side.[41] Frank Gallagher, the editor of the official Fianna Fail journal the *Nation*, tried to improve matters by offering space to the former Irish Parliamentary Party activist William O'Brien,

Table 2: *Republican Electoral Support (Fianna Fail plus Sinn Fein and Independent Republicans), 1923-27: Percentage of Popular Vote*

Constituency	1923	1927	Gains/losses
Dublin City North	17.6	29.1	+11.5
Dublin City South	21.1	32.0	+11.1
Cork City	22.7	22.7	0
Dublin County	13.6	25.9	+12.3
Wicklow	18.4	21.7	+3.3
Kildare	21.3	29.0	+7.7
Meath	16.9	27.6	+10.7
Louth	27.0	28.2	+5.3
Monaghan	25.3	30.6	+5.3
Cavan	18.6	24.0	+5.4
Longford-Westmeath	31.1	30.2	−0.9
Laois-Offaly	27.3	28.9	+1.6
Kilkenny-Carlow	24.7	23.7	−1.0
Wexford	27.0	27.9	+0.9
Waterford	25.3	29.5	+3.2
Tipperary	29.5	36.8	+7.3
Roscommon	36.5	36.3	−0.2
Sligo-Leitrim	36.1	30.4	−5.7
Donegal	24.0	23.8	−0.2
Mayo North	39.9	42.7	+2.8
Mayo South	35.4	39.3	+3.9
Galway	33.4	37.9	+4.5
Clare	47.4	43.9	−3.5
Limerick	26.3	30.3	+4.0
Kerry	45.1	40.4	−4.7
Cork West	20.9	22.7	+1.8
Cork North	30.7	24.0	−6.7
Cork East	23.5	28.7	+5.2
University (National)	19.8	23.9	+4.1
Averages	27.4	29.9	+2.5

(*Source: Nation*, 25 June 1927)

then in the last year of his life, to denounce what he described as the 'two nations' philosophy of the Cosgrave government. But this reflected personal friendship as much as anything,[42] as Gallagher had been a part of O'Brien's Cork-based All-for-Ireland League on the eve of the war, and O'Brien's overall record – as a genuine advocate of conciliating Irish Protestant and unionist interests and as an initial supporter of recruitment for the British army in the First World War – left many Fianna Fail activists cold.[43] As Eamon Donnelly, a northern nationalist active in Fianna Fail at this time, noted in *Honesty*, 'There is no use shirking the fact that one of the biggest crimes to their [the Cosgrave government's] credit isn't a live issue by any means. I refer to Ulster.'[44]

At first, in the aftermath of the election, it seemed as if there could be no compromise with the treaty and the 'oath'. In late May de Valera claimed at Carrigallen, County Leitrim, 'They could no more recommend the Treaty than when they refused to work it, as they knew what it represented.'[45] The *Nation* insisted that in making the oath the central issue of the election Fianna Fail had not misinterpreted the feeling of the nation nor misjudged the national interests. The *Nation* argued:

> The Oath inflicts injury on the moral, material and national interests of Ireland. It is taken by three classes of men, those who intend to break it when the opportunity occurs to break the British connection: those who inspired by personal, party or misconceived national motives take it with the intention of keeping it, although disliking it, and the Imperialists who take it with joy.

Frank Gallagher concluded: 'Ireland cannot afford an oath which excludes from the legislature all but the dishonest, the weak and the imperially minded.'[46] Yet six months before these words were written, Dan Breen, an independent TD with a magnificent Republican reputation ('always physically fearless and perhaps he carries more wounds than any man living'[47]) had taken the oath. It was difficult to see how Breen could be placed in the category of the dishonest, the weak or the imperially minded.

Patrick Belton, a prominent agriculturist who had been elected in the Fianna Fail interest, became increasingly restive. In his previous campaign as an independent Belton had declared a willingness to take the oath,[48] and soon reiterated his adherence to this position, despite his own political change of clothes. Urging Fianna Fail TDs to take their seats, he insisted, 'Our supporters in Dublin, at any rate, are disgusted with us.'[49] Belton was immediately called upon to resign by the Fianna Fail organisation.[50]

De Valera, it seemed, would do almost anything to avoid taking the oath. At the beginning of August he told a meeting at Burgh Quay in Dublin that in exchange for the abandonment of such a political test, Fianna Fail 'will not press any issues involving the Treaty to the point of overthrowing such a government during the normal lifetime of the present Assembly'.[51] In the end the Free State government forced de Valera's hand. Responding to the assassination of Kevin O'Higgins, one of its most prominent members, it passed emergency legislation enforcing the oath as a *sine qua non* of participation in constitutional politics. Fianna Fail complied, whilst making it clear that they regarded the oath as an empty formula. Frank Gallagher could only tell his readers that the decision 'occasioned days and nights of anxiety'[52] – they can hardly have been surprised.[53] Soon, in a proclamation address, Fianna Fail moved to make a virtue of necessity:

To the People of Ireland

By its recent action in entering the Free State Dail, Fianna Fail has already given earnest proof that in the pursuit of its ideals, it is prepared to face and accept lasting realities. If returned to power with a majority in the coming election, and entrusted with power, it hopes to prove that hard-headed common sense is not incompatible with true nationalist idealism.[54]

The results of the election seemed to satisfy de Valera. In his first interview after the outcome became known, he declared that he had not expected to gain more than the fourteen seats which had been won. He had no doubt as to who the 'ultimate victor would be'. He seemed now to be firmly committed to the path of constitutional opposition and the *New York Herald Tribune* observed, 'De Valera's decision to follow a middle course has strengthened his political position.'[55] Fianna Fail's share of the vote rose from 26.1 to 35.2 per cent whilst Labour's fell from 12.6 to 9.1 per cent. The broad trend was established; increasingly Fianna Fail's language focused on economic and social themes: of particular importance here was the campaign against the payment of land annuities to Britain. In 1923 the then government of the Irish Free State had undertaken to collect and pay to the United Kingdom the monies due from tenant-purchasers – that is the annuities in respect of holdings purchased under the 1903 and 1909 British Land Acts. These annuities amounted to £3 million a year. In 1923 the Irish government resolved to collect the annuities from the tenant-purchasers and to pay them into the British government's Purchase Annuities Fund.[56] The Irish government's undertaking to pay the annuities was confirmed under the Ultimate Financial Settlement agreed with the British in March 1926. By this time the political sensitivity of the issue was indicated by the fact that the Free State government did not publish details of the settlement until eight months after it had been signed. A hostile commentator noted:

> The agitation on land annuities has been favoured by Mr de Valera ... largely because he believes that it will provide an effective controversial smokescreen under cover of which the last Fianna Fail deputy may withdraw from the Republic, without attracting attention.[57]

There were occasional aberrations – in March 1929, for example, de Valera declared that Dail Eireann was an 'illegal Assembly',[58] but the acceptance of state institutions was to become increasingly apparent. The Fianna Fail response had been a subtle one, in part determined by an astute evaluation of the weaknesses in the ideological heritage of Labour. In this a major, if only partially conscious ally, was that section of the leadership of the IRA associated with Peadar O'Donnell. To explain this it is necessary to look at the traditions of the Irish left in the 1920s.

Choices for the Left

The historian Emmet O'Connor has established the autonomous roots of the syndicalist upsurge of Irish labour in the period 1917-21, coterminous as it was with the rise of militant nationalism.[59] He demonstrates that class militancy was not, in any substantial way, a by-product of the national revolution and that the leadership of Sinn Fein was either cold or hostile to it. The substantial autonomy of the dynamics of the two processes of syndicalist militancy and national revolution had clear implications for the subsequent development of politics in the Free State.

O'Connor points out that in some senses Irish syndicalism was a caricature of the weaknesses of syndicalism generally, 'amorphous, incoherent and transitory'.[60] But was the labour militancy of the period with its disregard for 'politics' and the state simply symptomatic of the lacunae of the wider syndicalist movement? Or was there no alternative to a militant class-oriented strategy which attempted to maximise the possibilities of wage movements? There could be no conflagration as occurred in Russia in 1917 because the rural bourgeoisie was already firmly in control of the countryside. The discontent of the small farmer population, particularly in the west, would give rise to some localised and sporadic 'anti-rancher' manifestations but it had neither the social depth nor geographical reach to turn the countryside upside down. The small farmer and landless labourer were still mesmerised by visions of piecemeal land acquisition which were easily assimilable by anti-rancher rhetoric that had been the stock in trade of Irish nationalism since the days of the Land League.

The objective basis for a radical alliance between workers and small farmers was not a strong one, and therefore the strategic choice facing the working class was between a militant and necessarily 'sectional' defence of its interests within a predominantly conservative social and political order or some variant of a 'national' approach involving the search for support from other groups which would necessarily involve a dilution of the class strategy. Once the economy entered recession in 1921, however, the pertinence of the choice evaporated as the material conditions for syndicalist militancy disappeared. Yet a choice, of sorts, did remain.

The Labour Party chose the 'national' approach which

culminated in the severing of the link with the Irish Trades Union Congress in 1930 to demonstrate that the party was more than a political appendage of the trade union movement. But the party had in fact, in its gyrations between class and national vocations, done little more than concretise the fatal ambiguities in Connolly's legacy. For Connolly's own syndicalism had sat increasingly uneasily with his view of the leading role that the working class must play in the national revolution. The latter implicitly demanded a policy of alliances, yet Connolly's weakness in analysing rural Ireland meant that the nature of the unity of town and countryside was never specified. But clearly the possibility of allying working-class militancy and some substantial section of small-farmer Ireland was central to his thinking and to what became the common sense of the left after 1916. As long as this notion was not subjected to critical scrutiny it provided a major point of access for a populist nationalism.

It has often been argued that it was the failure of post-1916 Labour to challenge Sinn Fein for the leadership of the national revolution which consigned the working class to a subordinate role within the Free State. Yet once the new state had emerged what increasingly characterised both Labour Party and 'social republican' thinking was the need to build a popular alliance to achieve a set of 'national' goals which differ little from those of Fianna Fail. The left critique, identified with Peadar O'Donnell, took the form not of an assault on Fianna Fail objectives but rather of the claim that Fianna Fail had not the capacity to achieve the goals which it proclaimed. O'Donnell was capable of a rhetorical socialist critique of Fianna Fail; as we have seen, he attacked the protectionist-industrialist policies advocated by Sean Lemass as still accepting the framework of production for 'profit' not 'use'.[61] O'Donnell nevertheless acquiesced in nationalist assumptions – to the extent of supporting an Anglo-American war that might be turned to Ireland's advantage[62] – in ways that went much deeper than in his revealing acknowledgement of the 'very high level of personal integrity' in the Fianna Fail party.[63] For O'Donnell the main objective was to push Fianna Fail to the left. The annuities campaign was a means of increasing the pressure of popular as opposed to 'middle-class' or 'bourgeois' influences on the leadership. But much of the project could only have succeeded if the bulk of the people had perceived Fianna Fail's project of 'nation-building' to be irrelevant – something which Ireland's weak place in the international order always militated against. As Frank Gallagher replied to O'Donnell in the socialist republican paper *An Phoblacht*:

> We are in the trough of the wave. A large section of the Irish people are embittered, cynical. The nation's strength is sapped by emigration ... If the people are at present weary and indifferent it is not pandering to their sense of defeat to give them a task they can do. Rather it is breaking their self confidence still further to give them a task that they not only cannot do but to which they are repugnant.[64]

In early 1927 O'Donnell began to organise the peasantry on the annuities issue following approaches from small-holders in Donegal who were no longer able to pay.[64] Fianna Fail's response was a sympathetic but also a nervous one. Eamon de Valera always insisted that Colonel Maurice Moore, a former Free State Senator who soon joined Fianna Fail, had initiated the agitation rather than O'Donnell.[66] De Valera's one appearance on an annuities platform was marked by evasive irrelevance of the highest order.[67] More generally, de Valera discouraged Fianna Fail members from sharing platforms with O'Donnell, but was ignored by Patrick Ruttledge, who as an IRA commandant had a personal history of agrarian radicalism,[68] and by western branches.[69] Explaining all this, Sean Lemass told O'Donnell frankly, 'Damn it, man. Can't you see what we stand to gain from your agitation if we can't be accused of promoting it?'[70] O'Donnell wryly concludes:

> The only person who ever acknowledged my role in the thing was Paddy Hogan [Free State Minister for Agriculture]. When Fianna Fail was elected [in 1932] he said that de Valera rowed in on a crest of a wave promoted by the communist Peadar O'Donnell.[71]

But while there is a kernel of truth in Hogan's observations, it does require some elaboration. By the end of 1927 O'Donnell was exhausted and needed the support of Fianna Fail to sustain the agitation; part of the reason for this, he admitted, was the suspicious attitude of the Irish working class towards yet another agitation of the 'grasping' peasantry. Fianna Fail colonised the annuities campaign to give itself a suitably radical gloss – it should be noted that Hogan, with his usual insight, is arguing that Fianna Fail exploited O'Donnell; it was certainly not the other way round. To explain this it is necessary to look more fully at Fianna Fail's agrarian policy.

Notes

1. PRO CO 904/140/280.
2. PRO CO 904/120/199.
3. CO 904/120/303, County Inspector's Office, 24 January 1917.
4. *Mayo News*, 1 June 1935.
5. Joseph Lee, *The Modernisation of Irish Society*, Dublin 1973, p.152.
6. Ibid, p.151.
7. See Paul Bew, *Conflict and Conciliation in Ireland*, Oxford 1987, Ch.5.
8. L.P. Curtis, 'On Class and Class Conflict in the Land War', *Irish Economic and Social History*, Vol.VIII, 1981.
9. *An-t-Oglach*, 26 October 1918.
10. *Mayo News*, 5 June 1920.
11. See C. Townshend, 'The Irish Railway Strike of 1920: Industrial Action and Civil Resistance in the Struggle for Independence', *Irish Historical Studies*, Vol.22, No.83, March 1979, pp.265-82.
12. This is based on Paul Bew, 'Sinn Fein, Agrarian Radicalism and the War of Independence', pp.217-34 in D.G. Boyce (ed.), *The Revolution in Ireland, 1879-1923,* London 1988.
13. See David Fitzpatrick's brilliant *The Politics of Irish Life 1914-1921*, Dublin 1977, pp.182-4 and also the very interesting essay by T. Varley, 'Agrarian Crime and Social Control: Sinn Fein and the Land Question in the West of Ireland' in M. Tomlinson, T. Varley and C. McCullagh (eds), *Whose Law and Order? Aspects of Crime and Social Control in Irish Society*, Belfast 1988, pp.54-75.
14. PRO CO 904/120/854/218. Return of Agrarian Outrages reported to the Inspector/General RIC, 8 June 1920. Very slightly different figures are given in SPO, Dublin Castle, Police Reports, Carton no 5, 1917-21.
15. PRO CO 904/121/55.
16. *An-t-Oglach*, 1 October 1920.

17. E. Rumpf and A.C. Hepburn, *Nationalism and Socialism in Twentieth Century Ireland*, Liverpool 1977, pp.21, 53 and 55.
18. PRO CO 904/114/317, Inspector General's Report for January 1921.
19. PRO CO 904/114/587, Inspector General's Report for February 1921.
20. PRO CO 904/114/625, Inspector General's Report for March 1921.
21. PRO CO 904/114/318. See also on this topic the valuable study by Denis Kennedy, *The Widening Gulf,* Belfast 1988.
22. Maurice O'Regan, 'When the IRA Split on Class Issues', *Labour News*, 21 August 1937. See also, for general confirmation, the very interesting survey by Dan Bradley, *Farm Labourers: Irish Struggle 1900-1976*, Belfast 1988, pp.43-72.
23. PRO CO 904/116/480, Chief Inspector's report from Mallow, 31 August 1921.
24. PRO CO 904/116/640.
25. For a recently scholarly account see M. Hopkinson, *Green Against Green: The Irish Civil War*, Dublin 1988.
26. *Mayo News*, 6 May 1922.
27. R.F. Foster, *Modern Ireland 1660-1972*, London 1988, p.515.
28. *Modern Ireland*, p.520.
29. *Leader*, 29 January 1927.
30. *Nation*, 26 March 1927.
31. *Nation*, 30 April 1927.
32. *Nation*, 25 June 1927.
33. *Mayo News*, 14 May 1927.
34. Martin Mansergh (ed.),*The Spirit of the Nation: The Speeches and Statements of Charles J. Haughey 1957-1986,* Dublin 1986, p.198.
35. Peter Mair, *The Changing Irish Party System*, Manchester 1987, p.17.
36. *Irish Times*, 6 February 1987.
37. Sean Cronin, *The McGarrity Papers*, Tralee 1972, p.141.
38. Peter Pyne, 'The Third Sinn Fein Party 1923-26', *Economic and Social Review*, Vol.1, 1969-70, pp.24-50, 229-58.
39. 'Socialism and Irish Nationalism' in James Connolly, *Socialism and Nationalism,* Desmond Ryan (ed.), Dublin 1948.
40. Brian Reynolds, *The Formation and Development of Fianna Fail 1926-1932*, DPhil, Trinity College Dublin 1976, p.138.
41. G. Walker, 'Propaganda and Conservative Nationalism During the Irish Civil War 1922-23', *Eire-Ireland*, Vol.22, 1987, p.103.
42. *Nation*, 3 March 1928.
43. For O'Brien, see the extended treatment in Paul Bew, *Conflict and Conciliation in Ireland*, Oxford 1987.
44. Quoted in *Mayo News*, 4 June 1927.
45. *Leader*, 28 May 1927.
46. *Nation*, 4 June 1927.
47. *Leader*, 29 January 1927.
48. *Leader*, 28 May 1927.
49. *Leader*, 30 July 1927.
50. *Nation*, 30 July 1927.
51. *Nation*, 6 August 1927.

52. *Nation*, 20 August, 1927.
53. On these developments see Owen Dudley Edwards, *Eamon de Valera*, Cardiff 1987, pp.110-2. See also Jeffrey Praeger, *Building Democracy in Ireland: Political Order and Cultural Integration in a Newly Independent Nation*, Cambridge 1986. This is an interesting interpretation, aspects of which are challenged in the second issue of *Irish Political Studies*.
54. *Nation*, 10 September 1929.
55. *Nation*, 8 October 1927.
56. See Deirdre McMahon's excellent *Republicans and Imperialists*, New Haven and London 1984, pp.38-41.
57. *Star*, 5 January 1929.
58. *Star*, 23 March 1929.
59. P.E.J. O'Connor, *Syndicalism in Ireland 1927-1923*, PhD, Cambridge 1984. This thesis is shortly to be published by Cork University Press.
60. Ibid., p.292.
61. *An Phoblacht*, 12 March 1932.
62. *An Phoblacht*, 31 May 1930.
63. *An Phoblacht*, 12 March 1932.
64. *An Phoblacht*, 10 August 1929.
65. See, for more detail, two pieces by Henry Patterson, 'Fianna Fail and the Working Class in the Inter War Years', *Saothar*, Vol.13, 1988, and the chapter 'Land Annuities and Left Republicanism 1926-32' in *The Politics of Illusion: Socialism and Republicanism in Modern Ireland*, forthcoming.
66. *Mayo News*, 15 June 1934.
67. See Patterson, 'Land Annuities and Left Republicanism'.
68. C.D. Greaves, *Liam Mellows*, London 1970, p.313; *An Phoblacht*, 2 April 1932.
69. *Connaught Telegraph*, 14 August 1932, for evidence that O'Donnell spoke at Newport in response to a local Fianna Fail invitation.
70. *Monkeys in the Superstructure*, Galway 1986, p.26.
71. Ibid.

2   Fianna Fail Hegemony, 1932-1966

In 1932 Fianna Fail won the general election with 44.5 per
cent of the vote and, in an atmosphere fraught with tension
and wild rumours of 'coups' and 'counter coups', took office.
The losers in the civil war were now, ten years later, the
winners of the political competition for the allegiance of the
Irish electorate. O'Donnell believed that radical republicanism had successfully provoked Cumann na nGaedheal
government and the Catholic hierarchy – which had
produced a strong anti-radical pastoral letter in late 1931 –
into exaggerated acts of repression; in consequence a
popular revulsion had been created:

> The government did not just fall, it broke its neck after losing its
> head ... The arrests steadied the country. Up till then every
> townland was aware of the 'fact' that there was a murderous
> crew in the next parish all out for the shutting of churches, the
> hanging of bishops and the utter confusion of the community.
> Mere talk of that sort can live and breed unrest in rural Ireland,
> but once it touches the earth and arrests are made, then men
> and women have the measure of things. All the arrests made
> proved that all the talk was just a mean way of attacking folk
> that were well known to their neighbours as fighters for
> freedom.[1]

It is worth noting, however, that the Free State government
lost support even amongst those who supported its anti-IRA
stand. The *Leader*, for example, supported the general
position of the Cosgrave government: 'Our view was ... that
... the Treaty position ... should be worked for all it was
worth, and oaths and republics should have been put on the
long finger.'[2] Nevertheless, from early 1930 the *Leader*
insisted that 'Hogan must go',[3] and, despite a personal liking

for Hogan's frankness, it spoke repeatedly of 'the nation-killing policy of our Minister for Grass'.[4] In the end even a Free State intellectual like Professor Tierney was forced to take refuge in the most vacuous Catholic nationalism:

> the government they heard so much attacked was a government of ordinary plain native Irishmen like themselves – Catholic Irishmen, mostly reared in the country, educated in National schools, representative of the Irish people and of no one else.[5]

Much of the rhetoric of the government was narrowly based and defensive. Even at the level of polemic only James Dillon was in any way effective: 'Fianna Fail policy is introspective. It tells you to turn in upon yourselves. It might be compared with an ingrowing toenail. It causes a vast amount of discomfort without getting very far.'[6] With only this to recommend it, it is hardly surprising that the Cosgrave government lost the 1932 election. Fianna Fail, committed to a programme of nationalist industrialisation and major land reform, was elected. But what *was* the real nature of Fianna Fail's agrarian radicalism in this period? While O'Donnell claims an initiating role for himself he does not claim that he could impose any terms on the Fianna Fail organisation when it adopted his ideas; quite the reverse, Fianna Fail's support appears to have saved the land annuities campaign from extinction. This gives us a clue: Fianna Fail was able to adapt and mould the themes of the annuities campaign with other pre-existing themes of its discourse on the land question to create a broadly radical stance on the agrarian issue – a stance, however, which even in the late 1920s and early 1930s had some notably conservative elements.

As Rumpf has pointed out, in June 1927 Fianna Fail, like the republican Sinn Fein party in 1923, drew the great weight of its support from the west of Ireland, while in Dublin it was significantly more successful in the working-class districts than in other sections of the city. But, beginning with the September election of 1927 and its decision to enter the Dail, the party seemed to do better all round. Its continued expansion in the west is less remarkable than the 50 per cent increase in support in the counties of Longford, Westmeath and Monaghan, the 90 per cent increase in Waterford and the remarkable 100 per cent increase in East Cork.[7] In short, following the election of September 1927 Fianna Fail had powerful electoral reasons to sustain its new-found relatively broad basis of social support by adopting policies which appealed not only to the poorest section of the Irish farmers concentrated in the west but also to more 'solid' members of the farming community. All major Irish agrarian movements had faced this problem since the Land League. An exclusive emphasis on the western demand – land redistribution – would have alienated stronger farmers in the south and east. In 1880, therefore, the Land League movement increasingly focused on rent reductions; in 1900 the United Irish League emphasised peasant proprietorship and in the late 1920s and early 1930s the new theme was that of agricultural de-rating which Fianna Fail adopted as policy in February 1929. As before, there were those who detected a rightward shift, but then opponents confidently exploited the rhetoric of earlier 'heroic' struggles. The resolution in favour of agricultural de-rating at the Dublin Agricultural Committee of 1931 illustrates the point. Patrick Belton, that *enfant terrible* who had initiated Collins into the Irish Republican Brotherhood, arguably initiated Fianna Fail into the Dail in 1927 and then resigned, gave a typical rebuttal to those who, like the agrarian radical *Mayo News*, felt that there 'should be no derating of holdings over £25 valuation':[9]

Mr J.P. McCabe asked, was the resolution [in favour of de-rating] to refer to tilled land only, or was the Committee urging the subsidising of men with grass land which had not been tilled for years, like the grazing farmers of County Meath. Were they going to relieve the people with the big mansions and the broad grass farms and going to make the small farmers pay for it?

Chairman (P. Belton): Isn't it the greatest boast of your life that you stood on the platform with Davitt and Parnell, and did you ever hear any distinction made between the big farmer and the small farmer for the reduction of rents?

McCabe: That is a different thing.

Chairman: The day you make that distinction both are beaten. Anyway if tillage is made pay there will be enough tillage as a result ...[10]

Belton had already set out on the path which was to lead to his election as Cummann na nGaedheal TD in 1933 and a subsequent eccentric sponsorship of ever more rightist causes; here, however, he is accurately reflecting the real history of the Irish agrarian radical tradition. But there were those who remained stubbornly unimpressed by these calls for unity. The *Connaught Telegraph* posed the question acutely:

> What affiliation have the congests of the west with the Farmers Union which is composed of the men monopolising the grazing ranches of the country? How will de-rating affect the thousands of congests in Mayo with the 14 shillings worth of land as compared with the grazing farmers having hundreds of acres, of which he tills not a sod?[11]

Naturally, this had important implications for Fianna Fail with its strong roots amongst the rural poor in the west. Sean T. Ruane made the same point at Mayo County Council:

> The de-rating proposal was in effect a suggested Grazier's Relief Bill. The propaganda engaged in ... was directed to get relief for the big graziers of Meath, who dug graves on their ranches when they heard the people of Connaught were to be sent up there. If the people of Connaught were sent to the midlands the graziers were afraid they would have to work harder.[12]

Nevertheless, Fianna Fail supported, albeit without any great show of enthusiasm, the demand for agricultural de-rating, and did so in a way which linked it to the question of the annuities. As Tom Derrig, a representative figure of the Fianna Fail leadership, explained at Mucklagh and Killeigh:

> De-rating his party supported, but it should be financed out of millions sent annually to England as Land Annuities. De-rating would be a great benefit to the big farmers but not so much to the small farmer that his party would like to bring relief.[13]

Even on the issue of land annuities, however, after the election of the Fianna Fail government in 1932 the party's leadership found it more and more necessary to distance itself from O'Donnell themes. The problem lay partly in the fact that the annuities – although they might be seen from one point of view as an iniquitous imperialist burden – constituted the only real title to land in Ireland. If they were affected, or worse still abolished, all Irish rural property relationships would be thrown into disarray. This is the point made in a Ministry of Finance memorandum for the de Valera Cabinet in the late autumn of 1932:

> With regard to the proposal to completely remit all purchase annuities, the problem of legal title on land must necessarily arise. The land is vested in the tenant under various land purchase acts and this vesting carries with it the statutory obligation to pay annuities. If it is decided to absolve the tenant from this obligation, legislation carrying a new title in land will be necessary. The introduction of such legislation will immediately raise in an acute form the problem of landless men.
>
> It will give point and purpose to the agitation which is being carried on by Peadar O'Donnell's organisation for the non-payment of annuities. It is possible that behind the ostensible object of this organisation there may be a further purpose, that of creating that insecurity of title that would justify the appropriation of all land by the state ... every labourer would be demanding five or ten acres, and the question of land distribution would certainly arise in a revolutionary form.[14]

Such arguments reinforced de Valera's intention not to erase land annuity payments altogether but simply to retain them in Dublin – for Irish governmental purposes – instead of passing them on to Great Britain. The agrarian radicals in the Cabinet fully accepted this logic. In Letterkenny, County Donegal, P.J. Ruttledge, the Minister for Lands, who had apparently been close to O'Donnell, described O'Donnell's supporters as 'people' who 'were not acting in the interests of the Irish nation'.[15] De Valera told the Fianna Fail party conference:

> I tell the farmers that the man who suggests to him not to pay his annuities is taking from him one of his greatest securities. Pay for your land and it will be yours, cease to pay for it and I think your title will be a very tenuous one.[16]

Therefore the annuities had to be paid – albeit on a lower scale as a result of the political bidding unleashed between the two main parties in 1932-33 – but Fianna Fail always insisted that the money would then be 'repaid' to the tenant farmers. Or, as the *Nation* put it, 'to help tenant farmers and to facilitate the purchase and distribution of land ... with special reference to the Gaeltacht and Congested Districts'.[17] Such proposals eventually displaced the annuities issue from the centre of Fianna Fail's agrarian radicalism and replaced it instead with the theme of land redistribution. This was anyway a much more pressing issue for the party's western supporters.

The basic assumptions of Fianna Fail's agrarian policy are clear enough. Out of 378,000 Irish agricultural holdings, some 255,000 or 67.5 per cent were valued at under £15 per annum.[18] For the radical wing of Fianna Fail the political implication was obvious: the land of Ireland should be divided and peopled by agriculturists on holdings from £20 to £50 in valuation. 'This', the *Mayo News* declared, is the most immediate and pressing reform required in Ireland.'[19] The paper went on to state that:

> The spoken and written statements of Eamon de Valera, our great chief, openly and candidly convey to the ranchers that this state of things which keeps our people in poverty must end, as a consequence they are putting forth every effort to defeat him. Those men who lock up God's storehouse have the acres, but they have not the votes.[20]

But what about the obstacles to this new dispensation? The purist *Mayo News* was surprisingly blithe on this point:

> Roughly we have agriculturists living on land valued at two million pounds. They are our only originating source of wealth, and all other classes in the community are directly or indirectly deriving their income from them. There are a small number of men occupying land of valuation of £5,500,000 whose sole

occupation is, as the late Michael Davitt put it, watching cows' tails growing. They confine the land to growing blades of grass. They are practically worthless as an originating source of wealth to the community. The loss to the community per acre of such land is the difference between the life sustaining capacity of an acre of tilled land and of an acre of grass.[21]

Apart from a heavy moralism which happily dismissed the mainstay of Ireland's exports as 'practically worthless', this passage also ignores important political realities. It was one thing to target, say, the top 8 per cent – the 33,000 rich farmers who allegedly owned half the agricultural land valuation of the Irish Free State – quite another to place the top 32.5 per cent in this category. Yet, implicitly, this article identifies Fianna Fail with two-thirds of the Irish farmers and against the third at the top. However much some western radicals might like such an approach, the Fianna Fail leadership as a whole was careful to avoid it; their adoption of agricultural de-rating was a sign of their willingness to compromise with the larger farmers.

Nevertheless, it remains a fact that in 1932 and 1933 Fianna Fail pledged itself to speed up land redistribution. The Land Act of 1933 was crucial here; under it, the land commission was empowered to expropriate, with compensation, any property which seemed suitable and distribute it among very small farmers and landless men. Even at this point there were radicals (like 'Romanus' in the *Catholic Bulletin*) who saw the 1933 Act as accepting the premisses of the Cosgrave government's 1923 Act and who doubted Fianna Fail's intentions and spoke of a 'betrayal' of the 'moral law'.[22] Frank Aiken, Minister of Defence raised hopes, however, when he declared at Drogheda in February 1933: 'If there are people who want to keep their land in grass and dismiss their workers the government will deal with them and see that their land is in the hands of those who till it.'[23] The *Drogheda Argus*, traditionally a supporter of strong farming interests, anxiously drew attention to 'these ominous statements ...statements which give the farming community food for reflection'.[24] The emergence of the Blueshirt movement was to be intimately linked with these anxieties.

In this context it is also important to recall that the election of the Fianna Fail government led to a rapid deterioration in Anglo-Irish relations. The withholding of the annuities provoked English tariff reprisals on Irish exports which, in turn, intensified protectionist policies in Ireland. Amidst much ill-founded euphoria about breaking with dependence on England, Fianna Fail was launched upon a programme of protected, 'nationally' controlled industrialisation linked with agrarian radicalism. But the substantial drop in cattle exports in the first month (August 1932) of the operation of the new policy – was to mean hard times for many farmers. Senator Joe Connolly, a radical member of the Fianna Fail leadership declared:

> If the continuance of the cattle trade with Britain meant that we were to continue to export people as well as cattle, and that we were to continue to have the best lands of the country in the hands of a grazier who employed a herd and a dog, then I would thank God that such a market was gone.[25]

Such language sent shivers down the spine of wealthy Irish farmers.

The Emergence of the Blueshirts

The Blueshirt movement originated in the anti-republican Army Comrades' Association (ACA) founded in 1931. In the aftermath of Fianna Fail's victory in 1932 the ACA opened its membership to the general public, and at its height in 1933 claimed a membership of 100,000. In March 1933 de Valera called a snap election which increased his parliamentary majority, and in the same month sacked General Eoin O'Duffy, Cumann na nGaedhael's appointee as Chief of Police. O'Duffy was a popular figure – his views on athletics were praised in the Fianna Fail press only a few days before his sacking – and he quickly made himself the focus of the ACA which he renamed the National Guard. O'Duffy intensified this fascist style when he instituted the fascist salute and the wearing of a blue shirt as uniform. The vast majority of those who rallied to the Blueshirt cause were wealthy cattle farmers and their families – especially in Limerick, Cork, Waterford and Kilkenny.

At first O'Duffy steered clear of the traditional leadership of the opposition. His rhetoric was hostile to all forms of party politics, so much so that he immediately attracted criticism from traditional conservative elements. The *Drogheda Argus*, for example, was a bitter critic of Fianna Fail's agrarian policies, yet it was also highly critical of O'Duffy's anti-parliamentarianism:

> It is rather late in the day for that, General O'Duffy is discovering that the present parliamentary system is anti-Irish ... We do not see how General O'Duffy's plan, even if it were a workable one, would be any improvement on the present parliamentary system which under PR is the fairest and most democratic in Europe ... a dictatorship is the only real alternative.[26]

In the south of Ireland, however, O'Duffy had more uncritical support. The *Cork Weekly Examiner*, for example, declared, 'No one with a particle of understanding could envisage a dictatorship being set up by General O'Duffy.'[27] When a massive Dublin demonstration – in honour of the dead pro-treatyites, Collins, Griffith and O'Higgins – was successfully banned by the government, O'Duffy cleaved to the traditional politicians: in September 1933 a new political party, subsuming the Blueshirts, was announced. Fine Gael, or the United Ireland party, as it was known at first, had O'Duffy as its leader in the country, and the Blueshirts behind it on the platforms, but on the parliamentary level it was essentially a union between the old Cumann na nGaedhael and a small centre party.[28]

At this point the *Drogheda Argus* noted that O'Duffy had placed himself at the head of an imposing array of political talent. It welcomed what it saw as a 'move towards the right, a party intended to attract the support of the more conservative elements who have held aloof from politics'.[29] In fact, the conservative elements later tired of O'Duffy's demagogic leadership and abandoned him with impunity. Yet for a year from the autumn of 1933 to the autumn of 1934 O'Duffy had seemed to be a formidable force. Why

was his challenge so easily defused? To explain the collapse
of the Blueshirt movement it is necessary first to look at the
ideology both of the Blueshirts and of their opponents. The
Blueshirts and their republican enemies both claimed to
inherit the great Irish tradition of patriotism. In particular
both sides claimed the Land League motif. O'Duffy
declared at Clonmel: 'If Parnell or Davitt were alive today
they would lash those who are driving the Irish farmers into
a destitution greater than slavery.'[30] James Dillon made the
same point at Athlone:

> I want to say publicly that I challenge de Valera to contradict
> me that the Fianna Fail Land Bill takes from the small farmers
> of the country what Parnell, Davitt or O'Brien secured for them
> in the days of the Land League. I say to them that the Fianna
> Fail government can take any farmer whether he has 200 acres
> or 10 acres and put them on the side of the road at their own
> sweet will.[31]

In July at Borrisosleigh in Tipperary Richard Mulcahy
referred to a famous Land League incident when he
declared 'the people were asserting themselves ... the spirit
of the men who drove the RIC over the bridge at Thurles
was re-echoing. Their shirt today was a simple blue shirt.'[32]
In the same month, a 'very large meeting' at Straide in Mayo
heard that politicised priest Revd Felix Burke declare:

> 'The Fianna Fail speakers, when they come to Straide, boast of
> their attachment to that great Irishman and Straideman, whose
> bones lie in yonder graveyard. They state that if Michael Davitt
> were alive today, he would be on the Fianna Fail platform. I
> don't believe he would,' said the Rev Chairman amidst cheers,
> 'his son Dr Robert Davitt, is, thank God, alive today, and he is a
> Cumann na nGaedhael representative for the constituency of
> Meath, a seat once held by his patriotic father.'[33]

M.J. Morrisroe, Cumann na nGaedhael TD for North
Mayo, argued, with scant respect for Davitt's support of
land nationalisation, that:

> Because of the efforts of Michael Davitt and those associated
> with him, the farmers were made the undisputed owners of their
> holdings, but today I regret to say that the present government
> is trying to undo all that great work.[34]

The following week Dr Robert Davitt emphasised the point
by addressing a large rally at Kiltimagh, County Mayo,
attended by hundreds of Blueshirts gathered under a banner
headed 'Ireland or Russia'. The pro-government *Mayo
News* gasped in disbelief, 'They actually claimed they were
continuing the struggle for which Davitt gave his life ... was
Mr Fitzgerald-Kenney [a former Free State minister,
wealthy farmer and target of agrarian radicals] ever on a
platform in Mayo with Michael Davitt?'[35] But with casual
effrontery O'Duffy himself claimed the Davitt tradition: he

> paid a tribute to the Parliamentary leaders of the past, Parnell,
> Redmond, Davitt, Dillon, who won the land for the people and
> said that the Land Bill of the present Government was directed
> against the tenants.[36]

The Blueshirts argued that the traditions and practices of
agrarian radicalism – which may have been permissible
under the Union – were no longer acceptable in an
independent state. As M.R. Heffernan TD explained:

> The old tradition which proved effective in the past was
> misrepresented to delude them into thinking they were doing
> laudable actions when taking part in these night raids ... actions
> which were morally justifiable when we had only minority
> representation in an alien and hostile parliament are no longer
> justifiable when we have a freely elected parliament ...
> Agitations which had simply for their ends the running into of
> all holdings above a certain size should not be encouraged. Such
> a policy was simply disguised Bolshevism.[37]

There can be no doubt that the republican side in the 1930s
was more in tune with Land League rhetoric. As Joseph Lee
has argued, the appeal to 'spurious historic rights' was a
defining and original feature of the Land League
movement.[38] Blueshirt supporters were openly con-
temptuous of these alleged historical rights; they dismissed
the Land League notion of a Gaelic Garden of Eden. The
pro-Blueshirt *Cork Weekly Examiner* was provoked in 1933
by 'talk of the people's land' to ask 'when did the people
ever own land in Ireland? ... the [Gaelic] tribesman paid
rent and heavy rent to his chief.'[39] It is arguable, however,

that the Blueshirts were more in tune with the inner logic –
as opposed to radical froth – of the Land League revolution
which had consolidated the power of a rural bourgeoisie in
Ireland.

One pertinent symbol: in 1880 one of the most celebrated
Irish agrarian conflicts had been directed against Captain
Boycott. By 1900 Boycott's farm was in the possession of
Bernard Daly, one of the largest graziers in Ireland. Bernard
Daly, the brother of prominent nationalist activist and
newspaper editor James Daly, who has been described as
the key figure in the early Land League agitation, was
obviously one of the principal victors of the land war: by
1900 he held some fourteen farms in Mayo, Kings County
(Offaly) and Westmeath! By 1934 the same Daly interest
was still prominent in Mayo politics in the form of Patrick
Daly who took the chair at Blueshirt meetings.[40] From the
boycott to Blueshirtism, the Irish agrarian revolution
reached its unromantic terminus.

It follows from this rhetoric that the Blueshirt ranks were
dominated by richer farmers and their sons, who had to bear
the full burden of de Valera's tariff war with England;
Blueshirt agitation was especially obvious in the south,
where, as a form of retaliation, rates payments were
withheld from the government on a large scale in 1934. It is
clear that Blueshirts relied on this group for much of their
dynamism, while many areas of traditional Cumann na
nGaedhael support remained relatively quiet.[41] In Donegal,
for example, O'Duffy commented bitterly on the lack of
Blueshirt support whilst there was still a strong feeling in
favour of Cosgrave, the former leader.[42]

Ernest Blythe, a former Free State minister who
embraced the Blueshirts more enthusiastically than most,
related the strength of Blueshirtism to the degree of pressure
from militant radical republicanism in a given area. While
this is by no means an infallible guide – O'Donnell had
devoted much effort to Donegal where the Blueshirts
remained weak – it is clear that large groupings of Blueshirts
and republicans did tend to spark off each other's activism.
Blythe, employing the pen name 'Onlooker', noted in
Blueshirt for August 1933:

The National Guard is spread very unevenly over the country. It is strong in Cork, in Tipperary, in Limerick and in Mayo, and moderately strong elsewhere but weak in the big cities and in one or two of the Eastern counties practically non-existent. It is an extraordinary and almost inexplicable thing that in Wicklow, Louth and Kildare taken together there are not more volunteers than might be found in one village in County Cork. Possibly one of the reasons is that the IRA and its bullying are not so generally familiar as they are elsewhere.

Cork, one of the counties listed as 'strong', had seen a major affray at a Mallow electoral meeting[44] and serious fighting following an ambush in Midleton.[45] In Mayo – another 'strong' county – there had been an extraordinary incident at Straide: the home of a pro-Free State parish priest Father Felix Burke was attacked with stones by what Father Burke chose to stigmatise as 'a small but hostile crowd of Bolsheviks' as opposed to 'respectable' Fianna Fail supporters.[46] This had been followed by a serious confrontation at Hangman's Bridge in June between ACA and republican supporters. Limerick had seen the critical Kilmallock meeting when ACA supporters inspired by a defiant Mulcahy and their enemies had the 'most serious' fight of 1932;[47] following a further political meeting addressed by de Valera in September 1933 some 33 were hospitalised in the city of Limerick itself. Tipperary also had seen serious disputes which – according to Seamus Bourke, Cumann na nGaedhael TD – underlined the necessity of movements such as the ACA to protect free speech.[48] On the other hand, tensions in the weaker republican areas seem to have found milder forms of expression. In Louth a fight between girls supporting rival candidates was the major outbreak of lawlessness to flow from the 1933 general election campaign.[49] Peadar O'Donnell openly admitted that his working farmers committees were relatively weak in Louth.[50] In Kildare Justice Reddin seemed to find the electoral disturbances more a matter of humorous comment than rigorous condemnation, 'I had hoped that the stage Irishman was dead but apparently he can occasionally be resurrected in Kildare,'[51] while in Wicklow, the local newspaper the *Wicklow People* reported little in the way of

violence.[52] Again, Peadar O'Donnell acknowledged that,
along with Louth, Wicklow was one of his four weakest
counties – the other two were Cavan and Monaghan.

These tendencies do on the whole imply that the Blueshirt
movement was essentially reactive. As Blythe admitted, it
lacked urban support and it lacked rural support outside
certain key counties in the south and west. Some of its rural
support was clearly related to clashes with volatile Fianna
Fail people or supporters of the wider republican
movement. These clashes merely allowed the government to
adopt a statesmanlike stance, more or less even handedly
dispensing 'justice'. In 1934, the military tribunal established
to deal with such disturbances convicted 349 Blueshirts and
102 IRA men. The republican movement, naturally enough,
bitterly denounced any action against it as a betrayal, but
there is no sign that this decreased the government's popular
appeal. Unlike other authoritarian mass movements of the
1930s, the Blueshirts' leadership failed to create a
broad-based coalition of malcontents: the movement was
too dependent on the key social group – wealthy farmers and
their sons. If doubts and confusion could be sown in this
category, it would soon be defeated.

The Defeat of Blueshirtism

Fianna Fail's stragegy towards those sections of the rural
bourgeoisie which had sympathy for the Blueshirt
movement was admirably complex. It included threats of
apparently radical change, which further unnerved those
strong farmers who wondered where the 'lawlessness' of the
Blueshirts might lead them if it went unchecked. In
particular, wealthy farmers may have feared the implications
for property rights. Violent opposition to rates collection,
annuity payments and cattle seizures may have been
permissible before independence but it worried many after it
– Michael Hefferman's remarks on this point cut both ways.
The government also offered material concessions to those
hit by the fall in exports. The money saved by retaining the
annuities was used in part to give rate relief to strong
farmers in reduced circumstances. It was an elegant

combination of the carrot-and-stick principle.

While the actual progress of Fianna Fail on the question of land reform was gradual there was no indication of any willingness on the part of the government to play down its rhetoric on this point in the spring and early summer of 1934. On 15 April de Valera addressed a large gathering at Clonmel. He struck the appropriate traditional note by referring to the views of nineteenth-century novelist and Fenian leader Charles Kickham, 'Kickham would tell them it was the big grazing farmers who were the ruination of that town.' According to the report:

Pointing out that the government policy was to cut up the big grass farms, he said that there was no county in which there were a greater number of ranches to cut up than Tipperary. There were, some time ago, no fewer than 550 farms of over £300 valuation in this county. During the past month in which the Land Act had been operative they had divided in that county between 4,000 and 5,000 acres, and by the end of the month there would be 6,000 acres divided, or at the rate of 1,000 acres per week. They had not a staff sufficiently large to deal with the whole country at the same rate at once, but they were going to tackle those counties which needed division most, and where most was to be gained by it, and they were going to work intensively in these areas.

The *Mayo News* was 'very pleased' by this pronouncement but noted sadly, 'It is a matter for regret that in great part the halving of annuities and grants for relief of local rates have gone to graziers and have helped to maintain them in the evil grazing system.'[54] The Minister for Defence, Frank Aiken, kept up the pressure in Dundalk at the end of May:

Drastic action will have to be taken against those who are cornering the land, using it to produce cattle that they cannot sell, and who won't use it to produce the wheat that the Irish people require. If the bullock has to be put away to make room for men, we will put the bullock away. If the farmers who have the land at the moment won't use it, we will see that farmers are put in who will use it.[55]

O'Duffy felt sure that this rhetoric of Fianna Fail would give him a major electoral victory in the July 1934 local government elections and made ever more enthusiastic predictions of a major reverse for Fianna Fail. As O'Duffy argued:

There are farmers in Westmeath who voted Fianna Fail at the last election; there are farmers in Westmeath who came to Mullingar to cheer President de Valera a month ago. Are these farmers still satisfied? Were they pleased with President de Valera's speech? Will they vote for Fianna Fail candidates next Tuesday week? If they do they are not only letting their neighbouring counties down, they are not only making paupers of their neighbours, but they are false to themselves and to those depending on them.[56]

But the results did not justify O'Duffy's optimism. The Fianna Fail-Labour alliance controlled fifteen councils while Fine Gael ran only seven. Fianna Fail, still the majority party, took 782 seats, Fine Gael 596, Labour 185 and others 371. It was not an unimpressive Fine Gael performance in itself, as de Valera undoubtedly realised. It was O'Duffy's exaggerated rhetoric which made it look so poor and, in turn made a solid Fianna Fail performance look spectacular. Some Fine Gael sources attempted to minimise the defeat. The *Westmeath Independent* spoke of 'surprise – even astonishment' produced by Fine Gael's allegedly good performance in urban areas.[57] The *Nationalist* of Clonmel insisted:

There is no landslide to the government as Fianna Fail hoped, while Fine Gael have consolidated their position and laid the foundations for further successes. It is a notable fact that the President on realising the results at once broadcast a message expressing the government's anxiety about settling the dispute with England and promoting friendly relations.[58]

But only a few weeks before the same paper had spoken of the 'rising tide of public opinion' against the government of the people at large'.[59] The *Leinster Leader* was more frank, speaking of 'sensational returns', it noted:

In a country [Kildare] noted for its political conservatism the public were quite unprepared for a result which completely transferred the control of the public bodies to the combined forces of Fianna Fail and Labour.[60]

The *Mayo News* summed it up with some satisfaction, 'The county council and municipal elections in the Irish Free State have pricked and deflated the Blueshirt balloon.'[61]

O'Duffy immediately offered an arresting interpretation of his defeat. He had been deserted, he claimed in a Mayo speech, by a section of the strong farming community. In a further bitter comment, he declared in a letter to the *Irish Press*:

In a forecast of the result of the Local Elections, Mr Davin, General Secretary of Fianna Fail is reported to have said: 'The most spectacular gain for Fianna Fail will be in the ranching counties' and later Mr Norton referred to the striking gain in the ranching county of Kildare. The counties of Meath, Kildare and Wicklow are named. Cumann na nGaedhael only got one seat in each of these counties at the last General Election and the Farmers' party got none. It is obvious then that there were farmers in these counties who supported neither Cumann na nGaedhael nor the Farmers' Party then. They voted then for a continuance of the economic war and the bad markets.

After a further 18 months' experience of Fianna Fail administration they evidently have not recanted and are, in my opinion, more responsible for the destruction of agriculture, our main industry, than the Fianna Fail leaders themselves are. As leader of the Party which has made agriculture a major concern, I consider that in the interests of the farming community as a whole, responsibility should be placed where it lies.

You state that UIP [Fine Gael] farmers are 'bewildered' at my statement. The UIP farmers know where I stand in their regard: they know how the Fianna Fail policy has crippled them, and if they are bewildered it is because after two and a half years of hardship and distress they still see some farmers in the State who would allow themselves to be fooled even a third time by Fianna Fail.[62]

Peadar O'Donnell's *An Phoblacht* was inclined to support O'Duffy's analysis. *An Phoblacht* was in no doubt as to the meaning of the result which it headlined as a 'Blueshirt fiasco'. It proclaimed:

> The result of the Twenty Six County Local Government elections have proved conclusively that the Imperialist-Fascist organisation commands the support of only a minority of the people and even of those *who are largely composed of the people with a stake in the country.*[63]

Later, in the same article, *An Phoblacht* referred critically to the government's alleged tendency to placate opponents,

> This government's method of waging war was to make concessions and surrenders to the active allies of the enemy. By shouting around Merrion Street the ranchers got bounties on cattle exports, while the price paid to the small farmer was depressed to an insignificant figure.

Typically, the possibility that the defeat of the Blueshirts may have been related to the conciliatory element in the government's tactics – though implicit in the article – is never explicitly discussed. Instead, *An Phoblacht* argued that Fianna Fail deliberately magnified the Blueshirt menace in order to generate an uncritical popular unity behind the government.

There were others who were less inclined to agree with O'Duffy. The Labour leader, William Norton, disputed the Blueshirt leader's analysis:

> The fact was that his army was discouraged by the result of the General's bad tactics and vacillating policy. Whatever might be said about the ranchers of Kildare, it was unfair to them to deny that they supported General O'Duffy to the last. The ranchers had stood by General O'Duffy because they knew his policy was to continue the agricultural economy which made the bullock the lord of the land and drove the people to the emigration ship and the workhouse.[64]

Other radicals agreed with Norton and disputed the *An Phoblacht* view. The Communist Party of Ireland argued in the *Irish Workers' Voice* that the big business and ranching interests had declared themselves as Blueshirt and thus been

defeated by a popular mobilisation.[65] Conservatives too
were surprised by O'Duffy's analysis. Gerard Sweetman, a
key figure in O'Duffy's youth wing, declared: 'They had
seen how foolish and contradictory were the General's
references to the ranchers of Kildare whom he described as
touring the country with Fianna Fail posters.'[66]

M.J. Kennedy, a Fianna Fail TD for Longford-
Westmeath, announced an intention to attend an O'Duffy
meeting at Castlepollard, near Mullingar – 'he [O'Duffy]
will be surrounded by ranchers on that day' – and to force
O'Duffy to clarify his views on the grazing question.[67] In the
event, discretion once again triumphed over valour, and
Kennedy did not attend. Nevertheless, O'Duffy was forced
to offer, at least, bland phrases of reassurance. He declared:

> There are very few ranchers but the few there are, are entitled
> to justice and fair play. They are entitled to as much but not
> more consideration than any other decent citizen. I do not agree
> that the man who went in for stock raising where lands were
> naturally best suited for stock raising is an enemy of the
> country. Such men helped to keep our export and trade balance
> solvent.

But O'Duffy did admit, 'I would be opposed to a few men
holding huge tracts of land and using it in an unproductive
manner.'[68]

As conservative opinion mobilised against O'Duffy his
remarks were presented as further evidence of unreliability.
Yet it seems likely that O'Duffy had made a reasonable (if
typically overstated) point: Fianna Fail had managed to
induce a degree of uncertainty within the wealthy farming
class. The majority undeniably had remained electorally
loyal to O'Duffy but without wholehearted support from this
group, the cause of Blueshirtism was doomed. The
government's commitment to land reform had kept the
support of the other rural social classes, whilst its overall
strategy had managed to create a degree of uncertainty
within the strong farming element.

These doubts focused increasingly on O'Duffy's advocacy
of extra-legal action arising out of resistance to seizures
brought about by non-payment of rates. There seems to be

little doubt that a political element entered into the
non-payment of rates. At the beginning of 1934, for
example, South Tipperary had 78 per cent of its rates bill
outstanding – and this was an area where previously there
had been an excellent record of rapid payment. On the other
hand, South Mayo had a mere 36 per cent outstanding.[69]
Eamon de Valera was keen to exploit the issue:

> You know of the no-rates campaign in this and neighbouring
> counties. These are counties that are, from the point of view of
> the material wealth of the land, the richest in the whole country.
> Those who are responsible for trying to disorganise the local
> services by non-payment of rates are not the poor farmers of
> Mayo, Leitrim, and Donegal. They are relatively big farmers.
> They have been living literally on the fat of the rich lands. They
> had only to look out of their windows and see their cattle getting
> fat. Because those days hold for them no longer they want to
> disorganise the community as a whole. We tell them they will
> not be let do it. In Mayo, Leitrim, Donegal and Cavan 90 per
> cent of the rates are paid. It is rich counties like Cork,
> Tipperary, Limerick, Waterford and Kilkenny where we have
> arrears of the land annuities also. Some of the people who
> refuse to pay have fair, good balances in the bank. Wherever
> there is proved inability to pay the people are not being unduly
> pressed, but in these counties we believe that the non-payment
> of rates is the result of a deliberate campaign by those who want
> to stop the onward march of the nation, but they won't be let.
> I'm perfectly sure this is going to have the backing of the plain
> people of Tipperary (cheers).[70]

This was a bitterly disputed point. One Fine Gael TD, N.
Wall, claimed at least 75 per cent of the farmers were
genuinely unable to pay.[71] Another, R. Curran, declared,
'There is no such thing as a no-rate campaign in County
Tipperary. He had advocated, and he did so now, that those
who were in a position to pay their rates should do so.'[72]
Implicit in these comments is a fear of unnecessarily
provocative action by strong farmers. In the period after the
local government election, O'Duffy appears to have ridden
roughshod over such fears although they were, of course,
validated by the result of that contest. In a desperate
attempt to radicalise his support O'Duffy became even more

fervently committed to direct action. On 1 September 1934
An Phoblacht recorded that there was a pattern to various
agrarian incidents in Munster – threshing engines were
burnt, as were hay ricks and barns, and there were also cases
of violence against individuals.

> Our correspondents in the southern towns are reporting the
> incidents of what is now definitely exposed as a campaign
> against (1) Blueshirts refusing to dismiss non-Blueshirt labour,
> (2) Republican farmers, (3) Blueshirt farmers refusing to pay a
> levy to the newly formed Seizure Defence Fund which entitle
> them to the services of the Blueshirt movement to resist
> seizures. This is part of the campaign which Mr O'Duffy has
> designed and given rise to the split with the more conservative
> Cosgrave forces.

This was the terminal crisis of O'Duffy's leadership. Some
vacillated – as loyalist Patrick Belton repeatedly pointed
out, there were those who would advocate direct action one
day and pure legality the next. But enough of O'Duffy's
traditional conservative support turned against him to bring
about his resignation before the end of September 1934. The
conservative elements were particularly concerned by
O'Duffy's desperate last-minute radicalising themes –
non-payment of annuities and rents on labourers' cottages,
both proposals which smacked of radical republicanism.

One astute 'Irish Affairs' special correspondent offered a
perceptive account of the reasons for the General's fall:

> His critics complained that he was not tactful; others of the
> party disapproved of his proposals about the 'Corporate State',
> as not being practical politics and as giving an excuse to those
> who said that Fine Gael was opposed to democratic rule. All the
> time, too, there was a small but influential number who never
> quite fell in with the Blueshirt movement as savouring of
> Continental methods.

This writer, however, was sure that the principal difficulty
with General O'Duffy's leadership lay elsewhere:

> The chief criticism of late has come from those whose point was
> that a legal, constitutional opposition, however sympathetic to
> those who could not pay their annuities, should never be

committed to a policy of refusing to pay. Needless to say, on all these points, General O'Duffy had his ardent champions within the party, whether a majority or minority one cannot say.[73]

Were the Blueshirts Fascist?

There is, of course, no doubt that O'Duffy personally was a fascist, albeit one capable of striking a very traditional, rural conservative note that was almost bucolic in its simplicity.

> Our aim is to send the de Valera government to oblivion for all time and we want our time to deliver our policy. (Applause) It will be a great time again when farmers can go to the fairs and come home again whistling and singing – and having a little drink if you like. (Applause) We intend bringing back that time. (Applause) I deny that I am a Dictator'.[74]

O'Duffy was always careful of the need to advocate a specifically Irish path of development, claiming, '[he] did not want a Hitler campaign in this country, [he] wanted an Irish campaign.' Accusations of fascism at the time were bitterly denied. The *Cork Weekly Examiner* declared angrily:

> Mr Norton has no more right to call the leaders of the UIP party fascists than they would have to call respectable trades unionists Communists. We are sure that Mr Norton is not a Communist just as we are sure that General O'Duffy has no intention of proceeding along the lines of modern dictatorship as exemplified on the continent.[75]

But O'Duffy's acceptance of the need for a specifically Irish path was perfectly compatible with explicit support for the systems of both Hitler and Mussolini. In a riposte to the Labour leader, O'Duffy outlined his policy with reference to the corporate system:

> If Mr Norton could name one labour man living in Italy or Germany who would vote against Mussolini or Hitler he would retire from public life. When in Germany recently he noticed that every workman wore Hitler's badge. Under Hitler and Mussolini those workmen were getting their daily wage, and were not depending on doles. No power in the world could

induce the people of Germany or Italy to change. Hitler had done more for Germany than any other leader in the world had done for his country.[76]

Most observers tend to see the Blueshirt epoch as essentially a repetition of the civil war. Maurice Manning's *The Blueshirts* largely adopts this analysis, while F.S.L. Lyons has written that 1933-34 represented not the 'death-agonies of a Gaelic Weimar' but rather 'the nemesis of civil war'.[77] Rumpf and Hepburn claim: 'The emotions and bitterness were not really those of Europe in the 1930s but of Ireland in 1922.'[78] In a distillation of the conventional wisdom, G.C. Webber has recently written:

> In fact, it is difficult to know whether or not the Blueshirts should be classified as fascist. For the movement existed independently of traditional parliamentary parties only briefly, most of its leaders vigorously denied any association with continental fascism, and the emotions that the Blueshirts aroused did not really belong to Europe of the 1930s but to Ireland of 1922.[79]

While it would be absurd to deny the 'carry-over' effect of the civil war, these comments ignore the impact of fascist rhetoric within Ireland. In this context it is worth looking at some of the key texts of political Blueshirtism in its moment of crisis and collapse.

At the point when O'Duffy (in September 1934) was to be surprised by the resignation of Professor J. Hogan, party vice-president, from the UIP, Hogan criticised O'Duffy's hysterical and destructive style of leadership, but he also noted O'Duffy's support for the policy of 'universal non-payment of annuities and rents on labourers' cottages' and his demagogic utterances on Ulster. Hogan later expanded on the Ulster question;

> I am against any sort of attempt to force a solution on Ulster. I do not believe it is feasible even if it were desirable, which I don't believe either. General O'Duffy must have been perfectly aware that the Blueshirts were always a banned organisation in Ulster when he declared the other day that he was about to organise them there. This was in the nature of an act of war

against the present Ulster government and therefore was entirely counter to the policy of persuasion and reason which I believe to be the only policy possible of success.

I fail to see where such a policy as that advocated by General O'Duffy is different from that of the Irish Republican Army, which is also a policy of conquest. So far as I can see I am following in the footsteps of Kevin O'Higgins. He did not rush up to the Border and shake his fist at Lord Craigavon. He went and had a talk with Lord Craigavon and more good came out of that talk than out of idle and empty threats.[80]

O'Duffy's change of position on Ulster was a typical example of his incoherent style. Sometimes, he chose to be aggressively anti-unionist ('give them lead' was his famous phrase of 1922) and, at other times, the last word in pragmatic moderation. Once he drily pointed up Fianna Fail's ambiguities:

The longer the present government remains in office the more perplexing becomes their policy. It is only a few weeks ago since the Minister for Local Government – the great Sean T. O'Kelly – made the people of Phibsboro' shiver and tremble when he prophesied a bloody march on the boundary. Of course Sean T didn't mean it. An IRA leader said on Easter Sunday not to heed Sean T's bluff, that he was only stunting. Don't you think the IRA leader diagnosed Sean T's disease correctly? (Hear hear.) And on last Sunday the Minister for Education, speaking at Rathmore, on the Cork-Kerry border, told the people that those who imagined they could overcome the might of Britain and fight their way to a Republic against the hostile people of Ulster were suffering from the effects of something more potent than light beer. (Hear hear). Here we have two members of the Cabinet with diametrically opposite views on a major question of national policy.[81]

It is not difficult to see why Hogan should have been infuriated by O'Duffy's return to nationalist militancy on the issue. It clearly implied a profound absence of consistency or logic on the General's part, but it is important to note that Hogan's resignation was not made on the basis of anti-fascism. He stated explicitly, '*I am greatly in favour of the Fascist state*. While believing in the corporate state I am against the perversion of the corporate idea to serve the

Hitlerite ideal.'[82] Professor Michael Tierney, one of O'Duffy's key sponsors, similarly defended Mussolini's state in explicit terms.[83] Maurice Manning has written that O'Duffy was not a man of ideas and seemed unable to distinguish easily between the Catholic corporatism of Hogan and Tierney and some of the blatantly fascist regimes of contemporary Europe. In fact, Hogan's resignation statement and Tierney's polemics would suggest that – provided Mussolini, as well as Hitler, is included in the list of 'blatantly fascist regimes' – O'Duffy's inability to make such a distinction was hardly surprising. The truth is that the boundary between papal corporatism and admiration for Italian fascism was freely traversed at the time and not just by O'Duffy.

In recent years there has been a tendency to sanitise the Blueshirts. In the 1986 edition of his book on the subject, Maurice Manning has argued that 'while the Blueshirt movement had the appearance of fascism, it lacked all the elements of hard core fascism'. Such an argument, it is now clear, underestimates the admiration for fascist forms within Ireland's political class. The Blueshirts lacked the raw material for a successful fascist mass base, but they did not lack anything in establishment antipathy towards liberal democratic institutions. Revealingly, the main pro-Free State organ, the *Star*, sneered at the idea that de Valera could be a Mussolini, not because it would be a bad thing but because de Valera lacked the 'spiritual resources'.[84]

'Onlooker' in his first article in the *Blueshirt* appeared to validate this sanitisation when he denied that the Blueshirts were fascist and (less convincingly) anti-semitic, 'it is definitely in line with all that is characteristic in the Irish political tradition, and anything that may have been borrowed from abroad is accidental or subsidiary'.[85] It is worth asking (as Blythe did not) what is most 'characteristic' in the 'Irish political tradition'? Blythe merely gestured to the key historical experiences of modern Irish nationalism: the Land League, the United Irish League and Sinn Fein. Yet the predominant characteristic of all three is the way in which the rural bourgeoisie retained its dominance against challenges from the rural have-nots; normally, the rich

farmers were able to colonise key institutions of the nascent
nationalist 'state'. In 1932-33, with Fianna Fail in power and
the declaration of the economic war, it seemed for the first
time that the grip which the rural bourgeoisie had held since
1880 on the priorities of Irish nationalism was about to be
broken. This was the historic context – as much as the civil
war at least. It appeared that the nationalist leadership was
going to go beyond the traditional pieties about the need for
more tillage and breaking up the ranches; above all, it
seemed that the wealthy farmers were going to lose their
direct access to the British market, which had been the
foundation of their prosperity. The Blueshirt movement
represents their revolt against this possibility, ironically
employing many of the methods – resistance to cattle
seizures, etc. – which had previously been employed as part
of a wider nationalist strategy in the Land League struggle.
Many of the wealthy farmers were prepared to break with
parliamentary democracy and legality – to adopt, in short,
fascist styles and rhetoric to safeguard their economic
position. But it was this very narrow social basis which helps
to explain Blueshirtism's failure. O'Duffy, for all his
demagogic faults, recognised the need to forge a wider
coalition of malcontents. He blamed the old Free State
leaders:

> Fine Gael got the reputation of being a party that concerned
> itself more with the 'big men' than with the workers, or the
> small farmers or the poor ... Fine Gael, you may say, accepted
> the corporate thinking of the Blueshirts. Fine Gael, I say, did
> not ... [they] nominally, took it up at the time of the merger ... I
> believe we would have far more progress with the corporate
> system were it not for the fact that Labour suspected it once the
> Cumann na nGaedheal chiefs took it up.[86]

But in truth his problem was the nature of the Blueshirt
movement itself and its largely exclusive social basis. This is
revealed in Cosgrave's preference for the introduction of
restrictive educational qualifications for Dail members – a
very favourite theme also of W.B. Yeats. In a revealing

exchange in *United Ireland* in December 1933 Seamus T. Bourke argued:

> Perhaps modern democracy has served its purpose. But if we are to alter it here let it be done consciously and above board by the adoption of some form of minority rule through fascism in restriction of the franchise, and not in a furtive underhand way which gives no way out to a restive and class-conscious proletariat save the road to Bolshevism.[87]

But as one of Burke's critics, C.H. MacEoin, immediately pointed out, to be successful Irish fascism had to conceive of itself as a form of majority rule, and this was no easy task. In the view of a *New York Times* reporter, O'Duffy 'carried the Blueshirt organisation into the peasantry, Mr de Valera's own country, and planted it there whenever the economic war with England was engendering poverty and despair'.[88] But this was precisely O'Duffy's most crucial area of failure; he was never really able to penetrate 'Mr de Valera's own country', the small and middling farmers of Ireland.

The personal commitment to fascism of the Blueshirt leadership is not in doubt. In west Limerick Eoin O'Duffy declared: 'What the Blackshirts did for Italy, and the Brownshirts did for Germany, the Blueshirts will do for Ireland.'[89] But the raw materials for a successful fascist challenge for state power did not exist.

Anti-Blueshirt Ideology

But what was the nature of the ideology employed by grass roots Fianna Fail and socialist republican forces to oppose the Blueshirt movement? Angela Clifford has written polemically:

> It is best when dealing with the political history of the thirties to treat accusations of fascism between the major parties as meaningless debating points. There were strong elements of corporatist ideology in each party.[90]

The first point to make is that Labour and those often urban elements of Fianna Fail influenced by social democratic ideology *had* a clinical grasp of the nature of fascism: their accusations cannot be dismissed as 'meaningless debating points'. Nevertheless, it is also true that the forces of rural republicanism combined a strong hostility to the Blueshirts with a sneaking sympathy for fascism. To explain how this worked it is necessary first of all to outline the ideology of Irish agrarian radicalism as it existed in the 1930s. Above all, it was obsessed with land. A western priest calling for land redistribution insisted: 'There is no wealth like the land. Other things are in comparison very artificial.'[91] It opposed the Free State regime because it had sanctified the power of a rural bourgeoisie based on grazing interests which now engaged in mimicry of the unionist gentry. As the same clerical writer wrote:

> The very minute anyone becomes 'respectable', that minute he shuts his eyes on his own class and tribe and apes the English or the relics of the oppressors that are still left, and talks high sport, fishing, shooting, pictures, etc. The Land Question? Oh, that is the politics of Communism.

Rural radicalism was presented as the spontaneous ideology of the smallholder. There were, of course, lamentable cases of false consciousness.

> The man working five or six acres of cutaway bog in Connaught is also a farmer, or thinks he is, and thinking he is defending his own class, he sometimes joins the graziers in the struggle for the 'farmers'.[92]

As a sympathetic Mayo priest put it, 'Now, if the young fellows that have nothing, but are organised into this [Blueshirt] sham, only knew that it is to protect and preserve the graziers.'[93] This Jeffersonian vision of a rural smallholding democracy of republican citizens also entailed opposition to the growth of the state bureaucracy. In criticism of the Cosgrave regime it was said:

> They stereotyped graziers in the ownership of lands from which, under the evil landlord system, our people had been ruthlessly evicted, and perhaps even worse still, for the creation of jobs, they inflicted on our poor twenty six counties, of less than three

millions of people, all the expensive machinery for the government of an Empire.[94]

Opposition to the Blueshirts, therefore, was based on a sharp hostility directed against the pretensions of the grazing stratum, rather than a principled opposition to fascist or corporatist ideology as such. This was often linked to a popular religious theme:

> It is all very sad, and sadder still when it is recalled that the movement led by General O'Duffy and composed of so many prominent Catholics, has for its chief ally the Protestant Masonic element in our midst.[95]

The *Catholic Bulletin*, which supported the government in its struggle against O'Duffy, none the less denounced 'individualistic capitalism' as the enemy to christianity, small nations and the proletariat – the first of its seven deadly sins being its identification with Judaeo-Masonry. It called for a 'partial system of vocational representation' but, it insisted, 'not the fascist system'.[96] Others on the republican side were less scrupulous. The *Mayo News*, for example, believed it was perfectly legitimate to cite Mussolini, ('Every inch of Italian soil that will bear an ear of corn in future will be brought under cultivation') *against* the Blueshirts.[97] As late as February 1937 the *Mayo News* carried a leader commending Hitler's views on economics.[98] 'Romanus' in the *Catholic Bulletin* put it this way: 'German fascism has regimented population for the exaltation of Germany. Irish Nazism would regiment population for the exaltation of the Beast, in a United Ireland of the Beast.'[99] These formulations throw light on the nature of rural opposition to the Blueshirt movement. It was based above all on hostility to the alleged claims of the graziers and their allies – 'a Masonic camarilla of adventurers and ranchers'. O'Duffy's vision of the corporate state was decoded by his Irish critics in a way which revealed its hidden inner secret:

> Consequently the Corporate State will remedy these defects with the right to vote reserved only for those of proven non-communistic stock, something after the following manner:-

Three votes each for the distinction of having acquired a ranch through the evictions and deaths by starvation on the roadside of the rightful owners and their families. Same privileges for spies, pimps and hangers-on of the British Garrison, Castle hacks, pot-boys, execution squads and rent-office touts. Two votes each:- Bullock men, gaban generals who were under the bed in the Black and Tan war, Cosgravite slipper-lickers and various other Imperialists of lesser caste. No vote and the chain gangs for the following undesirables:- The remnant of those who fought the Land War, took part in the fight for freedom and were imprisoned from 1916 to 1928, and all the descendants of those who fought the British in every generation. The latter, however, will be given the benefit of occasional bedtime stories by the great, high and mighty starting-handle of the Corporate State – I Myself – O'Duffy, who being a master of the art of contradiction, should have no difficulty in switching back a few hundred years and resurrecting a seventeenth century audience, so essential to the success of the scheme.[100]

But it was this agrarian radicalism which was destined to be disappointed. As early as the Anglo-Irish coal-cattle pact of 1935 Fianna Fail intimated that it too was prepared to meet some of the graziers' concerns. Senator Joe Connolly, Minister for Lands, insisted in the west:

The land policy of the government was in no way altered by the agreement. It meant simply that we have a large surplus of cattle for disposal and that we must trade that surplus on the best terms available.[101]

None the less, this was to be a turning point. There were bitter ironic criticisms from *An Phoblacht* ('Another damned good bargain')[102], and the *Mayo News*, whilst avowing that the government was 'struggling very courageously' to deal with a difficult situation, noted sadly that

many other measures have been passed to help the grazing exporters of fat cattle by subsidies which we think are bolstering up the evil system against which Irishmen have so long inveighed.[103]

By August 1935 the same Fianna Fail *Mayo News* was lamenting

> They [the government] have toyed with the great and all important question of replacing agriculturists on the land and, as a result, we are yet far distant from that real foundation of independence – self-sufficiency.[104]

The author of this editorial was P.J. Doris, former friend of Michael Davitt with a proud 'national' record as a Fenian, Land Leaguer, Sinn Feiner and supporter of Fianna Fail. As the 'economic war' with Britain was wound down the government was clearly open to the charge that it was losing its radical nationalist tinge. The project of the 1937 constitution simultaneously allowed the government to maintain its new appeal to the centre with an attempt to massage sentiment in traditional heartlands. As Leon O Broin puts it in his superb autobiography *Just Like Yesterday*, de Valera was 'trying to placate left-wing republicans with national phrases and pious people with expressly Catholic bits'.[105]

The constitution, therefore, stresses the unifying elements of Irish political culture which were patriarchal Catholicism, nationalism (the claim on the North) and, hardly surprisingly in a nation of peasant proprietors, property rights and private enterprise. As Angela Clifford demonstrates in her recent book on the subject, there were very few discordant voices when the 'Constitution of a Catholic state' (Sean MacEntee) was being debated. She notes:

> The striking feature of the Dail discussion on divorce was that the legislators were indulging in the favourite Catholic practice of discussing the esoteric points of Church law, rather than examining the social results that would follow from the constitutional provisions.[106]

By February 1938 the Revd Dr Walshe of Tuam was going so far as to warn his flock against social intercourse with remarried divorcees – of whom there can not have been too many in the west.

Veteran Republican Thomas Hales (Fianna Fail TD for

Cork West) observed sardonically that those who were actually prepared to fight for Irish unity would find themselves imprisoned under Article 38 which set up the special courts. Eamon Donnelly, a Fianna Fail TD with strong northern roots, argued that Irish unity should precede the drafting of any constitution. Frank McDermott (Independent) was alone in stressing that the constitution would further alienate northern unionists; to achieve unity, he declared:

> We have got to offer them an Ireland in which a place can be found for their traditions and aspirations, as well as ours. Until we are willing to do this we are partitionists at heart, no matter how loudly we prate about unity.[107]

Fianna Fail in Power: An Overview

When in the early 1930s his opponents were making much of a supposed Bolshevik takeover of the IRA with links to the Fianna Fail party, de Valera was quick to point out the paltry number of Communists in the Free State. He also used the occasion to establish that the manifest economic and social problems which were the cause of 'extremism' demanded a solution but 'a solution having no reference whatever to any other country, a solution that comes out of our own circumstances, that springs from our own traditional attitude towards life, a solution that is Irish and Catholic'.[108]

But although the early radicalism of Fianna Fail was careful to distinguish itself from illegitimate anti-Irish creeds, it was for all that a radicalism which provided many hostages to fortune. In one typical example we have a report of a speech by de Valera at Irishtown in Mayo, where in 1879 the Land League had been inaugurated:

> The Ireland his party stood for was the Ireland of Fintan Lalor, an Ireland which still was their own from sod to sky. With the country's resources fully developed employment and a means of existence for a population of 20 million could easily be supplied.[109]

A hostile commentator gave this description of the first

election waged by Fianna Fail as a governing party: 'All the forces of economic discontent and extreme nationalism were directed to turn the election into a class war.'[110] In fact the IRA was at that time going through a leftist period and 'critically' supportive of Fianna Fail, had a better estimation of what Fianna Fail represented. An IRA Convention issued a manifesto on the same election, urging its members to support Fianna Fail, but noting

> with dismay the attempt to stabilise and build up an economic system, which for all that it relieves unemployment at the moment, will perpetuate the evils of social injustice. We are in favour of shutting out British goods, but this should not result in the enrichment of an exploiting manufacturing class here.[111]

But as prominent politician Sean Lemass, the architect of many crucial Fianna Fail economic policies from the 1930s to the 1950s, made clear, this was precisely what Fianna Fail intended to do:

> Fianna Fail if returned to power were planning a five year campaign ... to break the back of destitution and unemployment. The men who were providing capital for industrial enterprises were marking time as a result of this election, as they feared that if a Cosgrave government was returned, there would be no industrial revival.[112]

The radicalism of Fianna Fail defined the enemies of the Irish people as a small parasitic group of ranchers, import-export merchants and others with a vested interest in the existing nexus of economic relations with Britain. The bourgeoisie, actual and potential, was seen very much as an essential and progressive component of the 'people'. The function of the state was to avoid 'state absolutism' whether communist or fascist, and, in de Valera's words,

> to preside like a just father as the dispenser of social justice, to see that the natural resources of the nation were so distributed among private individuals, and among the various classes as adequately to secure the common good.[113]

The central problem for Fianna Fail was its clear commitment to end emigration and serious unemployment by its agrarian and industrial policies. Although when in power after 1932 the party did pursue a policy of land redistribution much more vigorously than its predecessor, there were clear limitations on what could be achieved. Crucially, it was agricultural exports which provided the resources to finance the increase in raw material and machinery imports which the protectionist industrialisation drive demanded. The Commission on Banking which de Valera had appointed was caustically critical about the negative effects of the land programme on the marketable surplus of agricultural produce.

But the pressure on Fianna Fail to appear to be doing something in this area was immense and in part self-generated. In contrast to the bitterly criticised *laissez-faire* policies of the previous government, de Valera had earlier committed the party to provide employment for all who could work.[114]

The onset of the slump in 1929 resulted in the closure of the United States as an absorber of emigrants – between 1926 and 1931 over 90,000 had gone to the USA out of a population of just under 3 million.[115] A large proportion of these came from the congested districts of the western seaboard. Their emigration had both removed pressure on available resources and through their remittances provided a major source of support for those who remained. A government committee estimated in 1938 that the congested districts – Donegal, all of Connaught, Kerry and part of Clare and Cork – accounted for 30 per cent of the population and 44 per cent of the total area of the state. However, although these were the most rural parts of the state (16.5 per cent of the population in towns and villages with a population of over 1,500 compared with 46.4 per cent for the rest of the country[116]), they accounted for only 34 per cent of the arable land and 26.3 per cent of rateable valuation.[117] Vast tracts of land were bogs, moors and mountainside and much of the remainder was land of very poor quality. In these areas there was only 53 per cent of acreage classifiable as arable land whilst 84 per cent of the population was dependent on land. In the remainder of the country the dependence on land was less but the proportion of arable land was much higher, at 81 per cent.[118] As the committee noted:

The general result is that an unduly high proportion of agricultural holdings in western counties are below economic standard, and incapable of affording a livelihood to present occupiers ... only emigrant remittances, pensions, unemployment assistance, county expenditure ... and the wages of seasonal labour in other parts of the country and in Great Britain, keep the standard in these districts above the level required to support a life.[119]

It was the congested districts that most clearly illustrated the continuing basis for rural discontent and demonstrated the limits of Fianna Fail's agrarian radicalism. The large ranches had long been a target for agrarian radicals, and an anti-rancher rhetoric was popular amongst the poor farmers in Fianna Fail's western heartlands. Under the Cosgrave administration small farmers and landless men had been very disappointed that the distribution of the large grass ranches had been undertaken so cautiously, in accordance with the principle of voluntary sale through the owner. With the onset of the world economic recession and the ending of emigration to the USA in 1928 there was a great intensification of the demand for the expropriation and distribution of the large ranches.

In its election campaigns and in the 1933 Land Act Fianna Fail responded to these demands. Under it the Land Commission was empowered to expropriate, with compensation, any property which seemed suitable and to distribute it among small farmers and landless men. A leading Fianna Failer and western radical, Paddy Ruttledge, was typical of the radical face of the party at the time:

The work of the land division in the country would empower the Land Commission to break down the walls of the big demesnes and remove all difficulties in the way of the Government placing all the landless young men on economic holdings.[120]

But despite an undoubted increase in the rate of land redistribution, by 1938 rank-and-file delegates to the party's Ard Fheis were complaining that the acquisition and division of ranches was proceeding much too slowly.[121] In the west there were sympathetic outbreaks of cattle driving in which groups of poor peasants forced the animals of rich farmers to move long distances, thus causing as much inconvenience as possible to their 'class enemies'. As Rumpf noted, there was in the persistence of land hunger a symptom of rural Ireland's chronic unemployment problem:

> It could only be solved by a general uplifting of the economy and a diversification of employment. Assuaging land hunger with land could be effective in dealing with the worst cases of hardship and exploitation ... But on its own it could not succeed, simply because a finite amount of land could not support an infinite number of people.[122]

This was partially recognised by the Fianna Fail government. Thus Frank Aiken in defending the 1933 Land Act could admit 'the utter impossibility of satisfying the desires of all the people who wish to get possession of land'.[123] However, it would to an important extent be local pressures which would determine the exact development of land policy in this period, in ways which often cut across the government's broader objectives.

Although the party would tolerate and even promote an anti-rancher rhetoric, it did not wish to appeal only to the poorest section of Irish farmers in the west. It had only been able to win the 1932 election by broadening its support in the midlands and the east to include more substantial farmers. Electorally, a too vigorous championing of the western smallholders could damage the party. It was also the case that these ranchers were in fact the mainstay of Ireland's export trade. It was not only Fianna Fail's political opponents who claimed that the policy would result in an overall decline in the efficiency and productivity of Irish agriculture, by the sacrifice of economic considerations to those of social and political pressure. Already by 1936 the Minister for Land was reporting that his department was getting many complaints that the limiting of the size of new holdings to between ten and fifteen acres was creating a whole class of holdings that were too small for the maintenance of a family.[124]

Of course the problem was that the demand for land was much greater than the amount available, and the government was hamstrung by its public commitment 'to settle as many people as possible on the land'. At this time it was estimated that there were 500,000 claimants for land equally divided between 'congests' and landless men and an estimated 720,000 acres available for distribution.[125]

Committed to redistribution, but also unwilling to antagonise the rural bourgeoisie which had already been damaged by the economic war with Britain, and faced with such substantial and often conflicting demands, Fianna Fail inevitably disappointed many of its small farmer and labourer supporters. Having decided to leave the fundamental structures of Irish agricultural production untouched, the agrarian policy increasingly ended up pitting one section of the small and medium peasantry against the other.

In the congested districts of the west it became apparent that much of the land redistributed had not gone to help the weakest farmers – 'a large amount of land which might have been used to relieve congestion has been used for other purposes'.[126] Fundamental here was the intense localism of the peasantry which demanded that those in the immediate proximity to land to be distributed be given priority over all other claimants. Often the most congested districts were not close to any land available for distribution, and those peasants to get access to new holdings became, in the terminology of the Land Commission, 'migrants'. The allocation of land to migrants often created much friction with local peasants who demanded the land for themselves. Thus in south Mayo, an area with a long tradition of agrarian agitation, the *Irish Times* reported a 'pitched battle', which led to seventeen arrests, between the police and villagers near Ballyhaunis when an official of the Land Commission attempted to distribute land to 'people from outside the district'.[127]

The Minister for Lands could inform the Cabinet that often land was distributed in ways that contributed little either to the relief of congestion or to the creation of economically viable farms. Thus small farmers were often given land up to two miles or more from their holding. 'The minister is definitely of the opinion that these distances are too great and that their adoption militates against land being utilised in the best manner.'[128] Local pressures could also ensure that land went to local notables like clergy, doctors and teachers despite the Land Commission's ruling that land should not go to those who had full time non-agrarian occupations.[129] Most crucially, it was felt that such pressures often favoured local landless men, with little or no experience of farming, over migrants who had such experience. When the initial statement of land policy was drawn up in the heyday of Fianna Fail radicalism 'landless men of a deserving class in the immediate proximity' came fourth in a list of five categories, migrants came last.[130] By 1936, because of intense criticism from the west, the list of priorities was changed and migrants became the fourth category and only then were landless men to be considered and these were more rigorously defined 'men of a good type who have experience of working the land and who have sufficient capital or stock to enable them to work the land allotted to them'.

Fianna Fail's agrarian policies in this period are revelatory of its political strategy. It sought to mobilise an agrarian constituency of small farmer and labourer aspiration and resentment. At the same time it confined this constituency within a national project which self-consciously eschewed class polarisation. Anti-rancher sentiment, quite prominent in 1932 and in the debates over the Land Act of 1933, never became an operational reality in agrarian policy. Hopes that a Fianna Fail administration would end the conditions of congestion and underemployment which characterised the west were inevitably frustrated. The resultant dissatisfaction was expressed in the temporary success of a western peasants' party, Clann na Talmhan (Children of the Land), founded in 1938 and winning 11 per cent of the vote and fourteen seats in the Dail election of 1943.[131] But although there was an undoubted erosion of support for Fianna Fail amongst the small farmers, its predominance with this group was never fundamentally undermined. Crucial here was the ingrained localism of the peasantry which, whilst it created many problems for the implementation of land policy, also meant, as Marx remarked of the French peasantry, that it could not represent itself and had to be represented. Fianna

Table 3: Number and Sizes of Holdings in Ireland (26 Countries) 1910-61

Year	Less than 1 acre	Above 1 acre and less than 5	Above 5 acre and less than 15	Above 15 acres and less than 30	Above 30 acres and less than 50	Above 50 acres and less than 100	Above 100 acres and less than 200	Above 200 acres	Total Holdings above 1 acre	Total all holdings
1910	68,335	48,274	115,882	103,547	58,728	48,524	20,486	8,602	404,043	472,378
1931	44,610	30,687	73,362	90,364	62,267	49,873	21,081	7,9549	335,583	380,192
1939	55,353	27,686	67,417	90,765	62,478	49,966	21,021	7,399	326,732	382,085
1949	60,939	26,360	62,423	86,983	64,453	51,287	21,772	7,270	318,548	379,487
1960	69,805	23,312	47,476	73,295	62,056	54,209	22,884	7,076	290,308	360,113

Source: 1910: *Agricultural Statistics of Ireland 1910* (Cd. 5964) p.xxvii; 1931: *Agricultural Statistics 1927-33* [P. No.1577) pp.1-2; 1939 and 1949: *Agricultural Statistics 1934-56* [Pr. 4335) p.2; 1960: *Statistical Abstract* (1961), p.100.

Fail both exploited this localism through clientelism, and transcended it by its appeal to the strong nationalist traditions of these areas.

Whilst its agrarian policies could do little fundamentally to alter the conditions in the west which continued to manifest themselves through emigration and population decline, they did attempt to shore up the party's western credentials by actions like the establishment of Gaelic-speaking settlements in County Meath in the late 1930s and early 1940s. These communities, which stirred up a lot of local resentment, were strategically filled with families from areas like Mayo where there was most dissatisfaction with government policies. Such low-cost but high-visibility policies (only 168 families were involved) represented the decline of the party's agrarian radicalism from a rhetoric which promised to reverse the agrarian and demographic trends of nearly a century, to policies designed to manage and massage the continuing decline of the rural Ireland of the small farmer.

It is not surprising that the most 'republican' section of Fianna Fail has come from the west, for it was the ideology of militant nationalism that provided a fundamental resource for the party when its substantive policies to regenerate the 'heartland' of Gaelic Ireland were producing meagre results. While winning new areas and social groups Fianna Fail sought at least to slow down the seemingly inevitable disappearance of this small farmer constituency. Many of its peculiarities as a 'bourgeois' party stem from the political imperative to maintain itself in part by propping up a class which from a strictly capitalist rationality ought to have been allowed to disappear much more rapidly. As Raymond Crotty's table on p.79 shows, Fianna Fail in the 1930s achieved a considerable stabilisation of small-scale family farming holdings, without reducing, however, the number of large holdings.[132]

Fianna Fail Strategy, 1938-66

In retrospect, the years of the wartime 'Emergency' seem like golden years for Fianna Fail. The inevitable isolation of Ireland imposed by neutrality suited de Valera. He ruled supreme as the philosopher king of Irish pastoralism and frugal comfort. Sean Lemass began to play an increasingly important role. There is no doubt that Sean Lemass represented the humane social-democratic face of Fianna Fail's modernising mission. *An Phoblacht* reported him frequently as speaking of the need for Ireland to industrialise without the negative effects (for working people) of that process elsewhere. When Cardinal Macrory in 1937 – at a Portadown fête – spoke of the need for 'proper' social conditions as the antidote to communism, Lemass leapt in to define these 'proper' social conditions (which the Cardinal had left rather vague) as a form of welfarism.

Lemass meanwhile performed efficiently enough the task of supplying the country with necessities. The economic strategy of self-sufficiency – which had come under increasing strain in the late 1930s – now seemed to be fully vindicated. The whole range of Fianna Fail slogans from protection to increased tillage seemed to be justified. By the general election of 1944 it was clear that the party had an unrivalled dominance in Irish politics.

But beneath the surface serious divisions about policy were beginning to appear within the party leadership for the first time. Sean Lemass and Sean Moylan began to argue for radical changes in agricultural policy. Lemass complained in increasingly bitter tones of the privileges and inefficiency of Irish farmers, and talked of state intervention to 'displace' the less productive. Moylan began to pour scorn on the results of much of the work of land redistribution. He was to proclaim openly in the Dail in 1946 that there were too many people on the land. Other more traditional elements in Fianna Fail, led by de Valera, resisted these arguments in favour of a rather romantic view of the joys of life on an Irish small farm. While the more radical ideas of the reformers – for example 'displacement' – were regarded as far too politically dangerous to apply, there is no doubt that this period saw the demise of that distinctive, though always ambiguous, appeal to agrarian radicalism (embracing even the land hunger of landless men) which so marked Fianna Fail in the 1930s.

The implication of such a development was that the

party's continued image· as 'progressive' would depend
largely on the relationship it worked out with the urban
working class. The party's electoral problems in the early
1950s were largely due to the fact that only Sean Lemass
within the leadership really grasped this fact. This realisation
is apparent in his general sympathy for the ideas of Beveridge
and Keynes. It was also evident in his industrial efficiency
legislation of 1947 – which would have given the trade unions
a much greater role. It is apparent in his speculations on the
1951 general election, when he alone interpreted Fianna
Fail's narrow victory as primarily the result of an increase in
support from the working class looking for economic expansion. MacEntee's massively deflationary budget of 1952
exploded such hopes. In the 1954 general election Fianna
Fail's strategy was based on the assumption that the party's
rural vote could be boosted enough to give it victory. When
this assumption was proved wrong de Valera seems to have
gained a new realisation of the importance of winning more
urban working-class support. Lemass was allowed his head
rather more.

Lemass began the business of elaborating a new progressive programme. In the 1930s Lemass had regarded the
penetration of foreign capital (especially British) as posing
grave threats to national independence. By 1945 his views had
altered somewhat. He now saw foreign capital and technique
as essential to Ireland's continued industrialisation. While on
a visit to America in 1953 Lemass specifically called for
foreign capital, commending Ireland's political stability to
potential investors.

It is not clear how this idea was received within Fianna Fail.
Certainly as late as the summer of 1956 de Valera and the
Sunday Press were still prating on about the old 'Sinn Fein
ideal of Irish ownership of Irish resources' and pouring cold
water on the Fine Gael-Labour coalition's rather nervous
efforts to attract foreign capital. Lemass's pronouncements
on the subject became rather cryptic, but it was nevertheless
clear to any moderately careful observer that he retained a
position in favour of foreign capital. Anyway, the soaring
emigration and economic crisis of the mid-1950s was to make
major change in economic policy almost inevitable.

By summer 1957 even the *Sunday Press* editorial and letter pages carried items in favour of foreign capital. Lemass also came out more and more strongly for an expansion of state expenditure – even in areas which were not, in the narrow technical sense, productive. In the general election of 1957 Fianna Fail was armed with a modernising programme based on vulgar Keynesianism and capitalised on disenchantment with the coalition's economic performance. It was perhaps Fianna Fail's last chance, but it was a chance that was taken.

The return to power in 1957 quickly demonstrated the strength of conservatism in the party's leadership. For, despite the rhetoric of Lemass during the election and the claims that Fianna Fail would 'put our men and machines back to work', the economic policies adopted were far from expansionary. The government's chief economic adviser was T.K. Whitaker of the Department of Finance. He had made it publicly known that he had little time for Lemass's 'simple Keynesianism'. His famous report *Economic Development*, presented to the government at the end of 1958, explicitly stated that it was 'quite unreal to approach the question of development from the aspect of employment'.

Like Garret FitzGerald, then the *Irish Times* economics correspondent 'Analyst', Whitaker wanted the 'modernisation' of Irish agriculture and industry to be based on the uncontrolled logic of capitalist market forces. This meant not only an end to protectionism and an opening up of the economy to foreign capital, but also an end to what were regarded as high levels of 'unproductive' government expenditure.

Both viewed Irish economic problems from the narrow point of view of the economic specialist and technocrat. Their analysis of the inefficient and uncompetitive nature of the Irish industry built up in the protectionist period was undoubtedly correct. It was also the case that from the point of view of the needs of capital it was 'unproductive' to invest money in housing, schools and hospitals. One of Lemass's colleagues, Erskine Childers, referred to the 1948-51 coalition's expenditures in these areas as 'slush'.

However, as Donal Nevin of the Irish Congress of Trade

Unions pointed out at the time, the hard-nosed free market approach of *Economic Development* would have little appeal to the urban and rural workers. It would arouse little enthusiasm to be told that if the proposals were implemented, real national income would be doubled in 35 years, especially as in the immediate future the proposals meant deflation.

But it was the conservatives in Fianna Fail who ruled the roost, at least until de Valera retired. Thus the First Programme for Economic Expansion (1959-64) provided for little increase in the state's programmes of capital expenditure and for real cuts in some areas. The starkest example was in housing where *Economic Development* claimed that needs were well satisfied. The government cut expenditure and as a result presided over a serious housing crisis in 1963 when a number of Dublin tenements collapsed and four people died. Lemass realised the deadly implications of these policies for Fianna Fail's support base amongst the working class. With the reunification of the trade union movement in 1959 after decades of internal division, he feared that if the reactionary approach of people like Childers and Sean MacEntee dominated Fianna Fail it would create the basis for the emergence of a social-democratic alternative. The image of Fianna Fail as a 'National Movement' of a progressive sort had to be preserved at all costs. From his accession to Taoiseach in 1959 Lemass set out to achieve this.

He approached his task with considerable skill. He realised that there was little sympathy amongst workers for the inefficient and often complacent bourgeoisie which had grown up during the protectionist phase. Employment and an end to emigration were the crucial needs as defined by the unions, and so Lemass went all out to convince them that Fianna Fail had serious plans for action. He initiated a gradual process of tariff reduction together with government-financed schemes for the modernisation and nationalisation of Irish industry. Lemass was careful to try and integrate union representatives into the various national and industrial committees set up to oversee this process.

At the same time he saw to it that government capital

expenditures began substantially to exceed the Whitaker projections. This incurred the anger of important sections of the bourgeoisie, particularly the banks, and was criticised by many of the government's economic advisers. However it served to cement a good relationship with the leadership of most of the important unions and to reinvigorate Fianna Fail's claim to be 'Ireland's Labour Party'.

His task was made easier by the weak and largely rural-based nature of the Irish Labour Party. In 1960 its new leader, Brendan Corish, had defined its programme as 'a form of Christian socialism. It is a policy that provides for all classes ...' Its lack of a coherent class perspective meant that the Labour Party was often forced into a position of merely reacting to Lemass's initiatives. Thus it ended up by pathetically attacking Lemass for moving towards the EEC. In the words of James Tully, '...it was quite obvious that if we entered the EEC we must drop our nationalism'.[133] In a situation in which the main opposition from the left was of a negative and nationalistic sort Lemass had little to fear.

Notes

1. *An Phoblacht*, 12 March 1932.
2. *Leader*, 20 August 1932.
3. *Leader*, 23 January 1932.
4. *Leader*, 27 February 1932.
5. *Leinster Leader*, 13 June 1931.
6. Quoted in *Westmeath Independent*, 27 January 1934.
7. E. Rumpf and A.C. Hepburn, *Nationalism and Socialism*, Liverpool 1977, p.107.
8. *Drogheda Argus*, 3 November 1934.
9. *Mayo News*, 14 January 1933.
10. *Leinster Leader*, 14 February 1931.
11. *Connaught Telegraph*, 22 February 1930.
12. *Connaught Telegraph*, 15 February 1930.
13. *Leinster Leader*, 14 February 1931.
14. Memorandum for the Cabinet from the Ministry of Finance, SPO S2888, 11 November 1932.
15. *Donegal Democrat*, 8 August 1932.
16. *Drogheda Argus*, 17 November 1934.
17. *Nation*, 28 January 1928.
18. *Mayo News*, 14 January 1933.

19. Ibid.
20. Ibid.
21. Ibid.
22. *Mayo News*, 24 February 1934.
23. *Drogheda Argus*, 11 February 1933.
24. Ibid.
25. Quoted in *Mayo News*, 16 February 1935. This is a clarification of Connolly's words. The *Sunday Independent* had reported him as saying, 'It has taken 100 years to establish the cattle trade; with God's help it will not take 100 years to kill it.'
26. *Drogheda Argus*, 29 August 1933.
27. *Cork Weekly Examiner*, 24 September 1933.
28. Rumpf and Hepburn, op.cit., p.130.
29. *Drogheda Argus*, 16 September 1933.
30. *Nationalist*, (Clonmel), 3 January 1934.
31. *Westmeath Independent*, 27 January 1934.
32. *Tipperary Star*, 22 July 1933.
33. *Connaught Telegraph*, 15 July 1933.
34. Ibid.
35. *Mayo News*, 22 July 1933.
36. *Munster News*, 26 November 1933.
37. *Nationalist* (Clonmel), 2 January 1932.
38. Lee, op.cit., p.94.
39. *Cork Weekly Examiner*, 29 July 1933.
40. Paul Bew, *Conflict and Conciliation*, p.40; *Mayo News*, 19 May 1934.
41. A. Orridge, 'The Blueshirts and the "Economic War": A Study of Ireland in the Context of Dependency Theory', *Political Studies*, Vol.XXXI, No.3, September 1983, pp.351-70.
42. *Donegal Vindicator*, 16 September 1933. Cosgrave was 'cordially welcomed' while O'Duffy was 'received with hostility' in many places.
43. *Blueshirt*, 19 August 1933.
44. *Tipperary Star*, 11 February 1933.
45. *Cork Weekly Examiner*, 28 January 1933.
46. *Connaught Telegraph*, 4 February 1933.
47. Maurice Manning, *The Blueshirts*, Dublin 1970, p.41.
48. *Tipperary Star*, 11 February 1933.
49. *Drogheda Argus*, 21 January 1933.
50. *An Phoblacht*, 11 July 1931.
51. *Kildare Observer*, 25 January 1933.
52. *Wicklow People*, 20 August 1933.
53. *Cork Weekly Examiner*, 21 April 1934.
54. *Mayo News*, 21 April 1934.
55. *Westmeath Independent*, 2 June 1934.
56. *Westmeath Independent*, 23 June 1934.
57. *Westmeath Independent*, 30 June 1934.
58. *Nationalist*, 30 June 1934.
59. *Nationalist*, 10 March 1934.
60. *Leinster Leader*, 7 July 1934.

61. *Mayo News*, 30 June 1934.
62. *Leinster Leader*, 14 July 1934.
63. *An Phoblacht*, 7 July 1934.
64. *Leinster Leader*, 14 July 1934.
65. *Irish Workers' Voice*, 7 July 1934.
66. *Leinster Leader*, 7 November 1988.
67. *An Phoblacht*, 8 September 1934.
68. *Leinster Leader, Westmeath Examiner, Midland Reporter* and *Westmeath Nationalist*: all 15 September 1934.
69. *Nationalist*, (Clonmel), 29 January 1934.
70. *Cork Weekly Examiner*, 21 April 1934.
71. *Nationalist*, 2 May 1934.
72. *Nationalist*, 2 May 1934.
73. *Enniscorthy Guardian*, 29 September 1934.
74. *Connaught Telegraph*, 14 October 1933.
75. *Cork Weekly Examiner*, 14 July 1934.
76. *Nationalist*, 5 September 1934.
77. F.S.L. Lyons., *Ireland since the Famine*, London 1971, p.531.
78. Rumpf and Hepburn, op.cit.
79. 'The British Isles' in D. Muhlberger (ed.), *The Social Basis of European Fascist Movements*, London 1987, p.149.
80. *Leinster Leader*, 1 September 1934.
81. *Cork Weekly Examiner*, 15 April 1934.
82. *Leinster Leader*, 1 September 1934. This passage of Hogan's is left out in Manning's account (pp.147-8), though Manning is clear about Tierney's admiration for the Italian model (pp.224-6). Our italics.
83. *Westmeath Independent*, 16 December 1933. For Tierney's decisive role, see *Sunday Independent*, 1 November 1987.
84. *Star*, 14 December 1929. But such enthusiasms are now passed over in silence; recently the *Irish Times* (12 March 1987) has described the 1930s politics of Desmond FitzGerald – Garret FitzGerald's father – who accepted O'Duffy's leadership as, quite simply, 'conservative'.
85. *Blueshirt*, 5 August 1937. Manning denies an Irish anti-semitic tradition but see Gerry Moore, *Anti-Semitism in Ireland*, University of Ulster 1984, unpublished PhD thesis. See also D. Keogh's, *Ireland and Europe 1914-48*, Dublin 1988. pp.46-55.
86. *Blueshirt*, 10 November 1934.
87. See on this point, John Heatley's excellent MSc thesis, *The Blueshirt Movement*, Queen's University Belfast 1987, p.66. Heatley also points out that the leaders of the leaders of the Jewish community in Cork were so concerned that they sought a meeting with O'Duffy.
88. *New York Times*, 8 December 1934.
89. P. Byrne, *Memories of the Republican Congress*, n.d., p.3.
90. *The Constitution of Eire/Ireland*, 1987, p.100.
91. *Mayo News*, 16 June 1934.
92. *Mayo News*, editorial, 27 October 1934.
93. *Mayo News*, 16 June 1934.
94. *Mayo News*, 24 August 1935.

95. *Mayo News*, 12 May 1934.
96. Ibid.
97. *Mayo News*, 27 October 1934.
89. *Mayo News*, 6 February 1927.
99. *Mayo News*, 24 February 1934.
100. *Mayo News*, 5 May 1934.
101. *Mayo News*, 16 February 1935.
102. *An Phoblacht*, 12 January 1935.
103. *Mayo News*, 1 February 1936.
104. *Mayo News*, 16 February 1935.
105. Dublin 1986. p.184.
106. Clifford, op.cit., p. 119.
107. Ibid., p.122.
108. *Mayo News*, 10 October 1931.
109. *Mayo News*, 10 January 1931.
110. *Round Table*, February 1933, Vol.XXXIII, p.301.
111. *Irish Times*, 10 January 1933.
112. *Irish Times*, 17 January 1933.
113. *Round Table*, May 1937, Vol.xxvii.
114. *An Phoblacht*, 19 November 1927.
115. Commission of Inquiry into Banking, Currency and Credit. Report No.2628, Dublin 1938, p.24.
116. Committee on Seasonal Migration S10191, p.25.
117. Ibid.
118. Ibid., p.26.
119. Ibid.
120. Quoted as an example of Fianna Fail's irresponsibility on the land question by Cosgrave, *Parliamentary Debates, Dail Eireann (PDDE)*, Vol.49, col.214, 18 July 1933.
121. *Irish Times*, 23 November 1938.
122. Rumpf and Hepburn, op.cit., p.125.
123. *PDDE*, Vol.48, col.12379, 13 July 1933.
124. S6490A memo to Cabinet, 11 November 1936.
125. S10191, Department of Finance's response to Interdepartmental Committee on Seasonal Migratory Labour.
126. *Irish Times*, 26 March 1938.
127. Memorandum from Minister of Lands to members of Executive Council, 21 August 1936, S6490A.
128. Ibid.
129. Statement on Land Policy drawn up by J. Connolly and sent to de Valera on 11 October 1932, S6490A.
130. Memorandum of Minister of Lands, 21 August 1936, S6490A.
131. Mair, op.cit., p.24.
132. R. Crotty, *Irish Agricultural Production*, Cork 1966, p.352.
134. This analysis of Lemass is based on P. Bew and H. Patterson, *Sean Lemass and the Making of Modern Ireland*, Dublin 1982.

3 Politics and Economic Transformation Since 1966

Factions in Fianna Fail

When Sean Lemass announced his intention to retire in 1966, the party faced, for the first time, the prospect of choosing a leader who would be drawn from its 'post-revolutionary' cadre. The aura of 1916 could not be used to simplify the question of the succession. Neither could it be used easily to legitimise policies like the free trade agreement with Britain and the radical break with traditional Sinn Fein economic strategy undertaken by Lemass.

There was a danger, perceived by some of the senior members of Fianna Fail, that the new economic policies and the economic growth associated with them, could threaten the party's portrayal of itself as a 'national movement' sensitive to the interests of the 'plain people' – workers and small farmers. De Valera had done much to establish the party's popular credentials by his care to maintain a personal regime of conspicuous asceticism – 'the noble example of the simplicity of his life' was how Countess Markievicz put it.[1] The contest for the leadership took place in the year of the fiftieth anniversary of the Easter Rising and the party's critics would make much of the comparison between the idealism and personal integrity of men like Connolly and Pearse and the current policies and alleged unsavoury business connections of the second generation of Fianna Fail leaders.

Much of such criticism focused on the role and activities of Lemass's son-in-law Charles Haughey, the then Minister of Agriculture, who was one of the main contenders for the succession. First elected to the Dail in 1957, Haughey had obtained a junior ministerial appointment in 1961.[2] He had been rapidly promoted, becoming Minister for Justice later that year, and soon developed a reputation for high intelligence and energy in running his department. Some senior members of the party had reservations about him, however, particularly over his alleged lack of decorum in mixing business and politics and becoming rich very rapidly in the 1960s.[3] He came to epitomise what critics and some party members saw as the dangerously 'organic' link between the party and the more unsavoury elements of the indigenous bourgeoisie based on building and property speculation who were profiting from the boom of the 1960s.

If Haughey was, in the word of an *Irish Times* leader, 'the modern man, essentially pragmatic and business-minded', his main opponent was easily identified as a 'chip off the traditionalist block'.[3] George Colley, who had only eighteen months' ministerial experience, was still clearly the favoured candidate of party elders like Frank Aiken, deputy Taoiseach and Minister of External Affairs and Gerry Boland, one of whose sons was a business partner of Haughey's and who had privately expressed the opinion that Haughey 'would yet drag down the Party in the mire'.[4] Colley had the advantage of coming from a strong republican family and was seen as the champion of the original pristine values, Gaelic and republican, of the party. Haughey's family came from an area in what was to become Northern Ireland and although his father had been in the IRA during the national revolution, he had gone with the pro-treaty side in the civil war and subsequently become a soldier in Free State army.

Lemass's own favoured candidate was the minister for Finance, Jack Lynch, a Cork TD who had entered the Dail in 1948 and held ministerial positions under De Valera and Lemass. He had no familial revolutionary pedigree, although this was somewhat compensated for by his record as an All-Ireland hurling player for Cork in the 1940s.[5] While Lynch had apparently not been interested in becoming leader when Lemass first approached him, the increasing dissolution of the party into rival camps for

Haughey and Colley, coupled with the late intervention of Neil Blaney, the powerful Donegal TD, threatened the party's reputation for fundamental unity – one of its most significant electoral resources. Lynch was then approached to reconsider and go forward as a unity candidate. When he accepted Haughey and Blaney withdrew and he easily defeated Colley.[6]

Colley's refusal to withdraw, despite the formal support of only one member of the government, represented the belief which he would continue to assert as late as 1969 that the party needed 'decisive' leadership that would reinvigorate its founding principles and traditions.[7] Lynch's own apparent initial lack of interest, his subsequent consensual approach to his government and the fact that the other ex-candidates for the leadership saw him as a 'caretaker' led to an unprecedented lack of cohesion in government on some crucial issues.[8]

One such issue was the party's special organisation, created in 1966, for eliciting financial support from the business community for electoral activities. Called Taca (Irish for support), it functioned through organising meetings and dinners for business people who, after subscribing £100 a year, could meet and socialise with government ministers.[9] It came to represent for the party's opponents, particularly on the left in the Labour Party and the recently radicalised Sinn Fein, obvious proof of the corruption of its founding ideals – as Mairin De Burca of Sinn Fein put it: 'The selfless idealism of Easter Week has become the self-seeking degeneracy of Taca.'[10] There was serious disquiet over Taca in the party itself. This was clearly articulated by Colley when he referred in a speech to the fact that 'some people in high places appeared to have low standards': Haughey was the politician most associated with Taca in the public mind.[11]

The Taca issue would figure very prominently in the government's failed attempt in 1968 to win a referendum on its proposal to replace the system of proportional representation with a simple majority system. Its opponents represented it as an attempt to cement in power a new corrupt alliance between Fianna Fail and the most rapacious section of the bourgeoisie.[12] The proposal was rejected by a decisive majority (60 to 40) and provoked a lot of speculation about the future of the party leadership.[13] For the first time since 1932 the party had failed to obtain more than 40 per cent in a national poll and there was evidence that many TDs and Senators had not campaigned for the government's proposal and that some had worked against it.[14]

The pressure for change to take account of the defeat and the Taca connection, which was commonly believed to have contributed to it, was particularly strong in Dublin where the challenge from the Labour Party was most substantial. It provided the impetus for a speech by Colley in December 1968 when he emphasised that 'under no circumstances can we allow big business to dominate or appear to dominate Fianna Fail' and outlined a proposal for 'the reconstruction and recovery of Fianna Fail which would review its adherence to the principles of the Republican, Democratic Programme of 1919'.[15] What aspects of the Democratic Programme he had in mind were not clearly spelt out and some of the programme's more radical and autarkic elements ('We declare ... the right of the people of Ireland to the ownership of Ireland and to the unfettered control of Irish destinies to be indefeasible ...'[16] would sit uneasily with the main lines of post 1957 economic policies. However his focus was on the inspiration which he claimed the programme had given to the social concerns of Fianna Fail:

> The party must demonstrate that it was adhering to the original tradition under which it tried to do justice to all sections of the community but with a special concern for the small man, the small farmer, the urban working man and the clerk ... If today's social order is not in line with the principles of 1919 then it is time to set about achieving the 1919 objectives.[17]

Colley's demands for a jettisoning of Taca and for a more vigorous promotion of the populist traditions and welfarist commitments of the party would be echoed at the Ard Fheis where there was much criticism of Taca by delegates – 'only complete abolition of Taca could save Fianna Fail the support of the man in the street' was a typical view expressed by a delegate from Dublin South-West. There was also a clear feeling that the party needed to demonstrate more clearly its commitment to the 'plain people of Ireland' through the development of a social dimension to its economic strategy. As a delegate from Dublin South-East, Frank Ryan, put it: 'to win the next general election with an overall majority, we have to do a hell of a lot more than retain the status quo ...' The party had to revivify itself as the organisation 'from which has emerged every significant national movement and social advance'.[18]

Lynch had already announced that Taca was to be restructured to open it up to 'plainer' people – membership was reduced to £5 a year – and it was to be much more clearly controlled by the national executive of the party. But although he claimed that these changes would remove all basis for the 'irresponsible and unscrupulous' attack on Fianna Fail and that 'no member of Taca has benefited in any way from membership', the changes were not sufficient for critics in the party and the organisation was quietly allowed to disappear.[19]

However, perhaps because the demand for a clearer commitment to the party's radical roots had become associated with Colley, who still obviously regarded himself as an alternative leader, Lynch adopted a different approach to the issues raised by left-wing critics and Labour Party pressure on Fianna Fail. This was to combine an accommodation to demands for increased expenditure on social welfare with a strident anti-communism. The first hint of the latter came in an otherwise unmemorable address to the Ard Fheis when he attacked a recent Labour Party policy document on industrial democracy. It was alleged to contain 'extreme socialist proposals'. 'Pernicious doctrines' were being preached in the name of workers and the underprivileged and these threatened 'our most precious freedom'. He appealed to the Irish working class,

> the descendants of those who, fifty years ago, so bravely and unselfishly helped to free our country from one invader ... not to make the mistake of facilitating or inviting, however unwittingly, another invader, an insidious tyranny to conquer the same land whose freedom was so dearly bought.[20]

The party's election campaign in 1969 would take its tone from this part of Lynch's speech and was characterised by an intense assault on the 'foreign' influences which had apparently captured the leadership of the Irish Labour Party. As Director of Elections Haughey gave it a dubious imprimatur when, in explaining why Fianna Fail did not deign to present the electorate with a manifesto, he proclaimed: 'Manifestoes have a Marxist ring about them.'[21] The Labour Party was commonly accused of wanting to impose 'Cuban socialism' on Ireland and Neil Blaney, not known for his subtlety of approach, asserted that Labour would like to invite the Soviet Union to set up nuclear bases on the Irish coast.[22] The Minister for Justice, Michael Moran, had asked the civil servant responsible for the Special Branch for dossiers on over 60 organisations 'of a subversive character' to help him highlight 'extremist' tendencies in the Labour Party.[23] He became obsessed with the role of a number of university-based intellectuals who had recently joined the Labour Party and some of who were prominent candidates in Dublin. He engagingly referred to them as 'the new left wing political queers who have taken over the Labour Party from the steps of Trinity College'.[24] Sean MacEntee, a founding member of the party and an ex-Minister for Finance, who had consistently opposed Lemass's attempts to reinvigorate Fianna Fail's radical image in the post-war period,[25] provided in an election speech in Dundalk a graphic example of how Fianna Fail attempted to identify itself as a radical populist party, while using appeals to nationalism and Catholicism to exclude alternative strategies as alien to Irish traditions. He emphasised his own role in 1916 and claimed that Fianna Fail continued to represent 'the twin causes of Patrick Pearse and James Connolly: freedom for Ireland and justice for the worker'. Connolly, he claimed, would have had nothing to do with the Irish Labour Party

> when he sees descending upon it a flock of strange birds from Queen Elizabeth's College of the Holy and Undivided Trinity, the college which she established in Dublin to wean the Irish from their traditional ecclesiastical obedience.[26]

Yet if anti-communism and assertions of the party's identification with nation and church were dominant themes, it is also clear that they alone could not to be relied upon. It was recognised that it was important for the government to respond to the demands associated with the growth of support for the Labour Party in Dublin and that simple use of the considerable ideological resources of Catholicism and anti-communism was not sufficient. The themes which Colley raised would have important effects on the government's balancing of the economic and social dimensions of its policies.

The need for more 'social progress' had first emerged in the final two years of Lemass's leadership. In 1965 both Fine Gael and Labour had struggled to make health and other forms of welfare central issues in electoral competition. Fine Gael's 'Just Society' programme had pointed out that the proportion of resources allocated to social welfare in the Republic was exceptionally low, even allowing for the fact that per capita income was lower than in other European countries.[27] The initial Fianna Fail response was to make increases in social expenditure dependent on economic growth: 'without economic progress there could be no social progress'[28] or to imply that growth itself would deal with the problem – Lemass's famous claim that 'a rising tide lifts all boats'.[29] But the government was forced to acknowledge the issue as a significant one and during the election campaign, Lemass declared that it would be possible to draw up a 'social development programme' linked to its economic development strategy.[30]

It was such a social development programme that Colley was demanding. In fact, the inner-party wrangles over Taca and the continuing leadership manoeuvrings tended to obscure the degree to which the government was moving, under pressure, in the direction of increases in social expenditure. This was after all, given the unprecedentedly high rate of economic growth throughout the decade, not a particularly painful option. A recent substantial analysis of the development of a welfare state in the Republic by Maria Maguire points out that 'It is only since the early 1960s that the Irish social services have developed in a rapid and

sustained fashion.'[31] She mentions the importance here of
the 'demonstration effect' of the considerably higher levels
of social provision in Britain, accentuated by the 1961
decision to apply for membership of the EEC, which
heightened awareness of the gap which had opened up
between Ireland and other European countries. But, as she
points out, such factors together with the economic growth
which itself encouraged greater expectations in the field of
social expenditure were mediated by political competition
and the greater salience which this gave to issues like health
care and social welfare. The government's 'Third Programme' for economic expansion was symptomatically
labelled 'A Programme for Economic and Social Development 1969-1972' and committed it to a reappraisal of social
services in the light of possible EEC membership
establishing the objective of bringing income maintenance
levels up to a 'European' level.[32] Thus although the party
would exert itself to ensure that the issue of expenditure on
health, education and social welfare was not given the class
inflection of the left but treated as a way of establishing
social harmony and of reasserting the party's responsiveness
to the 'plain people', there was no fundamental dispute over
the need to accommodate demands for increased public
expenditure in these areas.

If there had been such a debate the result of the 1969
election would have demonstrated the need for action. After
the resounding defeat in the proportional representation
referendum, the disquiet over Taca and the unprecedented
disarray at the top of the party, the Fianna Fail victory was a
major boost for morale and strengthened Lynch's position.
There was, however, little room for complacency – the
party's total vote was 2 per cent down on the 1965 general
election and, most crucially, its vote in Dublin had slumped
from 48.4 to 39.5 per cent, very largely to the benefit of
Labour whose share of the Dublin vote had risen from 18.5
to 28.3 per cent.[33]

The very intensity of the assaults on Labour may have
represented something of a displacement of the party's own
internal divisions. Dick Walsh has described the nature of
these divisions as 'less to do with politics and ideology than

with personal and professional considerations – friendship, local or regional loyalty, estimation of competence and vote-getting ability'.[34] There is much truth in this, but it is necessary to register the degree to which real questions of the party's strategic orientation to the working class were involved, if in a complex and refracted way. Colley's challenge to Haughey and later to Lynch represented a perception that corporatism *à la* Lemass, whilst it had rescued the party from the doldrums of the 1950s, needed to be developed and deepened if Fianna Fail hegemony over the working class was to be preserved. For a while the expansionary economic conditions allowed the serious questions he had raised to be responded to only partially. In the 1970s the onset of very different international economic conditions, together with increasing problems in the domestic economy, would force the party to confront the questions in a clearer and ultimately divisive way. But in the late 1970s, as in 1969 and 1970, divisions which had their basis in the economy and society of the Republic would be overlain and complicated by disputes over an issue which Lemass had probably hoped to have consigned to the margin of the party's concerns.

The Arms Crisis

The development of the civil rights movement in Northern Ireland from 1967, the crisis in the Northern Ireland state to which it massively contributed and the onset of serious violence brought the 'national question' back into the centre of Lynch's government's concerns in a way which was most unwelcome to a majority of its members. As *the* republican party, with the first of its seven constitutional aims being 'to secure the Unity and Independence of Ireland as a Republic', Fianna Fail was faced with an explosive problem when serious disorder developed in Derry and Belfast in August 1969 involving deaths of northern Catholics and the destruction of much property. It appeared that the whole 1921 'partition settlement' which it had execrated for decades was disintegrating and that inevitably raised questions about what Fianna Fail strategy should be in such an eventuality.

Lemass had reconstituted Fianna Fail's approach to Northern Ireland by emphasising the need to create economic and social conditions in the Republic which would make unity a more attractive notion for northern Protestants. Peter Mair has described the process well:

> A new nationalism and a new nationalist consensus began to emerge in the late 1950s. Nationalist ideology proved as potent as ever, and Fianna Fail remained the standard bearer *par excellence*, but the emphasis on territorial unity *per se* no longer played a crucial role ... the national aim was to be the achievement of social and economic self-respect in the 26 county state, rather than the achievement of territorial self-respect in a new 32 county state.[35]

Under Lemass and Lynch the focus of concern in Northern Ireland was the need for internal reform as a prerequisite for the essential transformation of attitudes which would ultimately allow a majority of Protestants to reconsider their British affiliations. Both maintained their formal fidelity to the cardinal party tenet that partition was wrong – 'a deep throbbing weal across the land, heart and soul of Ireland' was how the usually prosaic Lynch described it at the 1970 Ard Fheis. But there was no question of encouraging the notion that partition would be eliminated by some simple policy like British withdrawal or that there was any way around attempting to persuade Unionists to alter their attitude to unity.[36]

The northern crisis was a major check to this process of modernisation. It stimulated a strong upsurge of traditionalism, and not simply in border areas like Blaney's Donegal consituency and along the western seaboard where fundamentalist attitudes were strongest. There was a wave of sympathy for Catholic victims of what was commonly perceived as a state-sponsored pogrom and demands that the government take strong action to defend northern Catholics. In the aftermath of the August violence barricades were erected to defend Catholic areas and a number of Citizens' Defence Committees emerged. Representatives of these committees, who included prominent Catholic politicians and IRA members, travelled to

Dublin to demand aid, which often meant military training and guns.[37]

In the Cabinet a group led by Blaney and Haughey pressed for a more decisive response, while the majority led by Lynch did not favour anything stronger than criticisms of the Stormont and British governments and a demand that UN rather than British troops be sent in to defend the Catholics. In what must rank as one of the most startling abdications of leadership in the history of the southern state, Lynch, who was temperamentally and ideologically averse to playing a strong role,[38] allowed Haughey, as Minister of Finance, responsibility for deciding upon the size of a government fund for dealing with northern 'distress' and effective autonomy in allocating these resources. Haughey and Blaney were also key members of a committee set up to improve the government's profoundly inadequate knowledge of what was going on in the north.

In May 1970 Lynch would sack Haughey and Blaney, who would be subsequently tried and acquitted on charges of attempting to import arms illegally into the Republic for use in Northern Ireland. Kevin Boland, the other main protagonist of a hard line in the Cabinet, resigned in protest, as did a junior minister. The evidence from the court, a subsequent investigation by the Dail Public Accounts Committee and the accounts of some participants in the crisis indicate the development of what was in effect a para-state apparatus for involvement in Northern Ireland through an attempt to influence the main lines of development of Catholic insurgency.

This consisted of military intelligence officers, civil servants on secondment, businessmen allies of Fianna Fail and at least one prominent southern journalist. Its aim was to ensure that the members of the IRA who were playing a key role in defence committees, and would obviously be the core of any structure for the military defence of Catholics, were 'reliable'. This meant that they were single-minded in their role as a Catholic defence force and possibly as an agency encouraging radical constitutional change in Northern Ireland. The southern state, and particularly its Justice department, was well aware of the radicalisation which had followed the defeat of the IRA's previous military campaign, that of 1956-62. The IRA and its political wing, Sinn Fein, were increasingly seen as a threat to political stability in the Republic. The northern crisis, which had encouraged the more conservative sections of the IRA, particularly strong in Northern Ireland, to question the leadership of the radicals led by Cathal Goulding – Chief of Staff of the IRA – provided an opportunity to split the IRA and at the same time acquire leverage in Northern Ireland.[39] Neil Blaney, who as a Donegal TD was closely in touch with developments in Northern Ireland and a major exemplar of 'gut republicanism', had already anticipated later developments when he approached the commander of the IRA in the south of County Derry to sound him out on the IRA's military capacity in the event of a crisis and his attitude to the 'new politics' of the Dublin leadership.[40] After August 1969 such contacts multiplied as Haughey, Blaney and their representatives, sounded out attitudes and potentialities amongst northern republicans. Goulding himself was approached by Haughey and others and asked to re-orient his priorities from social revolution in the Republic to the possibility of a 'final push' in Northern Ireland.[41]

Haughey's role in what was a blatant usurpation of government policy-making in an area fraught with dire possibilities of diplomatic embarrassment and violence appeared out of character. He had no record of identification with traditionalists like Blaney and Boland, although his family's roots in Swatragh, County Derry, his father's role in the IRA and an uncle's internment by the northern government in the Second World War, may have had some influence on him.[42] However such biographical details had not prevented him in 1961, when appointed Minister for Justice, from pinpointing the crushing of the IRA as his primary objective and the re-activation of the Special Criminal Court as the means of achieving it.[43] But in 1961 the IRA had clearly and miserably failed to dent the northern state. By 1969, with the disintegration of that state, the increasing involvement of the British government and growing international concern, the context for IRA activity was radically different. Conor Cruise O'Brien, writing soon

after the events of the crisis, had Haughey clearly in mind
when he referred to

> ...one or two people ... who had not hitherto been suspected of
> more than conventional republicanism, but who now ... saw, in
> the resurgence of republican passion, a new political force ...
> capable of being harnessed in the service of political ambition.[44]

Haughey had fundamentally miscalculated. For although
Lynch was clearly caught off balance by the August events
and reacted weakly and indecisively – and this in itself
encouraged the pretensions of Haughey and Blaney – the
possibility of the northern crisis leading rapidly to some
wider political crisis, suitable for 'decisive leadership' of the
sort Haughey hoped to offer, was not great. By the end of
the year violence in the north had subsided and with it the
passions and inchoate demands for action in the Republic.
Lynch was able to reassert himself, secure in the knowledge
that his opponents had become dangerously exposed. There
was still a considerable space for a moderate interpretation
of the 'first national aim' as long as it could be plausibly
argued that the British state could be pressured and
persuaded to defend northern Catholics and reform
Northern Ireland. Haughey's own refusal to follow into the
wilderness Boland, who founded a short-lived 'pure'
republican party, or, like Blaney, to court expulsion, and his
own ignominious return to the backbenches demonstrated
that he was well aware that August 1969 had been a false
dawn.

However the *Irish Times* leader which recorded Lynch's
consolidation of support at the 1971 Ard Fheis, and claimed
that it signified 'the burial of some part of Fianna Fail', i.e.
its hardline territorial nationalism, was premature.[45] The
Arms Crisis illustrated that while popular passions could be
aroused by particular developments in Northern Ireland,
such passions did not, for the bulk of the electorate, displace
the more fundamental concerns with economic and social
issues. The north was not, and would not become an issue of
fundamental or realigning significance in the politics of the
Republic. Even in the 'republican' party, outside the west
and the border consituencies, it was not a major issue for

party members and supporters. It is not clear that if the machinations of the Haughey/Blaney para-state had reopened the national question that the masses in the Republic would have rewarded them, given the fears of the cost and contagion of northern violence that increasingly developed in the south. Yet anti-partitionism did remain the unchallengeable aim of the party, as well as a fundamental canon of the national consensus – an element of continuity with the struggles of 1916-21 and their 'incomplete' achievement. The national question would remain as a potent resource which Haughey would return to later in the 1970s. It remained so for two reasons. Firstly, the continuation of violence in Northern Ireland and the failure of successive British initiatives provided a fertile ground for the rejuvenation of nationalist appeals. Secondly, it could be used as a powerful, if secondary, issue in a renewed assault on Lynch at the end of the 1970s. That this resulted in a victory for Haughey was not fundamentally because of his manipulation of nationalist sentiment in Fianna Fail, but rather because it helped to amplify an attack prompted by the failure of Lynch's economic strategy. Haughey's victory in 1979, as much as his defeat in 1970, demonstrated the primacy of internal economic contradictions in determining political developments in the Republic.

Recession and the Limits of the Lemass Strategy

Crucial to an understanding of what from the late 1970s, would be increasingly termed the Republic's 'crisis' is an appreciation of the intensifying problems faced by the economic policies adopted in the Lemass/Whitaker watershed of 1957-58: the crucial decision to phase out protectionism in preparation for entry to the EEC, and the associated set of policies to transform the economy by the attraction of foreign capital to invigorate a stagnant industrial sector. The new policies enabled the Republic's economy to benefit from the last phase of the post-war period of capitalist expansionism, and by the end of the 1970s it had moved from being a predominantly rural and highly traditional society to a relatively industrialised and urbanised one.

Table 4: Change in the Social Structure of the Irish Republic[46]

	1951	1961	1971	1979	
Population	2.96	2.82	2.98	3.37	(millions)
Labour force	1.27	1.10	1.12	1.22	(millions)
Urban population	41	46	52	60	(percentage)
Farmers and farm workers	41	36	26	19	(percentage)
Industrial workers	24	25	31	32	(percentage)
Paid employees	56	60	70	74	(percentage)

The average rate of growth in industrial output of the Republic throughout the 1960s and 70s was above that of any EEC country. This growth was almost totally dependent on the attraction of new foreign investment in export-oriented industry. The Republic's Industrial Development Authority (IDA) aggressively marketed Ireland as the land 'where private enterprise is public policy', where there was a stable political climate and where manufacturing industry could expect to earn the highest rate of return anywhere in the world.[47] The existence since the 1950s of the system of tax relief on profits from exports,[48] coupled with very low rates of corporation tax on manufacturers, made Ireland a 'highly efficient place to accumulate profits on sales within the EEC'.[49] By 1980 foreign-owned firms, predominantly from the USA, but with a strong representation from Germany, Britain and Continental Europe, accounted for one third of manufacturing employment and 70 per cent of manufacturing exports.[50]

This massive influx of foreign capital was responsible for profound changes in the structure of the Republic's economy. Primary production, which employed 41.5 per cent of the employed population in 1951 and 36.9 per cent a decade later, had its share halved to 17.4 per cent by 1981.[51] Whereas in the 1950s the country's exports consisted mostly of primary goods – live animals, unprocessed meat, dairy products – by the early 1980s manufactured goods accounted for over 60 per cent of total merchandise exports.[52] It is the foreign sector which massively predominates in the export of manufactured goods now so crucial to the Republic's economy. Exports of goods and services which accounted for 25 per cent of national output in 1960 had increased their proportion to 63 per cent by 1985.[53] Foreign firms account for 80 per cent of the Republic's non-food exports and most multinational subsidiaries export the bulk of their output – 90 per cent in the case of US firms.[54] Because of foreign investment the Republic has the highest share of electronics in non-food exports in the OECD group of countries. At the beginning of the 1980s 40 per cent of manufacturing exports was in the high-technology category in areas like chemicals, office equipment and instrument engineering which are all heavily dominated by US firms.[55]

This veritable revolution in the structure and nature of the manufacturing sector has not, however, had the long-term effects on employment which its protagonists in the government and state had hoped for. Thus by 1985 manufacturing production was four times greater than in 1960, but the share of manufacturing in total employment was only a little higher than in 1960.[56] As one radical critic of dominant economic policies in the Republic has pointed out, manufacturing industry employed 212,000 in 1950 and 197,000 in 1984.[57] The new jobs in the foreign sector were increasingly counteracted by substantial job losses in the indigenous industrial sector. The dismantling of protection had 'snuffed out rather than stimulated' native Irish industry.[58] The older industries tended to be crowded out by both internal competition and increasing import penetration of the domestic market on which it heavily relied – imports in 1980 accounted for almost two-thirds of sales of manufactured goods in the Republic, compared with about a third in 1960.[59]

While the IDA could point to the development of the electronics sector as a success story for the new policies (from 7,750 workers in 36 firms in 1973 to over 16,000 workers in 200 firms by 1983), in the same period traditional industries like textiles, clothing and footwear had their workforces decline by almost 40 per cent.[60]

The industries were particularly hard hit in the international recessions after the oil price rises in 1973 and

1979. The Republic's entry to the EEC coincided with the beginning of the first recession and the results for indigenous industry were catastrophic in many cases. The IDA had estimated that there would be 17,000 job losses in manufacturing industry in the 1973-77 period, while in fact there would be over 57,000 in the first three years.[61] The Lemass/Whitaker strategy had envisaged a much more positive interaction between the new foreign sector and the indigenous bourgeoisie where moves to trade liberalisation and the new fiirms would encourage the modernisation of the traditional industries. By the early 1970s, however, economists were noting the lack of interaction between the foreign 'enclaves' and native industry and an increasing and unproductive 'dualism' in the Republic's manufacturing sector where the new high technology foreign plants had few, if any, linkages with native industry:

> The new foreign plants ... drew their technology from their parent firms and made little use of Irish research and development ... they relied heavily also on their overseas affiliates to provide markets for their products. The plants were little more than production platforms which were located in Ireland to take advantage of the generous industrial grants and tax concessions, political stability, access to markets, and the availability of labour at rates of pay well below the industrialised nations ... they had few links with the rest of the economy.[62]

The new foreign sector had little connection with the old, indigenous low-technology industries. In 1982 the Telesis Consultancy Group of management consultants produced a report on industrial policy for the National Economic and Social Council. It found that in 1976 only 8 per cent of the components and assembly work bought in by engineering, the largest foreign sector group, had its origins in Ireland. Few of the foreign firms located any research and development work in Ireland or included in their Irish operations any of the crucial stages in management planning and strategic decision-making. The branches in the Republic were typically satellites carrying out a few of the stages in a more complicated manufacturing process.[63]

The development strategy adopted at the end of the 1950s was increasingly recognised to have given rise to serious imbalances and dangerous dependence on a continuing high level of foreign, mostly US, investment. The new policies had certainly radically diminished dependence on Britain: as late as 1960, 75 per cent of Irish exports went to the UK; by 1984 this was reduced to 34 per cent and the United States had become a much larger source of capital investment.[64] The Irish economy had been radically opened up and the result was an internationalisation and diversification of the sources of its dependence, although within this diversification the US was undoubtedly the dominant force.

The failure of foreign industry to develop strong ties with the domestic economy meant that increases in employment depended on continuing high levels of new foreign investment. By the end of the 1970s this appeared more problematic as the Republic suffered a decline in attractiveness as a location for foreign industry. Some of this decline could be blamed on the international recession and a reduced amount of internationally mobile investment. However there was some evidence that the Republic was also suffering from increased competition for the shrinking pool of funds. The development since the 1960s of a number of low-wage, newly industrialising countries as politically reliable sites for investment, combined with rising labour costs in the Republic, inevitably eroded its attractiveness. Its pull as a low-wage export platform for US firms wanting access to the EEC has been further undermined by the recent accessions of Greece, Portugal and Spain. In the 1960s and 70s the proportion of US investment in Europe which went to the Republic was well above that which could have been expected on the basis of population or national income.[65] However between 1979 and 1982 the Republic's share of new US investment in Europe declined from 2.3 to 1.5 per cent,[66] and total US investment which amounted to $175 million in 1980 had declined to $170 million by 1984 and these figures mask the much more precipitous decline in new 'greenfield' investment.[67]

The positive impact of the foreign sector on the rest of the economy was further attenuated by practises like transfer pricing whereby components and services were bought in from branches of the same company in other countries at artificially low prices and the Irish product sold, again within the company, at as a high price as possible to maximise profits which were subject to tax relief.[68] A higher proportion of profits tended to be repatriated as many enterprises progressed beyond their start-up phase when investment was heavy. As the dollar strengthened in the early 1980s this process was encouraged – in 1983 only 20 per cent of the profits of European affiliates of US companies was reinvested compared to 67 per cent in 1979. In the Republic the repatriation of profits by multinational companies was running at £300 million in 1981, and by 1984 it had risen to £945 million.[69] The OECD pointed out the clear limitation of the dominant economic strategies in figures for 1983. In that year multinationals based in the Republic had sales of £5,000 million. However the impact of this on the economy was considerably reduced by the fact that £2,000 million was accounted for by imports of raw materials and other inputs and a further £1,000 left in repatriated profits.[70] By the end of the 1970s, therefore, the wager of the Lemass/Whitaker strategy on the role of foreign capital as agent of economic transformation and industrialisation was seen to have increasingly questionable results. Levels of unemployment were rising and at the same time what the *Economist* referred to as 'Ireland's bewildering array of grants and tax subsidies' for foreign capital was a major contributor to an emerging crisis in the public finances.[71]

Public Expenditure and the Crisis

The problems for the economic development strategy intersected with a profound social transformation associated with a major change in demographic patterns. One of the main indicators of the pathology of British rule for Irish nationalists had been the continuous post-Famine (1845) decline in population. The population of the area which is now the Republic was 6.53 million in 1841; in 1926 the first census of the new state showed it had dropped to 2.97

million.[72] Independence did not stop the decline, and neither did the protectionist policies adopted by the Fianna Fail government after 1932. In fact it was to be the heavy levels of emigration and clear evidence of continued population decline that were to impel the new direction in economic policy at the end of the 1950s. The preliminary report of the 1956 census disclosed that the population at 2.89 million was the lowest since independence, and in a famous editorial the *Irish Times* commented: 'If the present trend continues Ireland will die, not in the remote unpredictable future, but quite soon.'[73]

As we have noted in earlier chapters, at the core of the decline was an agrarian order which in the post-Famine period had come to be dominated by a rural bourgeoisie whose predominant activity was cattle production for the British market. Cattle farming was not labour intensive, and the desire of these large farmers to pass on their land intact to their eldest sons led to a pattern of reproduction which powerfully contributed to population decline as rural Ireland was characterised by a pattern of low marriage rates and the lateness of those marriages that were contracted.[74] High rates of emigration by those whom the rural economy could not absorb were inevitable. Fianna Fail, despite its tinges of agrarian radicalism, did little to alter the structures of the rural economy and the new protected industries were neither large nor dynamic enough to challenge the weight of a conservative, extensive agriculture. It took a new partnership between an activist state and foreign capital to begin to change the demographic patterns of over a century. The censuses of 1971 and 1981 registered population increases of 5.55 and 14.4 per cent respectively, and the 1981 census also revealed a net immigration of 100,000, a startling reversal of the post-Famine pattern.[75] The decline in the weight of rural Ireland in national life was also manifest in an increasing rate and falling age of marriage. By the beginning of the 1980s the birth rate at 21 per thousand was far in excess of the EEC average of 12 and the rate of natural increases in the 1970s was six times that of the EEC.[76]

Demographic changes coupled with the less favourable international economic situation in the 1970s put increasing pressure on the state's job-creating capacity. At the end of the decade it was calculated that 20,000 new jobs a year were needed just to deal with new entrants to the labour force. This compared with the annual average of 17,200 in the decade.[77] The problems of creating new jobs in industry are clear from the figures below, which show the substantial job losses in traditional industries counteracting the effect of IDA-sponsored new industries.

Table 5: Employment in Manufacturing Industry (Thousands)[78]

	1973	1974	1975	1976	1977	1978	1979	1980
Gross job gains	21.5	16.8	14.6	20.3	21.7	21.1	23.6	22
Gross job losses	11.7	20.0	27.4	17.5	16.1	14.5	14.9	22

As agriculture continued to decline in significance as an employer of labour, the increasing problems experienced in the state's industrialisation drive, together with the political importance of job creation in the recasting of Fianna Fail hegemony that took place after 1957, impelled the state itself to become a crucial factor in employment creation. As the OECD noted in 1981, Irish economic development in the previous two decades had as a central feature 'the increasing importance of the public sector both in its direct participation in economic activity and its indirect influence on other sectors'.[79] Governments in the 1970s, most starkly the Fianna Fail one which took power in 1977, expanded public sector employment to compensate for the failures of traditional industry and the inevitably limited employment capacity of the foreign sector. Thus half of new jobs outside agriculture in the 1970s were in the public sector.[80] During the decade public sector employment increased from 23 to 29 per cent of the total in employment.[81]

Public expenditure levels were also pushed up by the substantial increases in state expenditure on social welfare, health and education which took place from the mid-1960s. By 1980 the share of national output devoted to the welfare state in the Republic was close to the European norm, notwithstanding the fact that per capita GDP was well below

the European average: in 1981 social expenditure in the
Republic was 28 per cent of GDP (11.7 per cent in 1960)
compared with an OECD average of 25.6 per cent (13.1 per
cent in 1960). In 1981 Ireland ranked twentieth in the
OECD in terms of per capita GDP, but eighth in terms of
GDP share of social expenditure.[82] By then neo-liberal
critics of the 'over-extended state' and the 'dependency
syndrome throughout our society'[83] were pointing to the fact
that by the mid-1970s Irish welfare benefits had been
brought up to a level of near parity with British rates,[84] and
that 'neither the public nor politicians are willing to accept
that we simply cannot afford the standards that have been
achieved by our richer neighbours'.[85]

As Maguire points out, the economic growth which began
at the end of the 1950s itself created demands for expansion
of social programmes like the educational reforms of the
1960s (the most significant of which were the introduction of
free secondary schooling in 1967 and of a limited grants
scheme for university students in 1968. In similar vein the
increasing proportion of the labour force in waged
employment led to increased pressure for the expansion of
the social insurance system).[86] Maguire indicates, however,
that there was a more complex causality at work than simple
economic growth – from the early 1960s to the mid-1970s
social expenditure rose much faster than output.[87] One
important factor was the 'demonstration effect' of higher
standards and levels of benefit in Britain. Given the mobility
of labour between Ireland and Britain and the fact that in
Northern Ireland social services had developed broadly in
line with those in the rest of the UK, differentials in
provision between Ireland and the UK in areas like health,
education and levels and range of benefit were particularly
visible.[88] Garret FitzGerald, soon to become leader of the
second major party in the state, bewailed the 'demonstration
effect' in a Dail debate in 1976:

> We have the problem ... of a republic faced with the demand for
> imperial standards, because we were part of the UK at one
> time. The demonstration effect, because of the transparency of
> our economy [*sic*] with that of Britain remains, and our people

have come to expect the living standards, the social service
standards and the standards of every kind of service and facility
they see in neighbouring Britain. Britain, by European
standards is not a rich country, but it is sufficiently richer than
us to create pressures on us to achieve standards which at our
present levels of output we cannot attain.[89]

There is some irony here, for it was FitzGerald who played a
key role in making social welfare a major issue in the
political competition of the mid and late 1960s. It was his
struggle to make Fine Gael a 'social democratic' party,
together with the pressure from the Irish Labour Party, that
had forced the Fianna Fail governments to place more
importance on social expenditure, in addition to the
substantial resources that were already going into their
economic development strategy. The irony is expressive of
the very conflicting pressures created by the liberalising
economic strategy, with which FitzGerald was in basic
agreement. Economic growth stimulated demands for
higher levels of provision in a revolution of rising
expectations fuelled by the ruling order's own desire to
make the Republic a model European nation. The long
hegemony of Fianna Fail in Irish politics had developed a
political culture characterised by a responsiveness to popular
pressures which was amplified by the clientilist mode of
electoral politics encouraged by proportional representation
in multi-member constituencies. In the 1960s the main
assaults on Fianna Fail had been from the 'left', as the
government was attacked for neglect of social issues. The
result was the emergence of an effective consensus for an
activist and 'social democratic' state.

This consensus was bound to disintegrate as the boom
period of the 1960s gave way, after 1973, to much more
difficult domestic and international economic conditions.
Social democratic themes would be replaced by neo-liberal
ones as the growth in the size of the public sector was seen as
the cause of the increasingly serious problems of foreign
debt and oppressive levels of taxation. Between 1967-69 and
1974-76, total public expenditure as a percentage of GDP
rose from 33.7 to 49.4 per cent. In a ranking of the eighteen
OECD countries according to share of public expenditure in

GDP the Republic moved from tenth to third place in the same period.[90] This expenditure was increasingly financed by resort to foreign borrowing. Thus, whereas in the 1960s official foreign borrowing accounted for 9.5 per cent of net capital inflow, with private direct investment representing 40 per cent, in the five years prior to 1975 the positions were reversed with foreign borrowing by the state representing 41.2 per cent and private direct investment only 15.2 per cent.[91] The debt problem would intensify given the dynamics of a state-induced development strategy in a recessionary international environment. The effect of the 1973-74 recession was substantial redundancies and rising unemployment which the coalition government of Fine Gael and Labour (1973-77) attempted to deal with by continuing the previous government's much-criticised practise of running a deficit on current account and financing it by foreign borrowing.[92] The Exchequer Borrowing Requirement rose from 7 per cent of GNP in 1973 to 16 per cent in 1975.[93] The government forsook expansionary policies, contributing to the rise in the unemployment rate from 7.9 per cent in 1973 to 12.5 per cent four years later and to its decimation at the polls.[94] Returned to power on a set of expansionary policies, Fianna Fail was able to generate a sharp but short increase in employment, much of it in the public sector – between 1977 and 1979 the numbers at work rose by over 60,000.[95] The second set of rises in oil prices at the end of 1978 and the onset of a deep international recession radically undermined the government's economic strategy. Growth of real GDP which had averaged 6 per cent in 1977 and 1978 was reduced to 1.5 per cent in 1979, and unemployment and redundancies began to increase sharply,[96] as did inflation which began to climb sharply in 1979 and peaked in 1981 at 20 per cent.[97] At the same time public expenditure and borrowing climbed inexorably upwards. Total government expenditure rose from 47.9 per cent of GNP in 1977 to 65.3 per cent in 1982. In the same period the Exchequer Borrowing Requirement rose from 9.8 to 16.1 per cent of GNP. After 1981 attempts were made to correct these fiscal imbalances, but by 1984 the outstanding national debt had risen to 128 per cent of GNP, the highest in the

OECD area, while interest payments on debt amounted to 11 per cent of GNP and 20 per cent of current government expenditure.[98] Increasingly the focus of national debate shifted from questions of economic growth, job creation and social conditions onto the terrain dominated by an increasingly assertive neo-liberal current which transcended traditional party boundaries. A key, if contradictory role in this process would be played by Garret FitzGerald and Fine Gael.

Fine Gael and Social Democracy

A *Guardian* report on FitzGerald's accession to the leadership of Fine Gael in 1977 commented that

> Irish politics rooted in civil war divisions ... is slowly edging towards a left-right division. Dr FitzGerald has accelerated the possible development of a social democratic party formed by a majority in both Fine Gael and Labour.[99]

In fact Irish politics had long ceased to be about the issue of the civil war and, as we have seen, the construction and reconstruction of Fianna Fail dominance had little to do with constitutional issues or the 'national question' and much to do with issues of economic and social development. If that hegemony was to be challenged there would need to be a transformation in ideology and political strategy of the Republic's second major party. The debate on these issues had begun in the early 1960s when a new generation of party members began to be concerned about what one commentator in 1964 referred to as Fine Gael's 'unfavourable party image' – that it was 'the party which big farmers, professional men and merchants tend to join'. In no election in the previous quarter of a century had it been able to obtain more than 32 per cent of the first preference vote, whereas Fianna Fail had never got less than 42 per cent (Fine Gael's vote had fallen as low as 19.8 per cent in 1948).[100] Fianna Fail, reinvigorated by its sponsoring of economic programming and its transformed approach to the question of economic development, was also strengthened by lack of a credible alternative as neither Fine Gael nor

Labour could hope to form a government singly, and Fine Gael's traditional rightism coupled with Labour's public disavowal of coalition removed the possibility of any coherent alternative to Fianna Fail.

The champions of a new course in Fine Gael were led by Declan Costello, who argued that a real opening for advance was available by attacking the limitations of Fianna Fail economic 'programming' and putting forward a more directed strategy of economic planning, social welfare and even the talk, unprecedented for a party with such reactionary traditions, of redistribution of income and social justice. Thus the Fine Gael parliamentary party in 1964 adopted a resolution that

> There is an urgent need for economic and social reform in order to produce a more just social order ... [and] that such reform can best be brought about by a more effective management of our economy and a more equitable distribution of the nation's wealth.[101]

There was agreement on a new programme which, formally at least, put Fine Gael to the left of Fianna Fail and formed the basis for the party's electoral document, 'The Just Society', published in March 1965.

As Mair points out, the success of the social-democratic phase of Fine Gael had much to do with the economic expansion stimulated by Fianna Fail and its generation of a mild revolution of rising expectations –

> Resources had grown enormously in the 1960s – between 1961 and 1973 – GDP grew by an annual average of 4.4 per cent – and demands for a more egalitarian distribution of these resources also grew apace.[102]

Economic expansion would allow the 'radicals' to deal with predictable resistance from the more traditional sections of the party by portraying social justice as a painless product of the redistribution of the extra resources generated by economic growth. In the 1960s, they were assisted by important changes in the attitude of the Catholic Church to social policy as it moved away from the position of bitter opposition to the welfare state and state economic interventionism which had characterised its interventions from the 1930s to the 1950s.[103]

There was still serious opposition to the new line: the leader of the party, James Dillon, continued to emphasise that his party was still 'a party of private enterprise'[104] and an attempt made by FitzGerald and others in 1968 to have the party renamed Fine Gael – Social Democratic Party, was defeated at the Ard Fheis.[105] The party did however, continue to emphasise its social-democratic aspect in the 1969 and 1973 elections and when, after 1969, the Labour Party became prepared to consider entering coalition again the new themes made the construction of a common programme considerably easier.

The slowing of economic expansion and the sharp effects of two international recessions would make the party's social-democratic pretensions more and more difficult to sustain. The party's coalition manifesto with Labour had declared its aim to be to 'transform Ireland into a modern progressive society, based on social justice'.[106] In fact it was in the areas of social welfare and taxation that the coalition could register some modest achievements. Gross expenditure on social welfare rose from 6.5 per cent of GNP in 1973 to 10.5 per cent four years later, most benefit rates rose by 125 per cent (considerably more than wages and prices), the rate of house-building increased 50 per cent, expenditure on health services increased almost threefold and taxes on capital gains and wealth were introduced, as was a measure to make farmers liable for income tax for the first time.[107] Such social-democratic policies had in the 1960s rethink been assumed to have been developed alongside 'planned' economic growth and job creation. In the 1970s such planning proved difficult and ultimately impossible for the coalition as the recession put an end to hopes of a painless combination of economic growth and social reform. The substantial victory of Fianna Fail in 1977 demonstrated clearly that for the electorate, including a majority of the working class, issues of social justice and redistribution were very much less significant than employment and living standards.

On becoming leader FitzGerald began to modulate his social-democratic philosophy to take account of the recessionary environment and the strains it inevitably placed on a party like Fine Gael, a substantial section of whose membership and electorate favoured a simple conservative response of retrenchment in public expenditure when faced with the growing fiscal crisis. Capitulation to such opinion would finally foreclose on any possibility of Fine Gael escaping from permanent minority status. The need to maintain an opening for a future coalition agreement with Labour dictated that the language of the 1960s not be jettisoned, although it would be increasingly nuanced. FitzGerald increasingly defined 'social democracy' in ways divergent from the usual use in relation to European states where it means reformist governments with strong and often institutionalised links with the trade union movement. If there was anything approaching that type of relationship in the Republic then it was Fianna Fail that had cornered the market.[108] For FitzGerald it meant precisely a state that was unresponsive to the main interest groups in society, including the unions, but which could therefore counterpose its 'idealism' to the 'materialism' of the organised groups in the interests of the poor. In a major speech on the role of Fine Gael which he made soon after becoming leader, he characterised the Republic as a 'pluralist democracy' whose main defect was for competing parties to promise more than they could deliver and to 'appeal to the materialism of the electorate'.[109] There was a need for a new political alternative but it should not be a left/right conflict: 'We need new solutions to the avoidable conflict between the economic need for incentives to effort and the social need to care for those who cannot look after themselves.' Such bromides were in sharp contrast to the language of the 1960s when the representatives of the new policies had self-consciously identified themselves as on the left.[110] Now FitzGerald defined the question of the redistribution of wealth as 'between the 20 per cent of our population which lives in poverty ... and the reluctance of a majority of the people to accept a reduction in living standards in favour of the minority'.[111] This conveniently obfuscated the crucial question of class inequities of a very radical nature in the way different classes in his 80 per cent 'majority' were affected by the fiscal crisis.

For the increasing assault from the right on the burden which the 'unproductive' state sector placed on the shoulders of the Irish tax-payers tended to ignore the inequitable distribution of the tax burden on different groups in society. In the 1970s an OECD comparison of fifteen member countries showed the Republic to have the largest share of total revenue coming from indirect taxation.[112] The relatively low yield from direct taxation was not because the average rates were low, but because of the narrowness of a taxation base from which the class which made the 'national revolution' – the farmers – and the self-employed were excluded. Companies were able to reduce their tax liabilities by exemption of export profits from corporation tax and by the various depreciation allowances and capital grants available. In 1980 capital taxes made up 0.5 per cent of total taxation, a drop of 50 per cent on 1970. In 1974 the coalition had introduced a wealth tax, the least onerous of the twenty such taxes then in existence in the world. It was abolished by Fianna Fail in 1978 at the same time as it raised the exemption limit for capital acquisitions tax and reduced the effectiveness of capital gains tax.[113] In the early 1970s the OECD had predicted that unless the tax base was widened the increasing rate of public expenditure could only be financed by public borrowing or higher rates of taxation.[114] In fact the Republic got both. There was a significant increase in the tax burden for those paying personal income tax. Taxes on personal income rose as a share of total taxation from 30 to 45 per cent in the decade after 1970. The proportion of income taken from persons on average earnings increased sharply, for most taxpayers it increased by half, but the rise was much steeper for a married couple with three children living on average male industrial earnings.[115]

It was this sharp increase in fiscal pressure in a context of state acquiescence in the exclusion of the farmers, industry and the self-employed from any significant share of the burden (in 1982 the employee sector contributed approximately 87 per cent of income tax, while the self-employed provided 11 per cent and the farmers less than 2 per cent)[116] which provoked nation-wide strikes and massive demonstrations against the Fianna Fail government's taxation policies in March 1979. Maguire notes of the Irish tax protests that they

> have not included to any discernible extent the element of welfare backlash seen in a few Western countries in recent years ... The protest was co-ordinated by the trade union movement, which was careful to emphasise that the demand was for a more equitable distribution of the tax burden rather than a reduction in the overall level of taxation.[117]

There was scope for the development of a more substantial social-democratic politics here. This would have favoured both a widening of the tax base, a reordering of relative tax burdens, and a radical reassessment of the nature of current patterns of public expenditure, the results of which were clearly inequitable. Thus expenditure on education benefited higher-income groups disproportionately because of their relatively greater participation in university level education. The child of an Irish middle-class family was thirteen times more likely to enter higher education than the child whose father was an unskilled or semi-skilled manual worker. A recent study of social mobility in the Republic concluded: 'The degree of inequality of opportunity in Ireland was remarkably high by international standards.'[118] The Irish middle class also benefited disproportionately from the various subsidies available for owner occupation and the health system had an important element of regressivity.[119]

But to take up these issues would have been to risk a major internal row and the loss of substantial middle-class electoral support. Fine Gael's 'social democracy' would be attenuated rather than deepened in the late 1970s. The Anglo-US examples of the displacement of supposedly 'statist' and 'Keynesian' regimes by abrasive neo-liberal ones undoubtedly influenced the state of political and ideological debate in the Republic. The collapse of the revived corporatism of the Fianna Fail government in 1980, the escalating level of foreign debt and an increasing popular consciousness that 'something' had to be done about the economic crisis strengthened the influence of the right in the debate on the economy. Typical was a discussion among five of the country's most prominent economists in the month before the general election in June 1981. The consensus was for a large reduction in public expenditure: 'The real choice is between deflation and more unemployment now on the one hand, and financial collapse and vastly greater unemployment at some later stage on the other.' At the same time there was a despairing disdain for politicians: 'Our politicians are living in cloud cuckoo land and our political system is incapable of meeting this crisis.'[120]

Such jeremiads which dominated discussion of the economic crisis in the Dail and the media put strain on FitzGerald's desire to maintain some credibility for Fine Gael's social-democratic claims. He might tell the party's trade union conference that 'Fine Gael is now seeking to become the acknowledged party of the working man and woman,'[121] but his party's appeal was increasingly dominated by the conventional theme that social reform, like all other demands on the resources of the state, must await radical action to deal with the public debt. Up to the election of 1981 the predominant emphasis in the party's approach to the electorate was to emphasise its 'idealism', its independence of special interests and its promise to introduce sufficient austerity in office to deal with the problem of the national debt.[122] In its approach to the 1981 election there was no consideration of a pre-election coalition agreement (as in 1973), its declared aim was to overtake Fianna Fail and form a single-party government. Its manifesto offered large cuts in income tax to be paid for by increases in indirect taxation, increased health contributions and, with some obeisance to equity, an employment levy on larger salaries.[123] The results showed a significant improvement in the Fine Gael performance: its share of the vote rose from the dismal 30.5 per cent of 1977 to 36.5 per cent, its highest since the formation of the party in the 1930s. It still lagged behind Fianna Fail (with 45.3 per cent) but the gap was closing and in the second election in 1982 it almost reached 40 per cent.[124] Part of the success was due to the major reorganisation and development of party structures that FitzGerald had set in train in 1977. The party constitution was modernised and democratised to undermine the control of a group of older and traditional TDs. An image of energetic radicalism, with little effective content, was developed through the encouragement of a youth wing and the role in the party of a number of women who had played an active role in the development of the women's movement. In Dublin a group of younger, 'community'-oriented Fine Gael candidates were able to take working-class votes from both Fianna Fail and the Labour Party.[125] There is evidence of a real increase in working-class support for Fine Gael in the period leading up to 1982. Opinion poll evidence suggests an increase in working-class support from 19 per cent in 1969 to 28 per cent in 1982, the bulk of this increase coming after 1977.

In the period from 1977 to November 1982 Labour's share of the working-class vote dropped from 14 to 9 per cent and Fianna Fail's from 50 to 38 per cent.[126] The exact role of Fine Gael's fading social democratic pretensions in this increase of support is unclear, but there is some evidence that it was much more the promise of tax cuts which proved decisive. A recent analysis shows that it was amongst the skilled working class that Fine Gael significantly improved its position, there being only a slight improvement in its support among the unskilled.[127] It was the skilled workers, particularly those in the private sector who were most open to the appeal that their money incomes could be increased by cutting public expenditures going to support the 'unproductive' state sector and its 'overpaid' employees.[128]

The two coalition governments, the first a minority government which only lasted eight months before being defeated in the Dail in February 1982, and the second, majority coalition from 1982 to 1987, were much more seriously divided over questions of fundamental economic strategy than the 1973-77 government. FitzGerald would be bitterly criticised by an increasingly vocal section of his party for allowing the government to be 'contaminated' by the supposed left-wing philosophy of the Labour Party. The only element of reality in such claims was the fact that the Labour members of the government did exercise some restraining influence on the more swingeing proposals for radical cuts in public expenditure. But the restrictive and deflationary effects of the policies of the coalition governments were unmistakeable. In its report for 1985 the OECD described 1982 and 1983 as years of strict austerity in which private consumption fell by 8.5 per cent, something which had not happened in the Republic before, at least in peace time.[129] The real earnings of industrial workers which had risen on average 4 per cent per annum in the 1970s, fell by 3.5 per cent in 1981 and 4 per cent in 1982.[130] The coalition's budget in 1983 was bitterly attacked by the unions as 'retrograde and regressive'. It failed to index personal allowances and tax bands and imposed income surcharges and increased deductions for social insurance. A rise in the yield of income tax of 20 per cent was expected, the great bulk of it coming from the working class.[131] Such regressive and deflationary measures did succeed in reducing the Exchequer Borrowing Requirement from 16.5 per cent of GNP in 1982 to 13.25 per cent in 1983 and the inflation rate which had reached 20 per cent in 1981 was reduced to 6 per cent four years later.[132] This was, in combination with the international recession, at the cost of increasing redundancies and rising unemployment. In the three year period 1980-82 there were 57,000 redundancies, 24,000 in 1982 alone. By the end of 1983 unemployment was over 200,000 or 16 per cent of the workforce, the highest rate in the EEC and 6 per cent up on 1980.[133]

FitzGerald was increasingly reduced not to the language of social democracy but of 'supply side' economics: the need to create an appropriate business climate by removing such disincentives as high rates of taxation and 'rigidities' like too high union rates for entrants to the labour market and innovations like job-sharing.[134] In the crucial area of welfare expenditure the pressure of the Labour Party, and perhaps FitzGerald's own recollections of his earlier pretensions, had ensured that the initial impact of the restrictive budgetary policies was to halt the expansion of welfare provision that had continued during the 1970s, rather than to bring about any significant dismantling of social programmes.[135] However in its economic and social plan for 1985-87 the government made it clear that further fiscal adjustment would come much more through reductions in public expenditure than increases in taxation, and that this would mean real reductions in expenditure in areas like health, education and income maintenance.[136] The collapse of the social-democratic project, and the increasingly vocal rightism of a sizeable section of the Fine Gael party and government, helps to explain FitzGerald's increasing concern with his other main project – the development of a pluralist society in the Republic. As we shall see, his commitment to reform here was as unsuccessful as his flagging social democracy.

Corporatism and Irredentism: Fianna Fail 1970-87

In an article in the *Irish Press*, the paper established by de Valera to provide a daily sympathetic to Fianna Fail, the state of that party just after it had lost the 1973 election was perceptively and critically described. Its achievement of incorporating the major subordinate classes was seen as central:

> After sixteen years of continuous rule with only seven years in opposition since 1932, it is something unique in Western Europe that Fianna Fail has retained its overwhelming composition of small farmers, the working class and lower middle class. Its record is of industrial and social pragmatism with left of centre leanings.[137]

There was, however, a serious doubt about the party's ability to maintain this hegemonic capacity. This was partly because of the reverberations of the Arms Crisis, but more fundamentally because the social-democratic tendencies in Fine Gael and its move towards a coalition with Labour had produced a situation where 'all three Dail parties are agreed on most of the major national problems'.[138] The 'leftist' tone of the 1960s, the increased salience of welfare issues in political debate and the effects of this on Fine Gael had all combined to put pressure on Fianna Fail's capacity to portray itself as the only realistically progressive option. The party needed a 'new dynamic injected'. There would be little consensus on what such a dynamic should be.

For three years in opposition the party seemed to lurch opportunistically towards the right and away from Lynch's moderation on Northern Ireland. Colley, his invocations of the Democratic Programme behind him, now joined with Haughey in a major assault on the coalition's proposals for wealth and capital gains taxes. As Haughey presented the Fianna Fail case, there was a simple and stark choice between the policies that would stimulate economic growth and the taxation proposals, motivated he claimed by socialist dogmas: 'We are not a rich community with large accumulations of private wealth crying out to be redistributed in the name of social justice.'[139] In one sense his attack was typically shrewd. As he pointed out, the depth of the recession, the rapidly rising rates of redundancy and unemployment and high inflation could make the measures which would bring only a very modest return seem supremely irrelevant: 'The whole economic climate is gloomy and depressing. Against that background this passage of complicated measures is irrelevant.'[140] The new taxes – 'this socialistic juggernaut'[141] – were contrasted to the successful policies of the 1960s when the taxation system had allowed economic growth and social progress 'side by side' and not sacrificed growth to over-concern with social equality.[142] Barry Desmond, a Labour TD, described Haughey's statements as 'ultra right-wing Powellite policies; Mrs Thatcher is more progressive than Deputy Haughey'.[143] While other Fianna Fail members strained credulity in trying to maintain some strained and convuluted 'left' credibility,[144] Haughey was forthright in his articulation of the conservative instincts of Fianna Fail when confronted with any issue that threatens social solidarity. Arguing that 'the present economic crisis is the most deep seated and fundamental that this country has ever faced,'[145] he emphasised the danger of proposing measures on the basis of 'squeezing the rich for the benefit of the poor'.[146] The Republic was not capable of supporting 'some sort of super welfare state' and he castigated a government minister for 'boasting ... that we have the highest paid unemployed in Europe'.[147] True to one of the key characteristics of the national revolution and the earlier period of Fianna Fail hegemony, he was anxious to exorcise any distributional issue which threatened to pit one social group against another: 'It is no time for horse trading between different sections of the community.'[148] But, again true to the party's traditions, the success of such emphases on the need for national solidarity demanded other policies which made the label 'Thatcherite' highly inappropriate.

For while Haughey could attack state intervention in the field of distribution, he complemented this with a call for 'radical sweeping measures' to deal with unemployment and for a major government initiative involving state action that no neo-liberal economic philosophy would have found congenial. Thus he favoured a 'plan ... on a three, four or five year basis' with its main focus on employment creation. There was little evidence of a belief in the unsullied primacy of market forces in declarations like

> Let us be a little unorthodox and if the demand is not there ... for the products which our economy is capable of producing ... we should divert the productive potential of our economy into a vast programme of reconstruction, re-equipment and infrastructural development.[149]

It was a restatement of Lemassian themes, of a close partnership between an activist state and private capital, ignoring issues of social equity and even more importantly of whether the changed domestic and international economic conditions allowed scope for such a strategy. Its immediate political strength lay in its job creation appeal; its long-term weakness lay in its neglect of its implications for public expenditure and state finances.

The extent of the Fianna Fail victory in 1977 (50.6 per cent of vote, its highest share since 1938) surprised many commentators who had been predicting that its opposition to the coalition's taxation proposals would damage its electoral support amongst the working class.[150] Amongst businessmen who clearly favoured a return to Fianna Fail government, and were strongly sympathetic to Haughey for his perceived defence of their interests, a survey carried out just before the election showed that only 26 per cent expected a Fianna Fail victory.[151] An exaggerated fear that the masses were mainly concerned with questions of economic justice, encouraged by the 'socialistic' policies of the coalition, may account for such a serious underestimation of Fianna Fail potential.

In fact Fianna Fail had fought the election on a very expansionary manifesto, focusing on the central issue which undermined the coalition: unemployment – 71,435 (7.9 per cent) when it took office and 115,942 (12.5 per cent) four years later.[152]. The manifesto promises which included cuts in income tax, abolition of domestic rates and road tax, together with increases in social welfare and commitments to extra public service and building jobs, would according to one economist cost the equivalent of a massive 21 per cent increase in total tax revenue.[153] The government's economic strategy was set out in a White Paper, 'National Development 1977-1980'. Martin O'Donoghue, a Trinity economics professor who had been an adviser to Lynch and was now made head of a new Department of Economic Planning and Development, described the proposals as a 'gamble' – the use of a vigorous pump-priming strategy by the state to encourage private sector growth, after which the state's role would be lessened.[154]

The strategy was supposed to create 29,000 jobs outside agriculture each year to 1980, to halve inflation to 5 per cent and, despite a temporary necessary increase in expenditure and government borrowing, ultimately to cut borrowing as a percentage of GNP from 11 in January 1978 to 8 by 1980.[155] It depended for its success, according to its own calculations, on two crucial factors: ultimate export-led growth in a recovering world economy, and wage moderation by the trade unions. Neither would actually work in the strategy's favour.

There was a sharp but short increase in employment: between 1977 and 1979 numbers at work rose by over 60,000.[156] However the second large increase in oil prices at the end of 1978 and the onset of a deep international recession undercut some of the fundamental assumptions of the government's strategy. The possibilities of the private sector expanding to allow a recession by the state declined. In 1979, before the full deflationary effects of the oil price rise worked themselves out, O'Donoghue was still producing plans for annual growth rates of 6 per cent and the total elimination of unemployment by 1983.[157] The government, as external factors turned against its policies, was forced to give increasing emphasis to the one internal factor which it claimed could radically improve both the government's ability to control its expenditure and the private sector's ability to compete internationally. As an important critic of successive governments' expenditure and taxation policies put it. 'The main policy requirement of the Irish economy at present is to achieve a consensus on money income growth.'[158] This comment came in a period of economic growth but was based on the calculation that if government was to take radical action to create jobs through 'pump priming', even in a favourable international environment this would inevitably trigger substantial inflationary pressures unless there was an incomes policy. He was later to comment that the Republic needed 'a uniquely high degree of national consensus on limiting the rate in rise of real living standards' if the government's objectives were to be achieveable.[159] As international conditions deteriorated the pressures increased for moves towards a reinvigoration and deepening of the corporatist tendencies of the 1960s involving employers and unions in a 'partnership' with the state for economic growth.

The expansionary conditions of the 1960s and early 1970s had favoured a rapid growth in trade union membership, which was already high by international standards.[160] By the end of the 1970s, 60 per cent of those at work were in unions, the third highest rate of unionisation in the EEC.[161] In the 1960s Fianna Fail governments had striven to integrate the trade union leadership into their development strategy with some degree of success. Economic growth and job creation were offered in return for wage moderation. A central problem for the development of some variant of the 'democratic corporatism' strategy, characteristic of other smaller European states, was the absence of one of the three factors which the most serious study of the strategy defines as essential: 'a relatively centralised and concentrated system of interest groups'.[162] The trade union movement in the Republic was fragmented, with no less than 85 different unions in 1979.[163] The majority of these unions were affiliated to the Irish Congress of Trade Unions and under Lemass and Lynch a central objective of government policy was to persuade the ICTU to play a more effective role in moderating wage demands. But the evidence from the 1960s showed a union leadership with little effective control over its membership: in 1964 the Republic topped the world league in working hours lost through strikes, and rank-and-file industrial militancy was a marked feature of the decade.[164] The 1970s were marked by new departures in government/union relations. Free wage bargaining had already been replaced by centralised collective bargaining between the ICTU and the employers' organisations in National Wage Agreements. The government did not play a formal role in these negotiations although they were influenced by budgetary policy and tax concessions. However in the second half of the 1970s there was a move to formal governmental involvement in tripartite discussions which culminated in the National Understandings for Economic and Social Development in 1979 and 1980. These represented the most serious attempt to develop a corporatist relationship between the state and producer groups in the history of the Republic. They involved very complex trade-offs between union commitments to pay restraint and government action on a wide range of issues – health, education, taxation and employment.[165] Even before the onset of the recession, however, there were signs that the strategy was not working.

The economic expansion from 1976 stimulated wage militancy and industrial relations turbulence. This was fuelled by increasing urban working-class resentment at a farming community whose incomes had been substantially improved by EEC membership but still made a niggardly contribution to tax revenues. The pressures of an oppressive and regressive tax system encouraged an inevitable but self-defeating wage militancy. In 1978 average earnings in industry rose by 17 per cent, twice the figure allowed for in the National Wage Agreement.[166] In 1979 O'Donoghue admitted that the targets of government strategy on job creation would not be reached if the rate of pay increases was not substantially reduced.[167] Critics of the strategy in the business and financial community increasingly pointed out that Irish wage rates were rising at a substantially faster rate than those in Britain and Europe.[168] Such disillusion with corporatism would become much more articulate as the effects of the 130 per cent increase in oil prices destroyed most of the assumptions of the post-1977 economic policies. A 50 per cent decline in the growth rate of world trade (from 8.6 per cent in 1960-73 to 4.2 in 1974-80) had already created a decidedly less hospitable environment for corporatism in all those small European countries where it had flourished and which were, like the Republic, heavily dependent on trade.[169] One of the few Irish economists sympathetic to a broadly Keynesian and corporatist approach pointed out that such a strategy faced a major crisis in conditions where, although there had already been almost a decade of much reduced rates of economic growth, there was little evidence that popular expectations of continuous improvement had been affected: 'Judging by the sustained upward pressure on money incomes, there is little doubt that expectations have remained influenced by the favourable experience prior to 1973.'[170] The Republic faced a 'crisis of Keynesianism' and, although he clearly rejected a move towards right-wing solutions, 'no democratic government can survive for long if it fails to do all in its power to achieve full employment,' he had no clear suggestions for salvaging his preferred approach in the much more hostile conditions of the early 1980s.

The increasing consensus amongst economists, political commentators and an emerging current of opinion in both the main parties was a replication of the themes of Thatcher and Reagan. The state, it was argued, had become too big, it was crowding out private enterprise and initiative:

> The state has portrayed itself, particularly in the last ten years ... as the purveyor of virtually everything good and the preventor of everything bad. The state is seen in this country, as the place of first resort rather than, as I would see it, the place of last resort.[171]

This version of neo-liberal themes was given by Desmond O'Malley in March 1979, while he was still a senior member of the Fianna Fail government. That such a fundamental repudiation of the role of the state would be maintained by O'Malley, when Haughey was to first appear to support it and then quickly repudiate it in practise, would be one of the most fundamental issues that resulted in O'Malley's departure from the party and the formation of the Progressive Democrats. The right-wing radicalism of O'Malley's proposals was at fundamental variance with the development of Fianna Fail political strategy since the time of de Valera. The ability to portray Fianna Fail as a 'national movement' rather than a mere political party, a movement not tied to any particular class, but at the same time responsive to the 'plain people of Ireland', depended on a vigorous use of the state. However from the 1930s to the 1970s the role of the state was seen as auxiliary to, and facilitator of, private enterprise. The integration of the Republic's economy into the international economy after 1957 demanded an even more extensive state involvement, both economically and in terms of the increased social expenditure necessary to ensure social harmony. The slowing of growth in the 1970s, culminating in the debt crisis and the associated rise in demands for cuts in public expenditure, created a major political problem for Fianna Fail. Ideologically it had never questioned the ultimate primacy of private enterprise in its development plans. However the continuing crisis of indigenous industry and the limitations of the influence of the enclave of foreign industry on the rest of the economy, led inevitably to a substitutionism by the state in the struggle to create employment. This expansion of the state's role reflected the central importance of job creation and employment in the reconstitution of Fianna Fail hegemony that took place under Lemass. Until the end of the 1970s it had experienced no serious problem in reconciling the roles of state and private enterprise. From 1979 the twin poles of its developmental strategy entered into clear contradiction. It became increasingly difficult for the party to reconcile its role in the elaboration of strategies that would allow for the expanded reproduction of domestic and foreign capital and at the same time maintain its hitherto unchallenged hegemony over the working class. It would be this contradiction which underlay the vacillations and sudden reversals of policy under Haughey after 1979.

In his mobilisation of support in the struggle to succeed Lynch, Haughey had criticised the expansionary economic policies associated with the 1977 manifesto, and when elected leader he would abolish O'Donoghue's Department of Economic Planning and Development. Some of those who supported him in 1979 did so because he was identified as the potential leader most likely to push through right-wing policies, particularly large cuts in public expenditure.[172] In a television address to the nation in January 1980 Haughey, who had just become Taoiseach, declared: 'We have been living at a rate which is simply not justified by the amount of goods and services we are producing.' He appeared to commit the government to action to reduce its level of borrowing, but in the remaining months of office continued to spend and borrow in a typically 1970s fashion. In opposition to the short-lived coalition he would publicly castigate it for its 'Thatcherite monetarism'.[173] In office briefly in 1982 he would continue to echo very traditional corporatist themes:

> There are those who think that economic policies can be pursued on the basis of confrontation with the trade union movement. We do not subscribe to that in any way. We have every confidence in the responsibility and maturity of our trade union leaders, and will continue to develop our economy on the basis of taking fairly into account those trade union leaders and the trade union movement as a whole.[174]

Out of office from 1982 to 1987, Fianna Fail could blame the coalition for increasing unemployment and the return of substantial rates of emigration. It could attack the coalition from the left for its 'Thatcherism' whilst at the same time ultimately benefiting from the lowering of popular expectations which the recession and deflationary policies produced. The 1987 election campaign 'witnessed a substantial restoration of the corporatist imagery of Fianna Fail' with 'the emphasis on growth and the reassertion of the national interest; the attempt to incorporate the unions and the plea for social solidarity'.[175] The result was less than reassuring for the party: it recorded its lowest popular vote since 1961 and for the fourth time in succession it failed to achieve an overall Dail majority. It was still the case that the only region where its performance improved on 1982 was Dublin, and that this came from an increase in its working-class support.[176] This support reflected the party's refusal, while acknowledging the need for cuts, to specify them and its commitment to cuts that avoided hitting those most in need. It also reflected the alternatives available – a small and divided left and two other parties, Fine Gael and the Progressive Democrats, who competed in right-wing rigour.

The increasing fragility of a corporatist strategy in domestic and international economic circumstances of the late 1980s is apparent from a reading of the Programme for National Recovery which the new government negotiated with ICTU, the employers' and farmers' organisations in October 1987. The constraints were clearly set out: a GDP per capita of only 64 per cent of the European Community average; a national debt of over £25 billion (Irish), equivalent to one-and-a-half times the GNP, the servicing of which consumes one third of tax revenue; no overall growth in the volume of investment in equipment in the previous five years; an unemployment rate of 18.5 per cent – 242,000 people – and a net emigration rate of 30,000 a year, equivalent to the rate of natural increase.[177] The increasing recognition, particularly since the Telesis report, of the inadequacies of an industrialisation strategy geared so heavily to the attraction of foreign capital, is reflected in an emphasis on the need to strengthen and expand indigenous manufacturing industry. However the approach was exhortatory and lacking in any very specific ideas about how the fundamental weaknesses of domestic industry would be tackled in a way which would also create new jobs.[178] In return for such essentially empty forecasts of new jobs, union support was elicited for an attempt to hold down pay increases to 2.5 per cent in each of the three succeeding years and for a reduction in employment in the public sector, the only concession from the government being that it would attempt to see that redundancies were voluntary.[179]

As the problem of unemployment increasingly appears to be structural rather than cyclical – an Economist Intelligence Unit report estimated that it could rise to 23 per cent by 1992 – the viability of a corporatist strategy which excludes over a fifth of the working class and sends a growing proportion into permanent exile could be put into question.[180] If, as seemed the case increasingly in the first year of the new government, it is little more than a device for boxing off union criticism of public expenditure cuts in health and education then it will have ceased to act as a fundamental material basis for Fianna Fail hegemony. This will not, in itself, produce a major realignment of Irish politics, but it will, by weakening the grip of the party on the working class, create new possibilities of development for both right and left.

Both Mair and Walsh have suggested that the difficulties of maintaining a broadly corporatist approach in a period of recession accounts for a resurgence of traditional nationalism since Haughey became leader in 1979.[181] However there is no possibility of the 'national question' becoming a substitute for Fianna Fail's lack of a credible economic strategy. Thus to give some evidence from the 1987 election, a poll survey of five issues as to whether they were seen as 'very important' had the only related issue, the Anglo-Irish Agreement, come bottom by a large margin at 15 per cent, compared to 'reduce unemployment' at 97 per cent and 'reduce taxation' at 76 per cent.[182] The continuing instability and violence in Northern Ireland would have complex effects on popular attitudes. While it strengthened the nationalist assumption that only unity could bring a final solution, at the same time it brought home the intractabilities of the north and the unwelcome burdens and costs that moves toward unity could bring. One survey of the evidence of opinion polls sums up the contradictions:

> Three trends are immediately identifiable: first, there has been a noticeable increase in popular approval of Irish unity ... second there has been a noticeable increase in scepticism about the likelihood of unity; and third, there is a noticeable increase in the reluctance to do anything to achieve unity.[183]

Traditional anti-partitionism was still a major resource in the internal struggles in Fianna Fail after the Arms Crisis. Lynch's moderation, popular though it was with large swathes of the electorate, was seen as craven, particularly after the collapse of the power-sharing strategy in the 1974 Ulster Workers' Council strike. The Labour government's increasing lack of interest in constitutional innovation, and its apparent willingness to treat direct rule from London as the best possible way of running Northern Ireland, encouraged a traditionalist response in Fianna Fail. Already in 1975 Lynch had been forced to accept a restatement of the party's northern policy calling for a British declaration of intent to withdraw as a prerequisite for progress, although he quickly moved to attempt to obfuscate the new policy.[184] Haughey assiduously courted the most traditional bastions of gut republicanism in the constituencies along the border and on the western seaboard. In the 1979 leadership contest with Colley the latter got the support of only one TD west of the Shannon and along the entire west coast.[185] Opposition to Lynch's perceived 'anti-national' policies had simmered in these areas since 1970, waiting for an opportunity to express itself. Blaney, expelled in 1972, was a hero to many who remained in Fianna Fail and his substantial victory in the elections to the European Parliament in 1979, with more than a quarter of all votes cast in the constituency, was produced by substantial Fianna Fail defections.[186] However although this 'western rebellion' was an important precipitant of Lynch's resignation, it is doubtful if in itself it would have achieved it. Its limitation was clear in its most symbolic act of disaffection – a speech at a republican commemoration ceremony in Fermoy by Sile de Valera, the 'Chief's' granddaughter – which attacked Lynch's alleged weakness in standing up to the British. Although a sympathetic journalist could claim that her hard-line sentiments 'go right to the heart of the rank and file',[187] her own world view, which was obsessively traditionalist, would not have been an obvious basis for the party's electoral rejuvenation.[188]

If Lynch had not been weakened by the increasing problems of his post-1977 economic strategy he would not have been vulnerable to such an upsurge of primitivism. But it was precisely because of the increasing unpopularity of his government, as the 1979 European and local government election results showed in the most modernised and urbanised sectors of Irish society, that the traditionalists could assert themselves successfully. It was issues like the inequities of the taxation system, government moves to abolish food subsidies and a hard-line stance against striking postal workers which undermined its corporatist appeal and produced increased working-class disaffection. Thus, although for traditionalists it was Lynch's alleged willingness to be humiliated by Thatcher in the aftermath of the IRA's murder of Lord Mountbatten and his party in Sligo that sealed his fate,[189] much more crucial was the Fianna Fail defeat in two by-elections in Cork where the most significant feature was the large increase in support for left-wing candidates.[190]

Haughey's narrow victory over Colley in the leadership election inaugurated a period of intense internal turmoil in Fianna Fail. While the vast majority of his Cabinet colleagues had voted against him, Haughey had had the support of a substantial majority of TDs.[191] For Lynch loyalists like Desmond O'Malley, the Haughey victory was that of the 'yahoo' element, acceptable as foot-soldiers, but disastrous as an influence on policy. The veteran Irish socialist Noel Browne had commented in 1978 that 'The sick tragedy of Irish public life ... is the existence within Fianna Fail of this off-stage, silent conspiracy to silently destroy one another.'[192] For three years after Haughey's accession, the conspiracy was centre stage and far from silent. Three attempts to dislodge Haughey would all fail, in large part because the opposition was divided into rival camps. His major opponent, Desmond O'Malley, would eventually be expelled from the party in February 1985 and found the Progressive Democrats at the end of that year.[193] For O'Malley and other critics of Haughey he was taking Fianna Fail in an authoritarian, narrowly nationalist and illiberal direction. Its self-image as the natural party of government with monolithic party discipline has been irrevocably destroyed. Together with the weakening of its ability to maintain popular support through policies of a corporatist type, its neo-traditionalist emphases are an indicator of its weakening grip on popular politics. The implications of this will be considered in the following chapter.

Notes

1. Constance Markievicz, *What Irish Republicans Stand For*, pamphlet n.d., reprinted from *Forward*, Glasgow 1923.
2. T. Ryle Dwyer, *Charlie: The Political Biography of C.J. Haughey*. Dublin 1987, pp.16-25.
3. *Irish Times*, 4 November 1966.
4. 'The Berry Papers: The Secret Memoirs of the Man who was the Country's Most Powerful Civil Servant', *Magill*, June 1980, p.48.
5. Jack Lynch 'My Life and Times', *Magill*, November 1979.
6. *Irish Times*, 5 November 1966.
7. Ibid.
8. *Irish Times*, 19 October 1968.
9. Dwyer, op.cit., p.67.
10. *Irish Times*, 3 October 1968.
11. Dwyer, op.cit., p.68.
12. *Irish Times*, 10 October 1968.
13. C. O'Leary, *Irish Elections 1918-1977*, Dublin 1979, p.68.
14. *Irish Times*, 18 October 1968.
15. *Irish Times*, 6 December 1968.
16. The Democratic Programme of Dail Eireann, quoted in Dorothy Macardle, *The Irish Republic*, London 1968, pp.254-5.
17. *Irish Times*, 6 December 1968.
18. *Irish Times*, 29 January 1969.
19. *Irish Times*, 11 December 1968.
20. *Irish Times*, 29 January 1969.
21. Michael Gallagher, *The Irish Labour Party in Transition 1957-82*, Dublin and Manchester 1982, p.91.
22. Ibid., p.83.
22. Berry papers, p.50.
24. Gallagher, op.cit., p.93.
25. See P. Bew and H. Patterson, *Sean Lemass and the Making of Modern Ireland*, Dublin 1982, for the role of MacEntee.
26. *Irish Times*, 29 May 1969.
27. Bew and Patterson, *Sean Lemass*, p.161.
28. Ibid.
29. For an interesting discussion of Fianna Fail approach to welfare issues, see Peter Mair, *The Changing Irish Party System*, Manchester 1987, p.187-8.
30. Ibid.
31. Maria Maguire, 'Ireland' in Peter Flora (ed.), *Growth to Limits: The*

Western European Welfare States since World War II, Berlin and New York 1986, p.343.

32. Ibid., p.342.

33. Michael Gallagher, *Political Parties in the Republic of Ireland*, Dublin 1985, pp.156 and 158.

34. Dick Walsh, *The Party*, Dublin 1986, p.90.

35. Peter Mair, 'The Irish Republic and the Anglo-Irish Agreement' in Paul Teague (ed.), *Beyond the Rhetoric*, London 1987.

36. Lynch's speech to the 1970 Ard Fheis is quoted in Geraldine Kennedy, 'The Thoughts of Chairman Jack', *Magill*, February 1978.

37. For a balanced analysis of arms crisis see Dwyer, op.cit., pp.72-100. For a participant's view see Kevin Boland, *Up Dev!*, Dublin n.d., pp.142-9.

38. Dick Walsh, political editor of the *Irish Times*, pointed out Lynch's temperamental aversion to what he regarded as argumentative and intransigent Northerners of both 'traditions' in an interview with one of the authors.

39. Berry, op.cit., recalls a memorandum which he encouraged his minister to circulate to the government in July 1969. It gave a comprehensive analysis of the IRA and 'emphasised again that the time had become opportune to drive a wedge between the rural members – the old faithfuls – and the doctrinaire republicans, mainly based in Dublin, who were sedulously propagating the gospel of a "Workers' Socialist Republic" ', p.50.

40. Francie Donnelly, who had been approached by Blaney in the spring of 1969, was subsequently offered a wage and a car to organise 'reliable' republicans in opposition to the 'reds' in the Dublin leadership. Interview with one of authors.

41. Goulding went to London with Padraig Haughey, the minister's brother, selected by him to go to Britain to enlist support for the government's relief activities in the north. The Irish Special Branch believed he was engaged in buying weapons and Goulding returned from London with a substantial sum of money for that purpose. Dwyer, op.cit., p.76 and interview with Cathal Goulding.

42. See Dwyer, op.cit., pp.3-7.

34. See Berry papers, p.48.

44. Quoted in Walsh, op.cit., p.100.

45. *Irish Times*, 22 February 1971.

46. Damien Hannan, 'Ireland's New Social and Moral Climate', *New Society*, 18 November 1982.

47. Ken O'Brien, 'Investment Earns a High Return', *Times*, 25 February 1981.

48. Bew and Patterson, *Sean Lemass*, p.101.

49. 'The Poorest of the Rich; A Survey of the Republic of Ireland', *Economist*, 16 January 1988, p.17. An IDA booklet published in 1974 under 'Financial Incentives' listed 'Total freedom from tax on profits generated by exports until 1990' and 'complete freedom from government control over investment of profits'. As George Colley explained in the

Dail, 'I have had personal experience of dealing with potential investors. They were always anxious to know if we would restrict them from taking profits out of the country. ... It was always a matter of vital importance that we were able to assure them that they were free to do what they liked with their profits.' This was part of his attack on the coalition's Capital Gains Tax Bill: *PDDE (Parliamentary Debates, Dail Eireann)*, Vol.278 col.134, 11 February 1975.

50. J. Blackwell and E. O'Malley, 'EEC Membership and Irish Industry' in P.J. Drudy and D. McAleese (eds), *Ireland and the European Community*, Cambridge 1986, p.109 and D. McAleese, 'Ireland in the World Economy' in K.A. Kenedy (ed.), *Ireland in Transition*, Cork and Dublin 1986, p.21.

51. D.A. Gillmor, *Economic Activities in the Republic of Ireland: A Geographical Perspective*. Dublin 1985, p.31.

52. McAleese, op.cit.p.20.

53. Ibid. p.20.

54. 'The Poorest of the Rich', p.15.

55. McAleese, op.cit., p.20 and 'The Poorest of the Rich', p.16.

56. K.A. Kennedy, 'Industry: The Revolution Unfinished' in Kennedy (ed.), op.cit., p.40.

57. Raymond Crotty, *Ireland in Crisis*, Dingle 1986, p.100.

58. Kennedy, op.cit., p.44.

59. OECD, *Economic Survey: Ireland*, 1981, pp.40-1. In one sector dominated by native capital, clothing and footwear, imports were negligible in 1959 and by 1985 accounted for 75 per cent of the domestic market. McAleese, op.cit., p.24.

60. J. Fitzpatrick and J.H. Kelly, 'Industry in Ireland. Policies, Performance and Problems' in Fitzpatrick and Kelly (eds), *Perspective on Irish Industry*, Dublin 1985, p.xxi.

61. *Irish Banking Review*, June 1976, p.7.

62. Kennedy, op.cit., p.46.

63. 'The Poorest of the Rich', p.18.

64. McAleese, op.cit., p.21.

65. Ibid, p.26.

66. Fitzpatrick and Kelly, op.cit., p.xxiii.

67. 'The Poorest of the Rich', p.16.

68. Kennedy, op.cit., p.44.

69. *Irish Times*, 17 May 1985.

70. *Irish Times*, 24 May 1985.

71. 'The Poorest of the Rich', p.19.

72. Gillmor, op.cit., p.24.

73. Bew and Patterson, *Sean Lemass*, p.78.

74. See K.H. Connell, *Irish Peasant Society*, Oxford 1968.

75. Gillmor, op.cit., pp.25-6.

76. Ibid., p.27.

77. OECD, *Economic Surveys: Ireland*, May 1978, p.30.

78. OECD, *Economic Surveys: Ireland*, January 1981, p.11.

79. Ibid., p.34.

80. J.J. Sexton, 'Employment, Unemployment and Emigration' in Kennedy (ed.), op.cit., p.34.
81. Brendan Walsh, 'The Growth of Government' in Kennedy (ed.), op.cit., p.68.
82. Maguire, op.cit., pp.286-7 and p.345.
83. Joseph Lee, 'Whither Ireland? The Next Twenty-Five Years' in Kennedy (ed.), op.cit., p.160.
84. Sexton, op.cit., pp.33-4.
85. Walsh, op.cit., p.69.
86. Maguire, op.cit., pp.312 and 343.
87. Ibid., p.343.
88. Ibid., p.341.
89. *PDDE*, Vol.289, col.1087, 7 April 1976.
90. OECD, *Economic Surveys: Ireland*, May 1978, p.27.
91. Ibid.
92. See T.K. Whitaker, *Interests*, Dublin 1983, pp.104-8.
93. Maguire, op.cit., p.345.
94. Gallagher, *Irish Labour Party,* p.198.
95. Sexton, op.cit.
96. OECD, *Economic Surveys:Ireland*, January 1981, pp.6 and 13.
97. Maguire, op.cit., p.345.
98. Ibid., p.346.
99. *Guardian*, 4 July 1977.
100. Bew and Patterson, *Sean Lemass*, pp.148-9 and Mair, *The Changing Irish Party System*, p.30 table 1.2.
101. Mair, Ibid., p.186.
102. Ibid., p.187.
103. Maguire, op.cit., pp.339-40.
104. Bew and Patterson, *Sean Lemass*, p.150.
105. Ronan Fanning, 'The Life and Times of Alexis FitzGerald', *Magill*, September 1985.
106. Gallagher, *Irish Labour Party*, p.118.
107. Ibid., pp.200-4.
108. We are not suggesting that Fianna Fail is a social-democratic party or much influenced by formal social-democratic ideas, only that from the early 1960s, under the aegis of Lemass, its semi-corporatist approach to economic policy allowed it to develop a close relationship with the leadership of the trade unions.
109. 'Radical Intellect, Cautious Instinct', *Magill*, May 1978.
110. Thus Declan Costello, 'I believe that Fine Gael should move openly and firmly to the left,' quoted in Mair, op.cit., p.185.
111. 'Garret FitzGerald: Profile of Expectation', *Magill*, January 1978.
112. OECD, *Economic Surveys: Ireland*, March 1974, pp.287-9.
113. James Raftery, 'Patterns of Taxation, and Public Expenditure: Towards a Corporatist Approach' in M. Kelly, L. O'Dowd and J. Wickham (eds), *Power, Conflict and Inequality*, Dublin 1982, p.138.
114. OECD, *Economic Surveys: Ireland*, March 1974, pp.28-9.
115. Raftery, op.cit., p.133.

116. Maguire, op.cit., p.362.
117. Ibid., pp.362 and 363.
118. Christopher T. Whelan, 'Class and Social Mobility' in Kennedy (ed.), op.cit., pp.84-5.
119. Maguire, op.cit., p.366.
120. *Magill*, May 1981.
121. Mair, *The Changing Irish Party System*, p.213.
122. Stephen O'Byrnes, *Hiding behind a Face: Fine Gael under Garret FitzGerald*, Dublin 1986, p.73.
123. Gallagher, *Irish Labour Party*, p.235.
124. Gallagher, *Political Parties*, pp.156-7.
125. See O'Byrnes, op.cit.
126. Mair, *The Changing Irish Party System*, p.42.
127. R. Sinnott, M. Laver and M. Marsh, 'Patterns of Party Support' in M. Laver, P. Mair and R. Sinnott, *How Ireland Voted: The Irish General Election of 1987*, Dublin 1987, Table 1, p.102.
128. FitzGerald was typical in an attack on high levels of public sector pay in an interview in 1981, *Magill*, April 1981.
129. OECD quoted in *Guardian*, 24 May 1985.
130. Irish Congress of Trade Unions (ICTU), *25th Annual Report*. 1983, p.137.
131. Ibid., p.198.
132. ICTU, *26th Annual Report*, 1984, p.131.
132. ICTU, *25th Annual Report*, 1983, p.180.
134. FitzGerald speech to Ard Fheis, *Irish Times*, 20 May 1985.
135. Maguire, op.cit., p.351.
136. Ibid., p.352.
137. *Irish Press*, June 7 1973.
138. Ibid.
139. *PDDE*, Vol.279 col.1149, 6 March 1975.
140. Ibid., col.1141.
141. *PDDE*, Vol.280 col. 1153, 29 April 1975.
142. *PDDE*, Vol.279 col. 1149, 6 March 1975.
143. *PDDE*, Vol.278 col. 434, 11 February 1975.
144. Thus Gene FitzGerald, a Fianna Fail TD in a debate on unemployment: 'I believe in the best aspects of socialism ... in equal opportunity for all our people ... some of them can grasp it better than others if some of them, by hard work, enterprise and initiative, make a better success than others, then they, who in turn can help those who have not done so well, deserve to be assisted and encouraged by the state. Instead taxation was being employed to kill initiative and effort.' *PDDE*, Vol.280 col.624, 29 April. 1975.
145. *PDDE*, Vol.282 col.2140, 27 June 1975.
146. *PDDE*, Vol.279 col.1145, 6 March 1975.
147. *PDDE*, Vol.282 col. 2132, 27 June 1975.
148. Ibid.
149. Ibid., col.2141.
150. See an analysis by Jim Corrigan in *Hibernia*, 13 February 1976: 'The

party's opposition to the wealth tax and capital gains tax may attract to it some former Fine Gael supporters and financiers; but the image of protector of the rich is unlikely to recommend itself to the urban lower and middle classes.'

151. The survey was of 34 chief executives of 'leading industrial and business concerns.' *Business and Finance*, 16 June 1977.

152. Gallagher, *The Irish Labour Party*, p.198.

153. Sean D.Barrett, 'Lynch's Manifesto – Dangers in the Small Print', *Business and Finance*, 23 June 1977.

154. 'Will the White Paper Work?', *Business and Finance*, 19 January 1978.

155. Ibid.

156. Sexton, op.cit.

157. 'The Stuff that Dreams are made of', *Business and Finance*, 11 January 1979.

158. *Irish Banking Review*, December 1976, p.4.

159. Ibid., September 1978, p.13.

160. Bew and Patterson, *Sean Lemass*, p.189.

161. Michael Fogarty, 'The Two Faces of Irish Industrial Relations' in Kennedy (ed.), op.cit., p.114.

162. Peter J. Katzenstein, *Small States in World Markets*, Ithaca and London 1985, p.32: 'Democratic corporatism is distinguished by three traits: an ideology of social partnership expressed at the national level; a relatively centralised and concentrated system of interest groups; and voluntary and informal coordination of conflicting objectives through continuous political bargaining between interest groups, state bureaucracies and political parties.'

163. Maguire, op.cit., p.338.

164. Bew and Patterson, *Sean Lemass*, p.173.

165. Bill Roche, 'Social Partnership and Political Controls; State Strategy and Industrial relations in Ireland' in M. Kelly *et al.* op.cit., p.63.

166. *Irish Banking Review*, December 1978.

167. *Business and Finance* 11 January 1979.

168. See *Irish Banking Review* December 1979, 'In the past decade earnings in Irish industry rose 50 per cent faster than in the country's main trading partners.'

169. Katzenstein, op.cit., p.192.

170. Kieran Kennedy, 'Employment and Unemployment: Prospects in Ireland', *Irish Banking Review*, September 1980.

171. Dick Walsh, *Des O'Malley: A Political Profile*, Dingle 1986, p.57.

172. Thus Charles McCreevy, the Kildare TD whom Haughey had expelled from the Parliamentary party in 1982 for 'disloyalty' had played a prominent role in mobilising support for him in 1979 as the candidate most likely to curb 'profligacy' in the national finances see Vincent Browne, 'Charlie McCreevy: An End to Political Hedonism', *Magill*, January 1982.

173. *Magill*, December 1981.

174. *PDDE*, Vol.337 col.564, 1 July 1982.

175. Mair, *The Changing Irish Party System*, p.219.

176. Michael Gallagher, 'The Outcome' in Laver *et al.*, op.cit., p.70.

177. Programme for National Recovery (PI 5213), p.5.

178. Thus it states possibilities as if they were already facts: 'Tool-making – Output can be increased by £5 million per year ... giving about 1,000 extra jobs. ... Electronics – The indigenous electronics sector will be doubled in size within five years,' p.19.

179. Ibid., pp.9-10.

180. *Irish Times*, 29 July 1988.

181. Mair, *The Changing Irish Party System*, p.214 and Walsh, *The Party*, p.157.

182. Sinnott *et al.*, 'Patterns of Party Support', p.117.

183. Mair, 'The Irish Republic and the Anglo-Irish Agreement', p.89: in 1980 only 29 per cent found paying extra taxes an acceptable price for unity.

184. 'The Thoughts of Chairman Jack', *Magill*, February 1978.

185. *Hibernia*, 13 December 1979.

186. Ibid., 12 June 1979.

187. Ibid., 13 September 1979.

188. Ibid.: 'Her sole concern in Fianna Fail is the north and Fianna Fail's republican mission.'

189. Ibid., 6 September 1979.

190. Ibid., 15 November 1974.

191. Ibid., 13 December 1979.

192. Ibid., 16 February 1978.

192. See Thomas Lyne, 'The Progressive Democrats 1985-87', *Irish Political Studies*, Vol.2 1987, pp.107-14.

4   The Crisis of Social Democracy

> I gather from Deputy Tully that someone accused the Labour
> Party of going 'Red', which hurt his feelings very much. May I
> straightaway dissociate myself from any such suggestion? The
> Labour Party are, and always have been, the most conservative
> element in our community. Far from the Labour Party going
> 'Red', they are not going anywhere ... The Labour Party are a
> nice, respectable, docile, harmless body of men – as harmless a
> body as ever graced any parliament.[1]

The Irish Labour Party's formation in 1912 as the Irish
Trade Union Congress and Labour Party makes it the state's
oldest political party, and its foundation heralded the efforts
of the trade union movement to establish an independent
political voice for itself in the anticipated Ireland of Home
Rule. That the Home Rule legislation was drowned in the
euphoria of the First World War only temporarily blinded
the party to existing opposition to any form of Irish
independence or a labour party separate from the British
Labour Representation Council: similar feelings had already
thwarted plans to establish an independent labour party in
1900, 1907, 1908 and 1911. Undaunted, the Labour Party
endeavoured to weave an image of political neutrality
against a background of unionist participation in the British
war effort and nationalist support for the Easter Rising of
1916. Admirable as these efforts were, they were
increasingly difficult to uphold given that the political aims
of its founders, James Connolly and Jim Larkin, were to
provide a labour party for nationalist labour. Connolly's
claim was that the 'cause of labour was the cause of Ireland,
and the cause of Ireland was the cause of labour'. In
subsequent years the Labour Party's political fortunes
became more openly identified with desires for a 'republic':

once the Irish Free State was established in 1922 it abandoned its neutral stance on Irish unity and participated in the Dail, initially as the main opposition party. By June 1927 it had obtained 22 out of 128 seats, enough to fuel a rumour of a possible future coalition with Fianna Fail prior to the following September's elections.[2]

The Labour Party has been nurtured electorally and organisationally by the trade union movement ever since its foundation, although these links have at times been far from cordial. Structurally, the ties were broken in 1930 after several years of electoral decline, and for several decades thereafter relations between the two wings of the labour movement were strained. Accusations over the role of British-based trade unions in Ireland, culminating in the Trade Union Act of 1941, varying interpretations of the relationship between socialism and Catholicism, and responses to Fianna Fail's Wages Standstill Order of 1940 split both the Irish Trade Union Congress (ITUC) and the Labour Party along lines which, broadly speaking, depended on whether a union's headquarters were British or Irish-based.[3] The split meant that the first inter-party government of 1948-51 contained members from both the Labour Party and the breakaway National Labour Party.[4] Unity was restored to the unions and the party in 1955: the 1960s saw the three major general unions – the Workers' Union of Ireland (WUI), the Irish Transport and General Workers' Union (ITGWU) and the Amalgamated Transport and General Workers' Union (ATGWU) – reaffiliate to the Labour Party, thereby bolstering its financial reserves. Today fifteen of the Republic's 61 unions affiliated to the Irish Congress of Trade Unions are also affiliated to the party.

Internal conflict and suspicion have been a constant feature in the Labour Party's history, engendered by competing aims and class interests within and between its political and industrial sections. A compromise constitution in 1914 sought to pre-empt these difficulties by ensuring that the newly formed party remained an ITUC-sponsored one, that only trade unionists could be members and that the 'professional politician who was doing as much harm as good' was excluded.[5] Yet these relations imprinted a pragmatic view of socialism upon the party, for although the first party congress in 1914 urged that 'labour unrest can only be ended by the abolition of the capitalist wealth production with its inherent injustice and poverty,' the Labour Party offered only palliatives. Parliamentary activity, with its own set of priorities, exaggerated these differences and led to the opening of a new rift between the party and organised labour. In the mid-1920s the party admitted small farmers and other individuals. The split in 1930 between the ITUC and the Labour Party transformed a trade union party into a mass-based organisation. T.J. O'Connell, party leader between 1927 and 1932, reflected the view of many members:

> Our ranks must be as comprehensive as our policies, uniting farmer and town worker, wage-earner, salary-earner, professional man, shop-keeper, industrialist, housewife, in the bonds of genuine political conviction, realist patriotism and patient enthusiasm for social progress and reconstruction.[6]

In either organisational format Labour's view of socialism was principally one of 'social unity' not 'class solidarity'. In its eagerness to be seen as a defender of Irish nationalism and not as an advocate of a 'foreign' ideology, Labour relied heavily upon rhetorical images of a future united Ireland based upon versions of Connollyism, substituting the concerns of 'class' with those of the 'nation'.[7]

There is little doubt that the rise of fascism on the Continent and the struggles of 'Catholic' Spain gave vent to a particularly virulent form of anti-communism in Ireland. The Blueshirts represented one form of reaction. Another was Fianna Fail which came to power in 1932, the same year as the Dublin Eucharistic Congress, and linked the concerns of nationalism and Catholicism in the preamble of the rewritten constitution of 1937:

> We, the people of Eire, humbly acknowledging all our obligations to our Divine Lord, Jesus Christ, who sustained our fathers through centuries of trial, gratefully remembering their

heroic and unremitting struggle to regain the rightful independence of our Nation ...

In addition to such religious fanaticism the Labour Party encountered the difficulties of late industrialisation, a relatively small working class, a high level of (small) property ownership and internal factions and personality conflicts. Yet to dwell on these factors is to ignore what Peter Mair has called the 'logic of party strategy'.[8] Rather than choosing the difficult path of undermining the national consensus and constructing the basis of a distinctive class consciousness, Labour choose to emphasise its dedication to the symbols of consensus and class harmony.

In the late 1920s and 1930s Labour first sought support for and then an alliance with Fianna Fail. Later it strove to reclaim the Connolly mantle by declaring, in 1936, its objective to be a 'Workers' Republic'; this was deleted the following year under pressure from the primary teachers' union whose members were employed by religious-controlled schools. The inspiration for party policy was regularly located in papal encyclicals rather than socialist theory.[9] In the 1940s and 1950s it redefined its political role to be part of any alternative government to that of Fianna Fail, and duly formed coalitions between 1948 and 1951 and 1954 and 1957 with the remaining political parties, of which the former Blueshirt-affiliated Fine Gael was the dominant member. Its own members often complained that their trade union colleagues neither voted for the party nor bought its papers.[10] Even Labour deputies appeared to show no particular loyalty to the party: its electoral strength was principally rural-based, and those who 'had secured election depended essentially on a personal following'.[11] Its leaders reassured the public that Labour's concept of socialism would threaten neither profits nor property; Thomas Johnson wrote in the *Irishman* of 14 May 1927:

> We would not deprive the farmers of the ownership of their farms. We would not 'nationalise' all the land; we would not nationalise all the factories, workshops or stores; we would not repudiate the National Loan; we would not 'abolish the family' as the unit of social life; we would not, in short, subject the

country to the shock of a catastrophic revolution. Ireland is too weak to bear shocks of this kind. What she needs is a long period of recuperation, so much to reassure timid people who shiver when they think of Labour in power.

In this respect the Labour Party has more aptly fitted the mould of an

integrative political party, fulfilling systematic functions like representation and brokerage, demand conversion and aggregation, imbued with a conception of the social order as being basically unified rather than fissured, and effecting a compromise between the sectional interests of various classes in the society by means of policies 'in the national interest'.[12]

This conception of socialism has marked Labour's progress since its origins. In the 1920s and 1930s it stressed its formative role in the origins of the state, while in the 1940s and 1950s it translated its national duty to be part of government. Elsewhere socialism has meant the control of state power and the means of production, distribution and exchange by the working class. The Irish Labour Party, by contrast, views socialism as a belief in freedom, equality, efficiency and reason.[13] It has alternatively been described as the nation's social 'conscience', 'a strong force within our political system' or 'a nice, respectable, docile, harmless body of men'.[14]

Labour and Coalition

If the roots of Labour's 'integrative' policy lie in its formative years, it is equally visible in the period from the 1960s to the present. Lemass's First Programme for Economic Expansion in 1958 ushered in a new era of national consensus; Fianna Fail reconstructed its hegemony based upon a simple Keynesian model of state incentives for international capital, free trade and guarantees of improved living and working conditions. Fine Gael followed in May 1964 with its own version of the mixed economy later entitled 'The Just Society'. Labour, in danger of being left behind, began a similar process of reassessment culminating in its 1965 election manifesto. 'The Next Five Years'. Brendan Corish, party leader from 1960 to 1977, refrained from describing himself as a Catholic first, an Irishman second and a socialist third, as he had done earlier. 'Socialism' was cautiously mentioned, but left largely undefined and eclectic; its usage followed upon Corish's admission that it was now in current fashion. By 1966 the party agreed to join the Socialist International; there were calls for reorganisation – in recognition of static party membership and poor electoral results – but policy remained unchanged.

By 1969, however, much of this was to change. The appointment in 1967 of Brendan Halligan, an economist with executive experience in a semi-state company, initially as political director and then as general secretary, added a strategic dimension to internal party affairs. In *Hibernia* he asserted that future growth was well within grasp, citing, *inter alia*,

> the failure of the two major parties to move with the times; their lack of distinctive identities or *raison d'être*; the disappearance of the 'old guard' from the political scene and the electorate; the emergence of new voters without formed voting habits; the growth of Labour branches in the universities; the growing political consciousness of the unions, as evidenced by the increase in affiliations; the votes, money and psychological boost brought by these affiliations; and the new, acceptable image of socialism.[15]

Halligan's assurances were matched by increasing membership, most notably among what Corish termed the 'new impatient generation': intellectuals like Justin Keating, Conor Cruise O'Brien, Noel Browne and David Thornley and trade union officials such as Barry Desmond and Michael O'Leary all had high profiles,[16] and serious attention was given to party structures and electoral image. A series of policy documents was produced by 1969 covering such areas as industrial policy (the 1930s concept of a National Development Corporation was revived to become a key plank of policy into the 1980s), taxation, social welfare, health, housing, education, agriculture, local government, foreign policy and workers' representation on company boards. 'Socialism' was widely proclaimed, and Corish's 'New Republic' speech to the 1967 conference called for the party to challenge every aspect of society: 'Labour must be impatient for efficiency, for growth, for equality, for welfare.' The speech had a resounding impact on those in attendance as well as within Ireland: that the Labour Party could confidently and openly announce the aspiration that 'The Seventies will be Socialist' was surely a signal that Irish society was undergoing a profound change.

What accounted for this development? Michael McInerney, political correspondent of the *Irish Times*, sympathetically described Corish's speech as the 'most radical statement ever heard from a Labour deputy since Connolly', while Halligan claimed it represented a 'milestone in Irish political life'.[17] There seemed little doubt that the party wanted to be viewed as socialist, but such calls were still couched in the language of moral indignation and anger. State control of economic activity was heavily influenced by papal endorsement of collectivisation; such ideas had informed many national objectives since *Rerum Novarum* (1891) and *Quadragesimo Anno* (1931) sought to create a middle ground between 'state-dominated socialism' and 'anarchic capitalism'. Hence, Corish declared, in words similar to the former encyclical, 'All men have a right to participate in decisions affecting their livelihood, whether in the workshop, the office or the farm.'[18] Another intepretation cautiously expressed 'socialism' as being the willingness to consider public enterprise if private enterprise failed:[19] in this respect, there was little to differentiate Labour from either Fianna Fail or Fine Gael. Garret FitzGerald's 1968 book *Planning in Ireland* acknowledged the national consensus that placed economic planning and state enterprise at the centre of any 'rational approach to the problems of economic growth'.[20] Labour Party fortunes are more appropriately linked to changes in the economy and society generally, and it is to these that we should look for the reasons for both Labour's successes and failures.

The 'open economy' approach, adopted by Fianna Fail in the late 1950s, belatedly allowed Ireland to take advantage of the last phase of post-second World War capitalist expansion. Popular protest and social unrest were familiar images elsewhere. Before the outbreak of conflict in Northern Ireland in 1969 the 1960s were already set to be remembered as the *Decade of Upheaval*:[21] Charles McCarthy documented the increase in industrial militancy, but the impact was felt much more widely. University students transcribed the experiences of the American and French student movements into the Students for Democratic Action to protest over inequalities within Christian Ireland. Nowhere was this more apparent than in public housing; the Dublin Housing Action Committee (DHAC), an outgrowth of Sinn Fein's Citizens' Advice Bureau in 1967, provided the ready vehicle and focus for radical protest. Traditional republican activities were displaced, and the DHAC 'attracted many hitherto dormant left-wingers who had no political home to go to ...'[22] New-found social consciousness was reflected in television current-affairs programming, leading, in 1968-69 to reorganisation and resignations from RTE amid cries of political interference.[23] When Northern Ireland exploded the impact spilled over into the 1970s: a splintered left emerged from the split within the IRA in 1970, with the formation of Official Sinn Fein. Even farmers took to the streets, sat in at the Department of Agriculture and transformed themselves from the quiescent and multifarious National Farmers' Association into the powerfully united Irish Farmers' Association by 1972.

Many of these events were concurrent with policy changes within the Labour Party, and as such they illustrate the ease with which changes in Irish society allowed the party to adopt a socialist tag. Labour's acclaimed shift to the left must be viewed within the broad context of the existent national consensus; integrative concerns of Labour policy were not supplanted. Nor did Labour cease to see itself as a 'national' rather than a 'class' based party. The issue of coalition is the best example.

The concept of coalition had received a serious set-back in 1957; the experience of being a junior partner in the 1954-57 coalition government dominated by Fine Gael had had repercussions for Labour electorally, particularly in Dublin which was objectively cited as its most fertile ground (see Table 6).

Table 6: Labour Party Election Results, 1943-1989

	Dublin	Rest of Leinster	Munster	Connaught/ Ulster	Ireland	Seats
	per cent	per cent	per cent	per cent	per cent	
1943	16.2	23.1	16.2	8.2	15.7	17
1944	11.6	11.7	10.7	1.2	8.8	8
1948	9.7	11.4	12.2	1.2	8.7	14
1951	10.8	17.3	15.4	1.7	11.4	16
1954	13.2	18.1	16.0	0.5	12.1	19*
1957	8.1	14.3	12.6	0.8	9.1	12*
1961	8.4	16.5	17.7	1.7	11.6	16*
1965	18.5	19.2	18.5	4.3	15.4	22*
1969	28.3	17.4	16.0	5.8	17.0	18
1973	22.3	14.4	14.0	2.6	13.7	19
1977	17.5	13.6	11.7	2.1	11.6	17*
1981	12.2	11.7	12.0	2.0	9.9	15
1982 (Feb)	11.2	10.0	11.2	2.4	9.1	15
1982 (Nov)	10.5	11.8	11.3	2.3	9.4	16
1987	7.1	9.5	6.8	1.2	6.4	12
1989	9.5	13.5	10.9	2.4	9.5	15

* denotes figures include automatic re-election of the speaker of the Dail.
Total seats: 1943-58: 138; 1948-57: 147; 1961-73: 144; 1977: 148; 1981-87: 166.
Source: Gallagher, *Political Parties in the Republic of Ireland*, 1985, p.168; Gallagher, *How Ireland Voted, 1987*, p.67; *Irish Times*, 19 June 1989.

The 1967 Labour Party conference decided that the party would not again participate in government until it had secured a majority of the parliamentary seats. There was no serious attempt to revise this view until after the 1969 general election, by when Labour's electoral fortunes had improved. The party had undergone a reassessment of all major policy areas, and had reacquired major trade union membership. The groundwork had also been laid when the issue was tentatively raised in 1967 by Corish. An arch anti-coalitionist, he had then signalled the possibility of a rethink when he asked: 'What do we do in the event of no party having an overall majority at the next election?'[24] Between 1967 and 1968 Fine Gael made a number of approaches, both private and public, to Labour. Within Fine Gael the overtures were made by those most closely identified with the 'Just Society' document, but prior to the 1969 election these approaches had been only coolly received.

Gallagher argues, in *The Labour Party in Transition*, that just as Labour's policy reassessments of the 1960s made an independent socialist strategy inevitable, so the result of the 1969 election made favourable consideration of coalition likely.[25] Given the expectations of political change in the 1970s, the 1969 results were disappointing; Labour's electoral base had historically been among rural workers, often located in small towns and villages; farm labourers, forestry workers, railwaymen, post office and county council employees. Only in the 1960s did the party make any significant break-through in Dublin; the 1967 local government and the 1969 general elections registered dramatic increases. Yet, side-by-side with Labour's urban advance and its articulation of a go-it-alone socialist strategy, it lost heavily in its traditional strongholds of rural Leinster and Munster. Some seats were to be lost forever.[26]

If the adoption of the socialist mantle in 1967-68 can be represented as a coup within the party, then the reversal of the policy on coalition in 1970 was a counter-coup.

> With the benefit of hindsight, it is difficult to avoid the impression that the initial reaction of TDs like Tom Kyne, Dan Spring, Sean Treacy, Stevie Coughlan, John Ryan and Michael Pat Murphy – the 'rednecks' of the party as Michael D. Higgins was to describe them ... was that all this policy-making was a harmless enough activity which would not have any serious electoral effect and, moreover, kept some of these young radicals from attempting anything more dangerous ... [It was] natural for people who have been booted in the electoral midriff so savagely to look around for someone or something to blame, and the 'Munster Mafia', as they are generally known, were not slow to pick their target.[27]

It would be misleading, however, to view the debate on

coalition as merely an expression of an urban/rural divide
within the Labour Party, although there is little doubt that
the majority of supporters for coalition in 1970, and since,
were rural delegates to the special party conference, while
about 90 per cent of Dublin speakers opposed the notion.[28]
Instead, the coalition debate exposes the existence of quite
distinct groups within the Labour Party.

The 'socialist' and 'pragmatist' sections of the party
co-exist with each other, and have done so peacefully, for
varying periods of time because they both share a
fundamentally moderate, cautious and reforming conception of social and economic progress. This view is sustained
by the ambiguity surrounding Labour's particular view of
socialism: that understanding has focused principally upon
Labour's commitment to generating national prosperity in a
manner which suggests that national concerns and priorities
embrace the interests of the working class as well.[29] Hence
industrial growth is given priority as the only means of
creating full employment and significantly improving the
living standards of the entire population. A National
Development Corporation would actively seek out and
exploit growth sectors. Calls for nationalisation and
workers' control are softened by 'excluding the petit
bourgeoisie' and small farmers from the impact of such
measures:[30] suggestions that the Labour Party in 1969
advocated nationalising 'industries, the land, shops, the lot
in fact ...' were ridiculed as a 'Fianna Fail smear'.[31]

In a society that has often been characterised as
authoritarian, patriarchical, intolerant and anti-
intellectual,[32] the Labour Party has provided one of the few
vehicles for progressive social and political criticism and
comment in Ireland and, as such, it has housed some of the
major intellectual voices of contemporary society. Yet its
definition of political change operates within a very narrow
perception of parliamentary debate, defending rather than
challenging, initiating or campaigning.[33] A sense of moral
outrage and conscience continues to inform Labour's
redistributive concerns, while specific working-class issues,
such as how to extend its political and economic power, are
ignored. Its failure to recognise or challenge the limitations

of the welfare state as a means to end social inequality has helped pave the way for the New Right to attack with a growing degree of public acquiescence. Thus Labour seeks to control and reform capitalism in order that neither economic growth nor regulation is at the expense of either the wealthiest or weakest sections of the population. It seeks to achieve these ends by constructing a 'balanced political force representing all sections of the community',[34] believing that 'being in government and participating in government must always be on the Labour Party's agenda ...'[35]

Interpretations of Labour's 'integrative' policy have not been unanimous. Intense and often 'stormy confrontations' have occurred, ultimately provoking the formation of groups within the Labour Party. The Militant tendency, a Trotskyist group linked to its British namesake, operates as an autonomous section within the Labour Party with its own organising structure, newspaper and finances, while the Liaison Committee of the Labour Left (LCLL), existed from 1973 to 1978 as a recognised faction within the party. In 1975 the Administrative Council claimed that membership of the LCLL was incompatible with party membership and strategic efforts to block the nomination of Liaison candidates for the 1977 general election led to a wider rift, resignations and the formation of the short-lived and splintered Socialist Labour Party in 1977-78. Following Labour's third coalition term between 1982 and 1987 threats to disaffiliate came from prominent trade unionists, while in 1983 Labour Left emerged as a small but articulate group requiring financial contributions from its supporters. Officially, the Labour Party claims that the existence of such groups and internal debate is an indication of the party's open democratic structure. While there is no doubt that of all political parties in the Republic only the Labour Party engages in any form of meaningful discussion at its party conferences, often angry and bitter divisions, schism and personal attacks occur precisely because different views of party policy and 'socialism' must inevitably 'lead in different directions' in practice.[36] Coalition has long been the focus for such acrimony.

For those supporting coalition, the 'pragmatists', the

argument has rested upon Labour's national responsibility; its duty to help provide alternative government and, anticipating public reaction to forming a government with Fine Gael, the necessity of moderating the excessive conservatism of its partner.

> The Party's participation in the current government [1982-87] has safeguarded the main programmes of public and social services at a time of crisis in public finances ... Despite disagreements within the Party about the wisdom of being in government from a strategic standpoint this record is widely accepted as having been a positive one ...[37]

The sense of urgency that surrounded the debate in 1970 was fuelled by the scandal concerning Fianna Fail ministers in the Arms Crisis and Fianna Fail's general reaction to events in Northern Ireland after 1969; in these circumstances, augmented by Fianna Fail's presence in government for its second sixteen-year consecutive term, Labour, it was argued, had little alternative but to help provide government. Others argued that Fine Gael of the 1970s was ideologically different from that of the 1950s; its right wing had been replaced by the acceptable christian-democratic face of Declan Costello and Garret FitzGerald. Unless Labour grasped the nettle of reality and participated in government it risked marginalisation. David Thornley stated the case eloquently:

> Those of us who practise the vocation of politics must accept the realities of the context in which we work, with all its attendant frustrations, not invent a more agreeable fantasy ... it is a nobler role to embrace reality, and seek to change it even marginally than to stand apart from it in glorious and impotent righteousness.[38]

After all, read a Labour Party statement of 1970, Labour had a 'responsibility to the nation'.[39]

In contrast, the anti-coalitionists' case was grounded in the rhetoric and passions that had informed the policy revisions of the 1960s. Accusing the coalitionists of reneging on those ideals, and opportunistically over-reacting to the election of 1969, they claimed that Ireland stood on the brink of political change. Modernisation theory was employed and substituted for a materialist analysis: economic expansion and growth would, it was argued, inevitably lead to an ideological realignment and union between the dominant bourgeois parties of Fine Gael and Fianna Fail; Labour stood to gain as the sole inheritor of the potentially enlarged working class's allegiance. Moreover, any alliance with a party previously associated with the Blueshirts could only tarnish Labour's image and hinder progress towards the creation of a socialist society, and an examination of previous election results following coalition periods showed Labour the major loser. Many Labour Party members, however, opposed coalition simply on pragmatic or personal grounds. Within the context of a particularly narrow and predominately conservative ideological consensus in Ireland – from which vantage point anyone who even mildly criticised the status quo, let alone affirmed socialist principles, was often termed 'left-wing' – many within the Labour Party have been inappropriately so 'labelled' because of their stance against coalition. Similarly during the 1920s many had opposed parliamentarianism for narrow trade union reasons and not from any belief about its ineffectiveness or concepts of class collaborationism. This distinction was particularly pronounced by the late 1970s; by then the impact of coalition and personal electoral imperatives had merged to form a coherent band of anti-coalitionists. Typically, Halligan in 1976 assailed those who opposed coalition as 'not interested in access to power, in the reality of politics ... [as] more committed to doctrine than to its translation into policy' but wrote in 1982 that the decision to end the 'no-coalition' policy was Labour's 'kiss of death', setting it on a 'path of continuous electoral decline'.[40]

In that same interview with the *Sunday Press* in April 1976, Labour's general secretary Brendan Halligan – three years into a five-year coalition term – dismissed speculation about a 'coalition chasm' over Labour's proposals for a state development corporation. A pragmatist, Halligan went on to argue that Labour was in a stronger position than ten years previously; the experience of government, he said, had proven that 'Opposition is hell, it's sterile, and has no validity for a political party unless it's a time of preparation.'[41] Despite this claim, Labour's coalition experience of 1973-77 was unimpressive and electorally damaging. Its loss of only two seats nationally in 1977 obscured its massive decline in Dublin from 22.3 to 17.5 per cent of the vote.

Labour had four out of fifteen ministers in the 1973-77 Cabinet, with party leader Brendan Corish taking the portfolio of Health and Social Welfare as well as being Tanaiste (Deputy Prime Minister) to Fine Gael's Liam Cosgrave. Corish's chosen portfolios indicated Labour's preoccupations, except for Conor Cruise O'Brien's appointment to the Department of Posts and Telegraphs, which ultimately proved the most controversial. From a rural and traditional constituency himself, Corish's 'personal evolution' was notable for his ability to influence many within the Labour Party about socialism.[42] His own ministerial performance, however, was not particularly stirring. He ran into trouble virtually immediately with the medical profession for his proposals to extend the national health service, and withdrew after a brief but inconsequential encounter. No similar plans were ever mooted again.

Michael O'Leary, a former ICTU research officer and liaison between the ITGWU and the Labour Party after 1965 with a pedigrée that included being known as a 'dangerous revolutionary' while at university, headed the Department of Labour.[43] He has been credited with the most effective record of any of his Labour colleagues or successors in that department,[44] introducing changes in protective legislation, public holidays, unfair dismissals, worker participation, equality rights and other areas;[45] but even here he failed to take clear advantage of the situation and succumbed to mounting pressure from employers. The Anti-Discrimination (Pay) Act (1975) and the Equal Pay Act (1976) were introduced, in the main because of pressure from the European Commission, but were restrictive and fell far short of expectations. The government itself attempted to renege on implementing its portion of the equal pay deal by refusing to extend it to the public service, while to appease employers it accepted the provision that companies could plead inability to pay. Moreover, companies were extremely successful in altering job descriptions and segregating men and women so that claims of equal pay for equal work were frustrated.[46]

Justin Keating, a university don and RTE current affairs presenter with a Communist background, headed Industry and Commerce. He drew fierce criticism from within and without the Labour Party and the trade unions for granting favourable terms to private companies for oil/gas and mineral ore exploration rights, in which the state was not entitled to royalties.[47] He refused to contemplate any significant state role in the exploitation of Europe's largest zinc mine, discovered outside Navan in County Meath, by the State Geological Survey Office or in the oil and gas reserves off the south and west coasts of Ireland. In the particular instance of Bula Zinc mine, Keating, on behalf of the state, agreed to pay the Roche family £10 million towards the development of a lead/zinc mine, with few appending conditions; the mine never opened and was bought in 1986 by the Finnish state company Outokumpu. These actions compelled the Liaison Committee to form a vocal lobbying group along with members of Official Sinn Fein, the Communist Party and trade unions called the Resources Protection Campaign (RPC). Criticism over economic policy would ultimately bring these same groups together as the 'Left Alternative' which published a 14,000-word document in 1976.

Conor Cruise O'Brien drew the strongest criticism for his authoritarian approach to censorship; Section 31 of the Broadcasting Authority Act (1960) entitles the Minister to instruct the RTE Authority to

> refrain from broadcasting any matter that could be calculated to promote the aims and activities of any organisation which engages in, encourages or advocates the attaining of any particular objective by violent means.

In 1972 the decision to broadcast an interview with Seamus Twomey, Chief of Staff of the Provisional IRA, led to the dismissal of the RTE Authority. Under O'Brien there was further controversy leading in 1976 to amending legislation which allowed the minister to proscribe groups whose members could not be interviewed. This created the anomolous situation whereby newspapers throughout the Republic could interview such individuals; additionally, over one-third of Irish television viewers could receive British (including Northern Ireland) programmes where such restrictions did not apply.[48] O'Brien's actions were accentuated by his highly publicised criticisms of Irish nationalism which took on an added dimension in his capacity as government spokesperson on Northern Ireland; as a former diplomat he had seemed the appropriate choice for this post, a decision which conformed to the tradition of separating those duties from the Department of Foreign Affairs. His vituperative remarks about the IRA, republicanism and 'fellow-travellers', as well as his own stated willingness to recognise the legitimacy of the unionist position, inevitably brought him into conflict with members of his own party and more particularly with Fianna Fail. O'Brien became the nationalists' *bête noir*; one of the key intellectuals in the party and the Dail, he adopted the role as his own despite the fact that the position had been largely pioneered by O'Leary and Frank Cluskey before him.[49]

Labour's political difficulties were compounded by the occurrence of two events, both essentially external to the Republic, which coincided with its term in office and combined to change significantly the terms of political debate within the state. In the first instance continuing unrest in Northern Ireland posed a threat to the security and legitimacy of the southern state, while in the second the international recession and accompanying domestic fiscal crisis combined to undercut support for the welfare state, which had previously been the mainstay of social-democratic concerns upon which Labour Party policy was based. In both Fine Gael ministers on the right wing of that party were in charge; their decisions provoked distrust and disagreement within and about Labour but the party failed to act decisively or distance itself significantly to preserve its credibility.

The security of the Republic came under legislative

scrutiny following the IRA assassination of Fine Gael Senator Billy Fox in March 1974 and the British Ambassador, Christopher Ewart-Biggs, in July 1976. In May 1974 two no-warning bombs placed by the Ulster Freedom Fighters went off in Dublin and Monaghan killing 28 people. There were also repeated threats by the IRA during 1975 and 1977 to the lives of ministers and deputies in support of colleagues then on hunger strike in Portlaoise Prison. Patrick Cooney, Minister for Justice, endeavoured to meet the challenge by declaring a State of Emergency as allowed under Article 28.3.3 of the constitution. This section grants authority to the government, by way of a juridically impotent Dail, to declare a state of emergency under which civil rights known in the constitution as 'fundamental rights', are not binding; the first two amendments to the constitution in 1939 and 1941 had already extended the meaning and duration of a 'time of war' or 'national emergency'. In addition to the declaration, Cooney introduced the Emergency Powers Act (1976) which sought to restrict the rights of the accused and extended additional powers of detention to the police. In 1975 the Criminal Law Jurisdiction Act, originating from the Sunningdale Agreement (1973-74), had allowed for trials to be held on either side of the border for crimes committed in the other state's jurisdiction. The passage of the Emergency Powers Act and the declaration of a State of Emergency were swiftly advanced by the suspiciously timed but in the event harmless bombs that went off in Dublin during the debate, which had lasted eleven months.

The Dail and Senate debates were heated and acrimonious, ultimately provoking a minor constitutional crisis. The President of Ireland, Cearbhall O Dalaigh, a former President of the Supreme Court and subsequently a member of the European Court of Justice, chose to exercise his authority under the constitution and test the constitutionality of the Emergency Powers Bill before the Supreme Court. Patrick Donegan, Minister for Defence, and standing on the far right of Fine Gael, called O Dalaigh's action a 'thundering disgrace' during off-the-cuff remarks to an audience of army officers, of whom O Dalaigh was the

Commander-in-Chief;[50] on a previous occasion, Donegan
had remarked that the 'army was the muscle of
democracy'.[51] Cosgrave's failure to chastise publicly or
dismiss his minister, despite the latter's offers to resign, led
to an embarrassing political impasse. In the end O Dalaigh
felt forced to resign in order to preserve the integrity of the
presidency.

Fianna Fail, due to its nationalist allegiances and its role
as opposition, dominated the debate in both houses of
parliament and thereby enlivened its otherwise ineffectual
parliamentary performance. Outside parliament the main
opposition was led by the recently formed Irish Council for
Civil Liberties – a novel departure in Irish society, as the
country has a particularly poor history of concern for civil
liberties. The Labour Party's performance throughout the
legislative and presidential debates was notable for its
divisions and equivocations; there were 'murmurs of
discontent' within the parliamentary Labour Party when
Fianna Fail called for Donegan's resignation, but the party
line was kept and it voted with the government. In order to
rectify this image of public schism the dissident members
were threatened with loss of the party whip.[52] Of its TDs
only O'Brien spoke in favour of the proposals. As a party,
Labour confused its role in government with its political
principles and was unable to distance itself from the
authoritarian actions of its partner and took no adequate
measures to defend civil liberties. Its behaviour prompted
Charles Haughey to remark that 'The Labour Party always
wrestles with their consciences [*sic*] but I am afraid that the
Labour Party always wins.'[53]

Labour and Fiscal Crisis

The origins of the present economic and fiscal crisis in
Ireland must be linked to the internal character of Ireland's
development, most particularly in the 'solution' adopted by
capital and the state in the 1950s. Keynesian policies with a
more aggressive role for the state were, under Sean Lemass,
specifically linked politically to high levels of expenditure on
roads, schools, industrial development and hospitals. The

strategy spurred rapid economic growth and rising living standards in the 1960s, although this was ultimately inappropriate and inadequate to resolve fundamental deficiencies of Irish capital. Uncritical wooing of foreign capital replaced previous autarkic policies with little or no comparable expansion in the indigeneous manufacturing base, leading to problems associated with the increased openness of the economy and competition. By the mid-1970s popular criticism of household rates, car tax and rising unemployment forced the adoption of an economic strategy which substantially exacerbated the fiscal crisis. Thousands were recruited into largely unproductive jobs within the public service simultaneously with a drastic shrinkage of state revenues. While the politicised package of economic growth, social progress and industrial stability was similar to that which had framed most capitalist states since the Second World War, in the Irish case contradictions inherent within the Keynesian formula were exaggerated by the particular characteristics of Irish development and by international factors, such as the 1974-75 oil crisis and the emergence of the OPEC cartel, and alterations in international capital formations. In effect, the 'solutions' to the crisis of the 1950s, engendered by over-protectionism and severe uneven development and dispersal of resources, became 'problems' during succeeding decades.

Unemployment did not become a political issue until 1977. Despite this, the coalition years 1973-77 saw unemployment rise from 71,000 or 7.9 per cent of the work force to 116,000 or 12.5 per cent:[54] its growth was attributed to the combined forces of oil prices, high inflation, balance of payments deficit, increasing capital investment and significant alterations in demographic and labour force numbers.[55] The latter was due to the twin factors of increased immigration and a population explosion. A study by economist Brendan Walsh for the National Economic and Social Council postulated that Ireland would need to create approximately 30,000 new jobs annually in order to approach 'full employment' by 1986.[56]

Against this spectre, the coalition's performance in the economic arena was judged by *Business and Finance* as 'hardly glorious'. The magazine pulled no punches:

In many respects, it was deplorable. Unemployment is a festering sore, and despite the announcement of new industrial projects with heightening enthusiasm ... the race to provide the jobless and school-leavers with employment while maintaining existing jobs is not being won. Inflation is still too high. So are borrowings. The Coalition does not really dispute these facts. What it says, and says with some justification, is that given the world economic conditions of the last four years the government took the right decisions, and that huff and puff as they may a Fianna Fail government would have done much the same.[57]

Its response was a traditional Keynesian one of pump-priming the economy in the assumption that the crisis would be short-lived. By doing this the coalition did not depart in any significant manner from previous Fianna Fail economic strategies. Richie Ryan, Minister for Finance, described the pattern:

> In 1973 we borrowed to increase growth. This foreign borrowing was widely welcomed by the private sector as being expansionist. Then, in common with the rest of Europe, we were plunged into a recession by the Arab oil crisis. Then our borrowing policy cushioned the whole economy against the recession's worst effects.[58]

Increased public expenditure accompanied selective employment and training measures and wage subsidy packages.[59] Under some pressure from Labour, social and welfare reforms were introduced, along with wealth and capital gains taxes which earned Ryan the unlikely nickname 'Red Richie'.

The Labour Party did not have a strategy for coalition; its 1969 policy documents were based on pre-coalition assumptions of majority government. The hastily drafted joint document for a national coalition merely stated that the intention was to 'transform Ireland into a modern progressive society based on social justice'.[60] It contained proposals for a national development corporation, which had been one of the major platforms of Labour Party economic policy since the 1930s, but these became the source of public disagreement between Halligan and Corish, and Fine Gael's John Kelly (Attorney General) in 1976.[61] In the main, the idea was not radically different from that offered by either Fianna Fail or Fine Gael. Given the undeveloped nature of the Irish economy, state-propelled economic growth had been accepted since the late 1920s as an essential ingredient to economic progress.[62] As the crisis deepened, however, Labour's concerns for social and economic equality were distorted by the overwhelming national consensus in favour of capital regeneration. The inclusion of Labour's call for an Industrial Development Corporation (IDC), recast as a National Development Fund in the government Green Paper on *Economic and Social Development, 1976-1980*,[63] did not obscure the fact that the document contained a significant departure in economic strategy.

Since the origins of the oil crisis the Central Bank, along with business and banking interests, had been using the onset of the recession to renew its criticisms of Keynesian models of growth. Similar public disputes had arisen when Lemass's 1958 Programme for Economic Expansion overturned Whitaker's fiscally orthodox proposals.[64] *Business and Finance* documented the renewed conflict throughout 1974, noting that the government and the Central Bank, the latter now under the governorship of Whitaker, were headed towards a 'collision course': 'the unedifying squabble and back-biting going on in Dublin financial circles between the bankers, the Central Bank, and the politicians – both government and opposition ...'[65] sprang from the latter's unwillingness to trim its public expenditure sails. The Central Bank's unilaterally imposed credit squeeze was an indication of how seriously it perceived the link between public spending and high inflation.

The government Green Paper of 1976 reflected the influence of orthodox principles and the imperatives demanded by this economic strategy. Labour's proposals were minimised by greater emphasis on the need to improve the competitiveness of Irish industry through agreement between the social partners on income restraint, improvements in the tax system and other measures to encourage private investment. The complementary budget of 1977 was consequently greeted favourably by business and banking as a 'remarkable turnabout': 'The most important thing which has happened during the past year in the eyes of Irish management is that the voice of business has been heard by government.'[66]

Labour's difficulties sprang from its traditional, 'integrative' ideology which stressed the importance of preserving national (social) unity and providing the basis for economic prosperity. In an environment of economic rectitude Labour's partnership with Fine Gael forced it to reprioritise its policies. Indeed, Labour bore most of the blame and little of the credit for its period in office. Its supporters argued it did too little to halt rising unemployment and inflation or attacks on the public sector, while business claimed its concern for social reform and welfare programmes were the root cause of an escalating fiscal crisis. Vincent Browne, a leading conservative commentator on economic matters and later editor of *Magill*, explained Labour's dilemma:

It went along with the emasculation of wealth and capital taxes and the abolition of estate duties. It failed to establish a national development corporation. Although some progress was made on social welfare, it was almost entirely wiped out by the economic recession and the high levels of inflation. And then, of course, Labour collaborated in the repressive policies of Coalition, almost without demur.[67]

A former supporter of coalition concurred:

When Labour took the decision to enter the National Coalition in 1973, those members who supported this move, and I was among them, justified it as a temporary measure to provide, in the short term, a better government than Fianna Fail could offer, particularly in the area of social policy ... The record of the first year in office, in my view, justified this decision ... All these actions fell far short of Labour policy, but none could have been achieved by Labour in opposition. The mistakes which the Labour party made were firstly to fail to publicly debate the gulf between Labour policy and the compromises reached at Cabinet level, and secondly to remain vague as to where the line between continuing in government and leaving should be drawn ... Survival in government has become, to many, an end in itself.[68]

A key element in Labour's participation in government rested upon its relationship to the working class, and in particular organised labour. In this respect it offered Fine Gael, whose electoral strengths were primarily located among the business and corporate sectors and professional people, the possibility of constructing an opposing power bloc to that of Fianna Fail by forging vital links with the working class. For Labour, coalition with Fine Gael presented the only immediate possibility of government. As the severity of the crisis for capital became more apparent, the function of marketing the new strategy was borne disproportionately by Labour. Rather than the economic difficulties prompting greater defence of working-class issues, Labour moved to defend its government status and seek a compromise between competing class interests. In this respect, Labour readopted its historic role of restraining working-class militancy; since the 1970s it has been in the frontline of imposing policies geared at 'police-political management and control of labour'.[69]

During the coalition of 1973-77 Labour used its status to influence trade union opinion on wages policy and to articulate the view that, unless the unions complied with some restrictions on their claims, legislative action would be forthcoming. To some extent this was true. Mounting pressure from industrial and financial interests for a pay freeze in order to reduce labour costs had already prompted the government to renegotiate the 1975 National Wages Agreement (NWA); on 9 June 1975 the Minister for Finance, Richie Ryan, had issued a statement linking the NWA with economic growth. New terms, accepted by the Irish Congress of Trade Unions in July, included an embargo on special claims by the public sector and an increase in 'inability to pay' claims by employers. But the ICTU was itself under pressure from increasing trade union militancy and politicalisation: the Dublin Shop Stewards Committee (formed in 1973) and strong unions traditionally opposed to centralised negotiations were campaigning against the

principle of national wages agreements, which had formed
the bedrock of union and government policy since 1970. In
addition, Official Sinn Fein, whose members were becoming
active in the unions, albeit supporting unequivocally the
concept of NWAs, was highly critical of Labour.[70] Special
meetings between Labour ministers and the ICTU were
convened during the autumn with the intention of boosting
the image of both; Corish promised to represent the unions'
case with government.[71] More discussions followed between
the government and ICTU, although these were aborted
when ICTU withdrew. Negotiations on a 1976 NWA were
deadlocked by the time the 1976 ICTU Annual Conference
heatedly debated Labour's performance in government –
this in itself a notable feature – and Michael O'Leary's
request to address the delegates. As a former ICTU
employee and Minister for Labour with some legislative
achievement, he denied any intention to influence or salvage
the NWA talks. There is little doubt, however, that his
speech was calculated to dampen criticism of Labour and
win support for a strategy of linking capital regeneration
with wage restraint:

> There are still powerful elements in our business world who see
> the answer to all our economic difficulties in the imposition of a
> statutory policy on incomes. There are politicians waiting in the
> wings of opposition who are ready to carry out that design ... If
> we, in the Labour movement, fail in the period ahead to relate
> our objectives to the demands and particularly the employment
> demands of the present situation, then we are inviting those
> who do not share the ultimate objectives of the working people
> of this country to impose their solutions on us unilaterally.[72]

Fears of government interference were not abated by
O'Leary's intervention, nor did it alter evidence of a
growing rift between the Labour Party and ICTU; five years
earlier the Executive Report had noted that 'good relations
between the Party and Congress were maintained during the
year, and a number of meetings took place, mainly on an ad
hoc basis'.[73] Labour TDs had participated openly in debate
at ICTU annual conferences. In 1976 two of the speakers
opposing O'Leary's request to speak were high-ranking

union officials: Paddy Cardiff, General Secretary of the Workers' Union of Ireland from 1977 to 1983, and Matt Merrigan, a District Secretary of the Amalgamated Transport and General Workers' Union from 1960 to 1987, of whom only the latter had a reputation for being a maverick. Both became members of ICTU's Executive shortly thereafter.[74]

Trade union disappointment over Labour's performance was also generated by: lost opportunities in the legislative field – particularly equal pay; its failure to influence economic policy and utilise new found natural resources as a vehicle for an 'industrial revolution';[75] its broad acceptance of using the National Wage Agreement as a policy of wage restraint with no reciprocal control on profits; its sluggishness to defend workers in the public sector against suggestions to privatise; in its acceptance of conservative concerns with order and economic stability; and, finally and symbolically, in O'Leary's decision to appoint the last Monday in October as an additional bank holiday rather than May Day. Not surprisingly, Labour's electoral position declined; the 1977 election saw the Labour Party support among the unskilled and skilled working class fall from 27 to 11 per cent and 28 to 16 per cent respectively, despite Ireland's comparatively high level of unionisation among its work force.[76] Ironically, the results cast doubt on both schools of thought about Labour participation in coalition: firstly, that the Labour Party would be marginalised only outside government and, secondly, that extensive industrialisation would produce a more class-consciousness work force. In Ireland, Labour had traditionally been challenged by Fianna Fail for the allegiance of the working class; in 1977 Fianna Fail gained 54 per cent of the skilled and 47 per cent unskilled working class vote.[77] Among sections of the lower middle class the results were equally disappointing; a significant element in Labour's appeal to other classes has been its emphasis on social reform and economic equality while maintaining its commitment to national prosperity. Labour's relationship to the trade unions did not alter this appeal, but its failure to distinguish itself adequately from Fine Gael begged the obvious question, 'why not vote Fine

Gael?'[78] Fine Gael held onto its support among the 'upper, middle and lower middle' class, while Labour lost substantial ground.[79] Its electoral decline can be attributed to the manner by which the new economic imperatives of reorganising the relation of capital to labour threatened Labour's ability to represent contrasting interpretations of its policy to different classes.

Labour and the Unions

The changing nature of Labour's relationship with the unions reflects these political difficulties. Since the 1930s trade union organisation operated within a self-sufficient and protected economy and Fianna Fail, which had constructed a power bloc on the basis of a broad class alliance, was broadly sympathetic to the unions.[80] Its Trade Union Act of 1941 favoured the expansion of Irish-based trade unions at the expense of British-based unions, which had restrictions imposed upon them. A shared nationalist sentiment evidenced collaboration between Sean Lemass, then Minister for Industry and Commerce, and William O'Brien of the ITGWU. Its passage prompted a 'major split within the ITUC between those who maintained an essentially nationalist viewpoint [CIU – Congress of Irish Unions] and those who supported a liberal-socialist perspective [ITUC]'.[81] A compromise was eventually reached in 1958 forming the Irish Congress of Trade Unions or ICTU.

The establishment of the ICTU did not affect the structure of trade unions; it was, after all, essentially an ideological unity. Schregle, who was commissioned by the ICTU in 1970 to examine trade union structure and financing, reported that trade unionism in Ireland was characterised by a multiplicity of unions with comparatively high density among workers:[82] its historical origins accounted for divisions between Irish- and British-based, craft and general, amalgamated and breakaway unions, and those affiliated to the Irish Congress of Trade Unions, the British Trades Union Congress or both. The preponderance of small unions was augmented by continued fragmentation due to poaching, jurisdictional disputes and inter-union rivalries. The ICTU acts as a central co-ordinating body providing education, training, work study and mediation facilities, although it also has a remit to investigate trade union restructuring. Its autonomy is strictly limited, reflecting the reluctance of its constituent parts to transfer too much authority to the ICTU. In effect, its executive council, which is composed of leading trade unionists democratically elected according to union size, restricts and weaken its own actions. Charles McCarthy suggests that

> When Congress is inadequate, it is an inadequacy that springs from its leadership, not its constitution. When we come to consider the executive council, therefore, we can be confident that, if it does not always represent the trade union movement in Ireland, it very adequately reflects it.[83]

Consideration of what role the ICTU should play was asked by Denis Larkin in his presidential address to the 1974 ICTU annual conference: was the Irish Congress of Trade Unions merely an organisation established for the purpose of convening conferences, or was it the

> centre of trade union activity, the recognised and accepted spokesman of the Irish trade unions – the initiator and co-ordinator of trade union policies and programmes, acting with approval and support of its affiliated unions on matters concerned with the fundamental interests of Irish workers?[84]

Changes in the ICTU's role and image over the past two decades has had less to do with a considered response to Larkin's question than to the impact of key structural alterations within the economy. The dominance of craft unions has been reduced as industrialisation and deskilling have advanced.[85] Expansion of the state and private services sector have been accompanied by rapid unionisation among white-collar and public-sector employees, whose unions since 1970 have outnumbered craft union membership and thus form a very powerful section of the labour movement.[86] In turn, these alterations in the social composition of unions led to a 'change of emphasis' and a strengthening of the ICTU in the 1970s.[87] The introduction of a system of two-tier picketing, with the ICTU adopting a co-ordinating and mediating role, reduced the traditional impact of 'moral' pressure and occurrence of spontaneous industrial conflict. Centralised bargaining further emphasised the ICTU's prominence and professionalism while granting it policing rights: unions accused of poaching or dissenting from agreed procedures found themselves outside the Congress. Equally, if not more importantly, the ICTU was mounting support for tri-partite or corporatist structures that reinforced its centralising role: in the absence of a powerful political voice for labour many on the left have joined with Fianna Fail in casting the ICTU into a quasi-political party.

The 1970s witnessed a higher level of trade union prominence and legitimacy in Ireland than any other period; a decade later, however, the unions were facing severe problems on several fronts: falling membership, declining influence, low level of participation, a growing credibility gap between the top leadership and the rank and file, erosion of bargaining power, and difficulty maintaining workers' living standards.[83] Alongside the growing powerlessness of political and industrial labour, capitalism was restructuring itself both economically and politically. If the 1970s marked the ascendancy of labour, the 1980s noted the reorganisation and successful challenge of employer groups, crystallising on the political level in an unofficial alliance between Fianna Fail, Fine Gael and the newly formed, neo-liberal Progressive Democrats in 1987. These trends were broadly evident in most developed capitalist economies, yet Ireland's particular conditions and experience meant that the impact has not been directly comparable.

A key feature of Irish industrial relations has been the prominence of voluntary centralised wage bargaining, which emerged initially as part of a far wider Fianna Fail strategy for forging an enduring alliance with the working class. The ending of wage control, by means of the 1940 Wages Standstill Order, and the formation of the Labour Court in 1946

symbolised the advent of a more tolerant or supportive approach to trade unions on the part of the Irish state. A similar change in state strategy was responsible for the granting of recognition to public service unions and the establishment of the civil service concilitiation and arbitration schemes between 1946 and the early 1950s.[89]

Through the offices of the Labour Court a framework for wage negotiations, termed a National Wages Policy, was agreed between employers and unions; between 1946 and 1970 a series of 'rounds' produced steady wage increases. The existence of this formal structure for wage negotiation had a direct impact on the number of strikes in Ireland; in the 1950s self-restraint and economic sluggishness maintained a lid on wage increases and strikes.[90] In the late 1950s emigration figures had reached 42,000 a year. The 1960s, by contrast, witnessed the advent of national economic planning which fed expectations of rising incomes.[91] Unions with industrial muscle utilised the demands of rapid industrial expansion to regain lost ground. The period of 'unparallaled turbulence in Irish industrial relations'[92] was caused by

a very small number of strikes [which] account[ed] for the great bulk of man-days lost through disputes ... 29 strikes representing a mere 4 per cent of all strikes over the period, accounted for 83 per cent of total man-days lost ... By far the greatest loss of man-days occurred in the following strikes: banks 1970 (787,000), maintenance craftsmen 1969 (629,000), construction industry 1964 (419,000), banks 1966 (323,000), printing industry 1965 (315,000), paper mills 1966 (153,000).[93]

The increase in industrial conflict was also an indication of weaknesses within the mechanism of wage bargaining; its loose structure encouraged rivalry and bitterness between workers whose 'rounds' did not coincide; leaving some sectors losing ground after inflation. Nor could it take account of fluctuations in the economy; protracted talks over what became the tenth 'round' were only resolved when the ICTU's 'feelings of national solidarity' helped to foster 'restraint'.[94]

Congress has shown itself once again to be far less sectional in its approach than people seem to expect. It emphasized ... the great need to maintain confidence in the ability of the national economy to continue to expand.[95]

In 1970 state action, buttressed by a National Industrial Economic Council (NIEC) *Report on Incomes and Prices Policy, 1970* which argued that economic growth and unregulated collective bargaining were not compatible, secured the new-style National Wages Agreement after government threats of statutory controls in the form of the hastily drafted Prices and Incomes Bill.[96] Importantly, the NIEC document was not rejected by the ICTU; rather, a special delegate conference in 1969 had cautioned only against the use of statutory restrictions or sanctions.[97] The NWA was a watershed; it ended the long period of free collective bargaining and introduced a tri-partitite formula whereby the trade unions became 'social partners': the 'old boundary separating politics and industrial relations was now to be dismantled by both the state *and* the unions'.[98]

Between 1970 and 1980 eight further national agreements were accepted. By 1974 the basic features were clear: firstly, 'the centrality of tax concessions to quid-pro-quo arrangements between unions and the state'; secondly, 'the integration of government budgetary policy into national pay determination'; and thirdly, 'the difficulty of gaining acceptance of such agreements from Congress delegate meetings'.[99] The latter was due, in the main, to differences over the comparative advantage of free collective bargaining versus centralised bargaining, a view contingent upon individual union strength. Implicit within the concept of the NWA was the recognition of an integrated approach to economic problems. Pressure for stable industrial relations prompted the government increasingly to moderate its concern about balanced current budgets for wage concessions; this was especially the case after 1973, by which time the rest of Europe was introducing retrenchment policies and restricting growth. The traditional pattern of clientilist politics in Ireland additionally ensured that budgets remained stimulatory and expansionary, and that the ICTU's call for 'full employment' became integrated into Fianna Fail's 1977 election manifesto – the first such programme produced by Fianna Fail since Lemass.

The unions read the state's eagerness to make concessions to it as a mark of their own strength and the employers' weakness, claiming that: 'The only reason the employers made a renewed offer was their collective fear of our collective power in the ICTU,'[100] and 'We are now accepted as definite partners in the community. The trade union movement cannot be ignored.'[101] In turn, unions pressed to widen the terms of national agreements as disillusionment with pledges on employment and tax concessions coincided with growing disappointment with Labour in government. John Carroll of the ITGWU was one of many speakers at the 1977 ICTU annual conference who argued for new definitions of state-trade union relations:

> The time is now opportune for the trade union movement, the incoming government [Fianna Fail], and the employers to determine whether or not a national programme for economic development will be evolved with the co-operation of the three parties. I do not mean the political parties, I mean the *Social Partners* ... It is my view that a type of *social contract* over the next couple of years is imperative ...[102]

Even Matt Merrigan of the ATGWU, a long-time critic and one of the few speakers to ever discuss its 'corporatist' or 'quasi-legal character',[103] favoured a tripartite approach.[104] Others from the left of the Labour Party and within Sinn Fein-the Workers' Party (formerly Official Sinn Fein) argued that centralised negotiations illustrated and sharply exposed the class divisions in society by pitting organised labour against employers.

One of the most significant factors in the evolution of the National Wages Agreement into the National Understandings of 1979 and 1980, and the 1987 Programme for National Recovery was undoubtedly the re-election of Fianna Fail. In addition the election of Charles Haughey as Taoiseach and leader of the party in late 1979 resignalled the priority of the Lemass strategy of viewing the unions not as 'adversaries so much as potential partners in the national economic and social enterprise'.[105] In this respect Haughey's style in openly courting the unions was sharply contrasted with the coalition's stand-offish manner and, given international trends, with Margaret Thatcher's confrontational policy of isolating British unions.[106] This is clearly evidenced in his Ard Fheis speech of 1981:

> Our fundamental economic strategy is to maintain employment and investment at the highest possible levels in the face of the recession. That is the policy outlined to the Irish Congress of Trade Unions and which as an objective of the National Understanding has their full support. Anyone who advocates a different, monetarist type of policy must understand that by tearing up the National Understanding they risk plunging the country into social and industrial unrest.[107]

The ICTU Executive Report remarked that Haughey desired meetings 'about once a quarter with Congress for a general exchange of views and to provide a forum where matters of current general interest to either side could be raised'.[108] The strategy posed risks, however: with the onset of the second oil crisis and deepening recession concessions to the unions were increasingly disadvantageous to the employers. The terms of the second National Understanding were only communicated to the Federated Union of Employers (FUE) after they had been negotiated between government and the unions.

> The FUE is furious with Mr Haughey for undermining its negotiating position with the intensity with which he publicly desired a second National Understanding. 'We never saw the conduct of the negotiations quite so *political*.'[109]

The 1980 Understanding was the last centralised agreement until Fianna Fail returned to office in 1987.

The changed economic circumstances of the 1980s seriously eroded the power and prominence of the unions. Initially it had been the employers, facilitated and encouraged by the state, who had been keenest to reach accommodation on wages in return for industrial peace; in the 1980s a massive decline in industrial production, dramatic rises in unemployment, sharp acceleration in employment in 'private' or 'traded services' – particularly in those sectors hostile to unionisation with high levels of part-time and casual employment – as well as increased uses of technology led to a rapid decline in union membership.[110] On a political level the decline in union power was already evidenced in its inability to make any headway on the taxation issue, despite cumulative evidence pointing to tax inequality benefiting farmers and the self-employed. In addition, Labour was seriously split over its approach to the issue. There were prolonged debates over the definition of 'farmer' and 'worker' and whether the unions were engaging in 'farmer-bashing'.[111] Furthermore, a Dublin Council of Trades Unions (DCTU)-sponsored one-day strike and protest march planned for 21 March 1979 clashed with ICTU negotiations on the 1979 National Understanding. In contrast to the support given to an ITGWU Sunday demonstration, the DCTU plan was criticised by both Labour Party TDs and the ICTU as too 'political' and not in the 'national interest'.[112] At a special delegate conference of the ICTU its general secretary, Ruaidhri Roberts, cautioned delegates:

> There is a danger ... that if the proposed strike goes ahead it may become confused in the public mind with the kind of action which was proposed by the farmers. And, if that impression is created ... [it could] make it far more difficult for the government to engage in the kind of negotiations which we propose ... Protest strikes are characteristically resorted to in countries where the trade union movement lacked real bargaining power. We do not lack real bargaining power.[113]

Yet, despite the promises of the National Understanding,

> The labour movement had neither the power nor the resources to force the state to comply with its obligations on the socio-economic commitments ... The only real power that ICTU had was its influence over the level of pay; this remained important only as long as the government was prepared to negotiate on it.[114]

Coupled with a resurgence in the ideology of individualism and competitiveness, fewer workers saw any benefit in joining unions.[115] The decline in union power was matched by hardening attitudes by a reorganised FUE:[116] tougher stances towards employees, new management strategies and an insistence on 'realism' in the face of a seriously escalating fiscal crisis of the state.[117] Support for the latter was underpinned by a barrage of economic data from national and international sources and, by 1987, an emerging national consensus favouring tighter control over public expenditure.

Trade Unions and the State

The coalition government of 1982-87, with the advent of economic conservatives like John Bruton and Alan Dukes to the financial and industrial ministries, signalled a new departure; despite the Cabinet presence of four Labour TDs, including ministerial charge of the labour portfolio, the government's concerns were international competitiveness, export growth, balanced budgets and an efficient and substantially trimmed down public sector. These developments coincided with and, until 1987, saw the end of industrial negotiations on a national level and a return to decentralised bargaining. While stronger unions initially welcomed this, believing that 'there was little merit in moderating their demands further in the face of stiffer resistance from the other parties,'[118] they ultimately fared badly on the wages front. In contrast to Fianna Fail's tripartite formula, the coalition proposed a wider National Planning Board to include all interest groups: 'it is a matter of deep regret to me that the political labour movement is involved with that type of situation,' cautioned John Carroll.[119] On one level the return to and advocacy of decentralised bargaining among employers was a response to the changed economic priorities of capital in the 1980s; on another level, and more importantly, it was evidence of two distinct economic and industrial relations strategies: Fianna Fail's corporatism versus Fine Gael's and Labour's liberalism. This can clearly be seen in the return to power of Fianna Fail in 1987 when the economic difficulties for capital were far worse than during the coalitions' term in office.

As discussed elsewhere, Fianna Fail actively sought to incorporate the interests of organised labour within the boundaries of the state through a series of trade-offs. Not surprisingly, the trade unions have, in turn, responded favourably to such approaches. Indeed it could be argued that they have responded more favourably to Fianna Fail when in government than to a Fine Gael/Labour Party coalition. This is often little understood, as it is assumed that when Labour is in power the unions should have direct access to power. That this has occurred to only a limited extent owes more to the Labour Party's conceptions of the state than to other factors: indeed, it is the similarity between Labour and Fine Gael on this issue that probably goes furthest to explain the existence of coalitions between two ideologically quite diverse political parties.

Both Labour and Fine Gael share a conception of the state based on the liberal-democratic model; in this tradition, the state is seen as an amalgam of

> complex, autonomous institutions politically neutral and external to structurally-determined social forces. It is, then, 'up for grabs', to be 'captured' by elected regimes and used as an instrument for their own specific purpose.[120]

Both the Labour Party and Fine Gael advocate the principles of pluralism; in an Irish context this term is most often employed to suggest a separation between church and state and, in this interpretation, both parties are perceived as pluralist or 'liberal', meaning tolerant and modernising. A more expansive definition refers to democratic theory's insistence on the separation of economic and political interests. Both the Labour Party and Fine Gael share the view that the neutral state could be captured and made to operate in the interests of the whole community. In neither case did this mean accommodating the trade unions, as to do so would have threatened the delicate institutional separation between economic and political power. Labour

Party members have expressed concern about the role and power of trade unions in Irish society; a survey in *Business and Finance* as far back as December 1977 showed that 36 per cent of Labour Party members considered unions had too much power, while 38 per cent of union members were of the same opinion.[121]

From this perspective, one of the inevitable consequences of tri-partite or corporatist structures is that they

> diminish the authority of Dail Eireann ... the Dail is rendered less and less capable of not only framing policy but of fully grasping the implications of policy as it is presented to it.[122]

In place of elected politicians, bureaucrats and powerful interest groups decide national policy; the 1987 Programme for National Recovery was presented as a national plan even though it had been negotiated entirely outside parliamentary structures, in the main between government and the ICTU, and then forced upon the FUE and the Irish Farmers' Association (IFA). Given the view of the state held by both Labour and Fine Gael, it is not surprising that the coalition's periods in office have been marked by a decided attack on those groups which threaten to undermine parliamentary power: civil servants, pressure groups, the unions, and more recently, supporters of the current electoral system.[123] In this campaign they have been joined by Ivor Kenny, former chair of the Irish Management Institute, and Fergus FitzGerald, Garret FitzGerald's brother.[124]

Trade union relations with the Labour Party have as a consequence been contradictory and equivocal. Despite their origins, many union members feel as comfortable voting for Fianna Fail as for the Labour Party; part of the explanation rests on the absence of a strong ideological or class identity in Ireland. Yet, neither the Labour Party nor the unions have succeeded in fostering such an identity, although the latter might often criticise its absence. Michael Mullen, a former General Secretary of the ITGWU and former Labour Party TD, Senator and councillor, applauded the fact that

The Labour Party is not a class party ... Labour does not depend on any particular class for its support: our policies are for the so-called middle class, the working class, and the so-called upper class for that matter – and, of course, the farming community.[125]

Indeed, the party's strict rules prevent unions or their delegates exercising too much influence.[126] These ambiguities enabled the Labour Party in turn to present itself as a 'national' party: the canvassers' handbook for the 1969 election asked:

Isn't the Labour Party a 'one-class party' ...? This is completely untrue. One need only look at the National Panel of Labour candidates to see that the Labour Party is now a national party, appealing to and drawing suport from all sections of the community ...[127]

More importantly, it has been the alternative presence of Fianna Fail that has caused the greatest amount of public confusion and political embarrassment; Fianna Fail in government carries none of the responsibilities towards the trade union movement that the Labour Party has. Despite affiliations at official trade union level and an interchange of personnel, unions exercise a degree of autonomy that has given them the freedom to draw concessions from competing power blocks.[128] There is little doubt that this arrangement has been more beneficial to the unions than to the Labour Party; nevertheless, Labour's failure to win any real concessions while in government proved embarrassing, as did its hesitant and belated endorsement of the tax reform.[129] In the closing months of the 1982-87 coalition several unions faced motions at their annual conferences to disaffiliate from the party. Although they were defeated, these developments were potentially more serious than criticisms raised during the 1973-77 term in that they were not restricted to people easily identified as 'mavericks' or couched in cautious official expressions of concern:

The progress made in social development in the Republic was largely due to the presence in government of our colleagues in the Labour Party ... Much though we criticise their failings in office ...[130]

In an obvious effort to quell an impending storm, key union personalities endeavoured to bolster the Labour Party's input into the 1986 Budget to avert serious damage to important school examinations by teachers, to support its referendum on divorce, and to articulate the need for wage stability in return for economic planning. The interventions were ultimately insufficient to fend off Fianna Fail in 1987, although Labour proved far more resilient than imagined by its challengers from the Workers' Party (formerly Sinn Fein the Workers' Party).

These developments are in striking contrast to the practices of Fianna Fail, which has openly courted organised labour. In this respect corporatist arrangements have framed the assumptions of both Fianna Fail and the unions since the mid-1940s. As Fianna Fail offered greater opportunities for ICTU to participate at national policy level, the unions interpreted such moves as an indication of their own enhanced strength. Moreover, Fianna Fail openly endorsed the language of and gave practical application to the ICTU's concern for economic planning, quite literally publicising its documents at Fianna Fail press conferences. It was precisely this contradiction that marred the efforts of Billy Attley, General Secretary of Federated Workers' Union of Ireland (FWUI), to salvage the Labour Party in the dying days of the 1982-87 coalition; his suggestion that a deal could be done between the unions and the government were brushed aside by government and grasped only by Haughey.

> Given the political times that are in it, it is likely that the FWUI's man's speech was directed at least as much at Haughey as it was at Garret FitzGerald and at Attley's colleague, Ruairi Quinn. Certainly, Haughey was very quick off the mark in replying and in saying most of the things the unions wanted to hear. Many of the most experienced union leaders say the movement has consistently fared better dealing with Fianna Fail governments ... Congress sources ... were quick to indicate that something more than a predictably positive response from a Labour Minister would be required.[131]

The Labour Party's predicament was that its desire to be seen to deliver to the unions was handicapped by Fine

Gael's distrust of tripartite structures despite the latter's efforts to woo workers with its 'Bill of Workers' Rights and Responsibilities' in 1979.[132] Indeed, there is no history of any such arrangement having been struck between the unions and a Fine Gael/Labour party coalition. Under coalition governments centralised mechanisms were decidedly weakened, not least because the economic imperatives ran contrary to them. By contrast, all major initiatives on pay and economic planning have emerged when Fianna Fail was in government: centralised bargaining (1947), national wage agreements (1970), national understandings (1979), and the Programme for National Recovery (1987).

Eager to reconstruct his own and Fianna Fail's hegemony, the 1987 election witnessed Haughey making extraordinary overtures to the labour movement and, in particular, the Irish Congress of Trade Unions, with continued reference to the latter's *Confronting the Jobs Crisis* and the ideas of Keynes.[133] Haughey's appointment of Bertie Ahern to the Department of Labour was crucial to this strategy. Ahern's Dublin inner-city roots and folksy manner proved a welcome relief to unions used to dealing with less friendly predecessors, even if both Liam Kavanagh and Ruairi Quinn were Labour Party members;[134] part of the antipathy towards Quinn was due to his professional origins – a former student activist, he had no direct trade union experience. During and immediately after the election in February 1987 Haughey invited the ICTU to talks and had completed his programme by late September; the comparison with Thatcher is again striking. While British unions were left out in the cold, Irish unions had not only been invited to talks about the economy and wages but also formed an essential ingredient in the government's economic strategy. The concessions gained were balanced against union weaknesses and international trends. The unions were on the defensive, but the fact that the ICTU could negotiate a deal with Fianna Fail and not with a coalition government was both startling and a source of discontent; it was this contradiction that fuelled irate and personalised exchanges between the ICTU, the unions and the Labour Party in the autumn of 1987.

The confrontation manifested years of trade union resentment at being denied, as the industrial wing saw it, a seat at the table of social and economic decision making. 'We waited for years outside the door and you would not let us in, despite our repeated assertions that we were willing to participate in a programme for economic recovery,' runs the complaint being widely levelled against the Party by union officials ...[135]

Similar comparisons exist in reform of industrial relations legislation. Quinn's proposals lay dormant while Ahern's were favourably greeted by the unions in 1988, although the employers reacted angrily; Ahern's proposals sought to travel more slowly and less provocatively down the road of legislative controls on union activity, particularly in his determination to preserve the right of secondary picketing and, more recently, in his defence of part-time workers.[136] The use of ministerial interventions in industrial relations initially turned Ahern into an active participant, virtually overriding agreed industrial procedures and the Labour Court in order to find an arrangement favourable to the unions and without risk to the national programme. A similar case arose in the controversial and secret agreement worked out with striking Talbot workers in 1982; the factory was in Haughey's constituency.

For the unions the implication of its relationship with Fianna Fail has been extremely problematic. There can be little doubt that the gains made by Irish labour in the 1950s, 1960s and 1970s derived from the advantages of centralised bargaining. The reorganised ICTU emerged in the 1960s as a formidable body co-ordinating trade union affairs; given the existence of over 80 trade unions covering approximately 670,000 workers, of whom two-thirds are in the Republic,[137] the ICTU's status has been enhanced, but the effects are contradictory. Centralised wage bargaining has allowed the labour movement to circumvent problems inherent in the multiplicity of unions with conflicting interests, protect weak and non-unionised workers – of whom the majority are women – and ensure some degree of wage index-linking during periods of high inflation. In exchange institutional recognition has cast the ICTU into a policing and monitoring authority; dissenting unions were forced to comply under threat of explusion. Critics' comments that centralised bargaining would weaken individual unions has been evident; by presenting wage increases as if they 'came from Dublin or from Heaven'[138] it contributed to undermining traditional industrial and class militancy between workers and employers, both private and state.

The ICTU's image of representing a co-ordinated, unifying and powerful labour presence to the public, willing and able to negotiate with government – thus preventing it from employing legislative mechanisms – belies its weaknesses. In reality it has power only so long as individual unions wish to delegate authority to it; conferences might annually pass motions on a range of impressive issues, but the ICTU has been powerless in the face of chronic unemployment. Its mistake has been to assume that its involvement in the policy-making process is tantamount to increasing power; faulty analysis has placed too much emphasis on centralised negotiations presenting the clearest public division between social classes. Rather, the incorporation of the unions has been encouraged and facilitated by the state, at times emerging because of threats by the state to intervene directly in a coercive or regulatory manner in wage structures. Far from instilling a more class-consciousness vision among the working class, corporatist structures – especially when sold by the unions and the left – have become 'the vehicle for engineering, legitimating ('in the national interest') and administering the increase in exploitation necessary to sustain capital in the crisis'.[139]

The 1987 Programme for National Recovery found the unions accused of 'trading' concessions for those in employment with stringent economies in welfare and social services and general support for the government's package of orthodox fiscal measures. The negotiations procedure itself engendered suspicion and criticism, provoking a mini-revolt by some public sector workers; the ICTU's campaign against low pay has involved an element of seeking to deflect attention away from accusations of a 'sweet-heart' deal.[140] If the unions have felt cornered, health and teaching unions were particularly humiliated in succeeding months because their members felt the greatest impact of retrenchment policies and yet were unable to manifest any sustained public protest. Public ambivalence towards the 'welfare state' in Ireland has derived principally from its introduction as part of the political strategy of the bourgeoisie and not, as in the UK, as a result of a post-1945 compromise between labour and capital.[141]

A further example of union vulnerability was tax: ' "Did ye hear the Boss is going to pull a little stroke?" whispered the FF man furtively, "The word is TAX!" '[142] By 1988 the urgency for tax 'reform' derived not from union pressure but because the interests of capital and labour had converged to lower the costs of labour. The unions' campaign for tax equity – which at its height pulled over 500,000 people (about one-sixth of the population) onto the streets in 1979-80 – was altered and popularised by a mounting chorus of domestic and international business and financial interests as a demand for reduced personal income tax. The 1988 Budget, which skillfully highlighted these benefits, contained only marginal moves towards taxing farmers and the self-employed, and ignored the £500 million in public spending cuts announced within days of agreement on the national programme several months previously. Personal tax gains were minimal, yet, coupled with over a 4 per cent decrease in mortgage rates between December 1986 and August 1988, together with excessive media coverage of fiscal and economic buoyancy, residual labour dissatisfaction was effectively undermined. Union conferences defended the programme and acclaimed its success, while the ICTU president, Gerry Quigley, denounced those who sought to inflict the 'British syndrome' on Irish industrial relations.[143] For those who argued that labour had previously lost out by not being sufficiently integrative, the unions now appeared to be on the threshold of power. Yet, rather than viewing the 1987 Programme as a further union incursion into policy-making, as in the post-war trend towards 'social partnership', one observer of industrial relations more accurately commented that

There is every evidence that the Programme was designed as a back-up to the government's programme of expenditure cut-backs and income restraint; the intention was primarily to tie the hands of the trade unions in particular and make difficult any serious militancy in opposition to these policies. An interim judgement would have to be that this approach is working and indeed working rather well.[144]

Social Democracy in the 1980s

One of the staggering features of the crisis of capitalism in Ireland during the 1970s and 80s has been the relative lack of class conflict. The profound changes in social and economic life over these two decades were not reflected in the emergence of radical politics, industrial militancy or in any fundamental change in the nature of Irish society. Ireland remained a conservative society imbued with the values of Catholicism, nationalism and ruralism, although less stridently so than in earlier periods.[145] Feminism was an important liberalising influence on the dominant moral and social values, but, as the results of the referenda on abortion (1983) and divorce (1985) suggest, it did not always translate into the legislative arena, remaining principally an urban – if not south Dublin – phenomenon.[146] The only significant challenge to the political consensus came from the right – the Progressive Democrats – who argued for an Irish version of Thatcherism. On the left, the Labour Party remained dominant, often successfully challenged by the Workers' Party and occasionally by the much smaller Democratic Socialist Party. Left-wing politics, however, remained marginal and declined, failing to emerge as a popular force.

It has been a central argument of this chapter that an explanation for Labour's weakness resides, in part, in its integrative concerns. The Labour Party has survived, albeit in a minor role, by articulating various interpretations of social and economic planning, income restraint, social conscience and nationalist values to potentially conflicting constituencies. Effectively, Labour has successfully enhanced its integrative function by using periods out of government office to renew its links with the working class and organised labour through a reworking of its socialist heritage, arguing for Labour's social and national responsibility when elections were imminent. The message was a confused one, ideologically, but in a society in which the dominant party has only been successfully challenged by a coalition of all-the-rest, Labour has been able to maintain its residual role by acting as the 'conscience' of Fine Gael and Irish society. Given the gravity of the domestic economic crisis by the late 1970s, the ascent of orthodox fiscal measures and the corresponding collapse of the Keynesian programmes that underwrote social democracy, the problems Labour faced in the 1980s were inevitable.

The period out of office between 1977 and 1981 enabled Labour to re-structure. In-so-far as the debates over party strategy and definitions of socialism signified that the integrative concerns of Labour were not unanimous, it is clear that they dominated those who consistently challenged coalition and whose concept of socialism meant the 'ownership and control of the means of production by the workers'.[147] In 1977 the Administrative Council took its revenge on those who had plagued the party between 1973 and 1977, expelling former anti-coalitionists on the basis that they had contested the election as independents: in fairness, Labour had sustained a level of public and internal criticism about its performance that no other political party would have tolerated. Both Matt Merrigan and Noel Browne were political mavericks, the latter having been a member of virtually every political party since first a TD in 1948, but by the mid-1970s Browne had come to symbolise radical anti-clericalism and socialist principles. While the expulsions were the public face of ideological discord, a membership drain – some to Browne's short-lived Socialist Labour Party, others to the Workers' Party, single-issue campaigns or the political sidelines – had been evident since 1974, reversing only after 1979.[148]

The resignation of Brendan Corish as party leader was an essential part of the process; his performance had been anaemic and carried too many public memories of Labour's term with Fine Gael. It had been suggested that he would have resigned in 1976 if offered the presidency following the O Dalaigh crisis.[149] Frank Cluskey, a former butcher and FWUI official, beat off Michal O'Leary's challenge by one vote. In terms of party strategy, both were coalitionists, though Cluskey was less likely to commit himself to government with Fine Gael until the residual loyalty of the unions had been secured and more likely to be determined in government;[150] in contrast, O'Leary had alienated himself from Labour supporters by his playboy image and 'lack of the common touch'.[151] Cluskey's pedigree and previous role as parliamentary secretary to Corish between 1973 and 1977, marked him as the most ideologically committed of Labour TDs, as later events would prove. His performance as leader, however, was disappointing and lacklustre; his seat was precarious, and in 1981 he lost both the leadership and his seat in the Dail, regaining only the latter in February 1982.

Electorally, the party's results were a mixed bag; it fared poorly in the 1979 local government elections, but because of the inherent disproportionality of the Single Transferable Vote form of proportional representation used in Ireland it gained four out of fifteen seats – the same number as Fine Gael – in the European elections held at the same time.[152] Conscious that by-elections could endanger Labour's Dail seats, it exercised the right of members to sit in both the Dail and the European Parliament; yet, the weekly exodus of John O'Connell, Michael O'Leary, Eileen Desmond and Liam Kavanagh to Strasbourg significantly depleted the party's debating strength and opened the party to charges of milking the system, particularly when the European holders of seats changed hands rather frequently after 1981. By 1984 ten Labour members had at some point taken up the lucrative European posting; indeed a deal was struck granting O'Leary's seat to Cluskey in 1981 after his Dail defeat, in exchange for O'Leary's succession to the party leadership.

The 1980 party programme, a successor to the 1969 document, reasserted Labour's socialist credentials and adherence to a classless society, and Cluskey defined socialism as 'not another way of running this system but a different way of organising this country on the basis of justice, equality and solidarity'.[153] The mixed economy was dismissed as merely reformed capitalism, and the programme openly favoured nationalisation of the banks, and a new non-sectarian constitution with provision for divorce. The major difference with the earlier programme was its reference to an 'internal settlement in Northern Ireland'. In contrast the party's election manifesto for 1981 mentioned Labour's commitment to a 'Socialist Alternative' only in the context of its traditional role being essentially a 'moral' one, offering 'realistic policies' for a 'nation ... in crisis'; 'public control' of the banks would be extended through government share-purchasing.[154] Despite the party's claim that it would contest the elections 'on its own policies without any pre-arranged pact',[155] both the party programme and manifesto made little sense except in the context of being in government. Accordingly, while the 1979 Killarney party conference temporarily shelved the coalition debate by referring future strategy to a post-election conference, Cluskey effectively paved the way for the 1981-82 coalition when he signalled that 'Fianna Fail will not have a monopoly on government.'[156]

The *Programme for Government, 1981-1986*, drawn up between Garret FitzGerald and Michael O'Leary reflected, on the face of it, Labour's success in the negotiations – so much so that John Kelly worried whether Fine Gael would be 'contaminated'. Yet it is clear that Labour's principles were included only in a diluted form, and that as the economic crisis escalated it carried the weight of criticism. Fine Gael's own policy for economic recovery aimed at stringent economies, with a heavy reduction in public finances, tax increases and emphasis on the 'restoration of vibrancy and dynamism to Irish industry'; it was these ideas that framed government thinking. Labour failed to gain ground on expanding the tax base – especially problematic given the recent tax campaign and Labour's ambivalences during it; bank profits were levied but there was no wealth tax. The National Development Corporation was seriously underfinanced as initially proposed, and when it did finally appear, during the 1982-87 coalition, it was not the 'success' the party claimed but essentially a venture capital fund with little scope for economic development.[157] A youth employment scheme (YEA) was established – though not until 1982 when Fianna Fail was in power; by then unemployment neared 156,000 or 12.1 per cent of the population, and the myriad training schemes it offered were inadequate to deal with the amount of training required. The joint programme skirted cautiously around Fine Gael's desires to restrict union activities, but Labour conceded significantly on the need for central pay norms; 'between 1981 and 1984 the exchequer pay bill declined by 4.6 per cent in real terms.'[158] Moreover, of all the political parties most likely to have supported FitzGerald's constitutional crusade, Labour's response was noticeably lukewarm; Dick Spring criticised the proposed referendum on abortion as unnecessary but the party was split by its own rural deputies' defense of traditional moral values.[159]

By February 1982 the government had fallen; harsh budget proposals in January, which included a tax on children's shoes and increased indirect taxation, followed an earlier mid-term budget in July 1981 which had only narrowly passed the Dail. While Gallagher suggests that Labour was more assertive than its 1973-77 predecessors,[160] such revelations failed to assuage either the public or the party's Administrative Council (since 1978 led by the Labour left) which argued that Labour ministers were exceeding their mandate. The party's difficulties were compounded, not lessened, by the election: by attaching itself to Fine Gael and proclaiming its unwillingness to abandon its national responsibilities it was forced to defend its record in government, particularly the budget. The February election showed the party at its weakest since 1957, although it managed to retain fifteen seats. It continued to lose heavily in Dublin (see table on p.150), and repeated the performance of 1981 when it recorded an increase only in rural constituencies.

Coalition was again the major topic at the 1982 party conference; by then the Fianna Fail government was in decline and another election imminent. The 'Killarney Strategy' was challenged by O'Leary: his proposal for open-ended talks on coalition and no special delegate conference was rejected in favour of a compromise motion from Cluskey, thereby promptly, but unexpectedly, provoking O'Leary's defection to Fine Gael and the election of Dick Spring. Of those contesting the leadership in 1982, only Michael D. Higgins was a strong anti-coalitionist; Spring supported the O'Leary formula with the provision that he would not hesitate to lead Labour out of government if necessary. In 1981 he had taken over the Kerry constituency to which his father, Dan Spring, had been elected in 1943 and had been a junior minister in the 1981-82 coalition; his youthful image and apparent aloofness from past wrangles contributed to his election and the party's symbolic re-unification.[162]

Labour's dilemmas were, however, magnified during the 1982-87 coalition. Not only did its ministers preside over some of the most stringent economies in public expenditure, but even these measures were insufficient to fend off an escalating fiscal crisis. The cabinet was beleaguered by rifts over fiscal and economic policy: targets for the budget deficit, the extent of public sector cuts, the role and financing of the National Development Corporation, the privatisation of broadcasting and tax reform.[162] The government's decision to rescue the Dublin Gas company, the PMPA insurance company and the Allied Irish Bank's Insurance Corporation of Ireland all proved extremely embarrassing; none of the 'nationalisations' could be defended on social or socialist grounds, yet they never threatened Labour's membership of government. Cluskey presided over the PMPA rescue rushing in emergency legislation but chose, astutely, to resign over the gas company issue.[163] Of Labour's four ministers – Quinn (who replaced Cluskey), Kavanagh, Spring and Desmond – only the latter, in Health and Social Welfare, gained a reputation, no doubt aided by his pugnacious personality, for confronting consultants over private medicine and the Catholic Church over his reform of Haughey's limited contraceptive law of 1979. He was, nevertheless, assailed for major cut-backs in health and social welfare, the latter leading to Michael Bell's temporary loss of the Labour whip. A score-sheet of Labour's record, submitted by Spring to the party's Commission on Electoral Strategy in 1986, indicated that in twenty major policy areas, progress was evident in only two – a company Bill (significantly rewritten during

Fianna Fail's 1987 term) and the reduction in the use of state cars.[164]

Labour's political future had become inextricably linked to the success of coalition economic policy; Desmond's speeches on the national debt sounded uncannily like those of John Bruton or Alan Dukes. One commentator noted that:

> Having supported a budgetary programme which owed more to Fine Gael monetarist policies than to the social concepts of wealth redistribution and backed a Bill which actually took money from the unemployed – a policy which was anathema to the political left – Labour has firmly locked itself into a full term of government with Fine Gael. Their political futures are now more firmly intertwined than ever and having chosen the path of fiscal rectitude, they can only batten down the hatches and hope that in two years time an economic upturn will allow them to untie the national purse strings to pave the way for a successful general election.[165]

Labour's participation in coalition added to the fiscal crisis by influencing – negatively – the extent of retrenchment policies, yet had no overall impact on economic development or unemployment. Despite speculation that Cluskey's resignation was tactically designed to alter the terms of coalition by 'squeez[ing] even further concessions out of the Fine Gael side',[166] there is little evidence for this; within months of taking up office Spring had moved to assure sceptics that Labour would act within the 'constraints of participation in government'.[167] Its acceptance of the weakening of the National Development Corporation – the benchmark of Labour economic strategy for decades – was firmly in line with that pledge.

By 1985 the inner-party divisions that sprang from the conflict between the party's integrative concerns and its working-class roots posed a major threat; Cluskey's resignation had challenged Spring's leadership from the left, while those of Treacy and Bermingham from the right, and Robinson over the New Ireland Forum report openly signalled the range and depth of discord within the parliamentary Labour Party. The threat from key unions, such as the ITGWU, ATGWU and FWUI, to disaffiliate or cease operating the political fund 'to any prospective (Labour) candidate who supports coalition with Fine Gael'[168] highlighted the contradictory way in which Labour's relationship with the unions was both a condition for its success as a party and a constraint on its ability to fully act out its integrative role. In addition, Labour's percentage of the 'left' vote had fallen from virtually 100 per cent in 1973 to 63 per cent in the 1987 general elections due to increasing competition from the Workers' Party:[169] in the 1987 general election the Labour Party registered a national vote of only 6.4 per cent, its lowest since 1933. Its support among the skilled and unskilled working class fell to 4 and 7 per cent respectively, compared to Fianna Fail's 45 and 41 per cent.[170] Nevertheless, the party managed to salvage twelve seats, a drop of only four.

Internal feuds had dogged the party since the late 1960s, and while publicly they were seen to revolve around coalition, they obscured a more fundamental debate, defined by Emmet Stagg as 'the choice between democratic socialism and being the political wing of the Saint Vincent de Paul'.[171] Institutionally, the battle centred on control of the Administrative Council; chaired by Higgins from 1978 to 1987, his replacement and the process for electing the party leader – on which it was rumoured that Spring had sought Neil Kinnock's advice – signalled open war. The Commission on Electoral Strategy had been convened in 1985 as a means to deflect and contain this feuding and to tackle the public dissolution of Labour's social base by reconstructing Labour's image; its significance lies less in what it says than it what it attempted to do. In this respect, its 52-page report reaffirmed the need to forge a realignment in Irish politics into a clearly articulated left-right debate through a stronger identity with the Irish working class and an assertion of Labour independence – arguments pursued for years by the Labour left. Yet, as a compromise document, it consolidated the right-wing's position, redefining class and identity without sacrificing any of Labour's integrative concerns; reference to the 1980 party programme of 'Labour the Workers' Party' (a crude plagiarism of its then rival Sinn

Fein – the Workers' Party) went alongside a strong defense of Labour's coalition performance.[172] The decision to adopt a 'flexible' approach to coalition, which would be unlikely in the near future unless a threshold of 25 Labour deputies was reached,[173] had been determined as much by Fine Gael's closer alliance with the Progressive Democrats as by obvious electoral imperatives. As an attempt to forge a common unity, however, the commission was a failure; the left might have captured key positions on the Administrative Council at the 1987 conference, but Spring quickly reasserted his control and succeeded in ousting Militant – with whom Labour Left had often formed an informal alliance – from Labour's youth section and party branches.[174] By publishing his *Labour's Alternative: Job Creation and Fair Tax in Tomorrow's Ireland*, Spring ensured that his more timid and reformist vision of economic growth – and not Labour Left's alternative document – dominated the political agenda.[175]

The Impasse of Social Democracy

Labour's challenge has come not just from the left, but in the party's scramble for working-class legitimacy and trade union allegiance, the Workers' Party has been its rival.[176] The Workers' Party's origins reside in the split in Sinn Fein in January 1970, when the majority formed Official Sinn Fein. Under the leadership of Cathal Goulding and Tomas MacGiolla the party developed radical policies, becoming involved, in the Republic, in community issues like housing and community rights to fishing. It gradually shed its traditional nationalism, and offered a reassessment of Irish political economy, with an implied jettisoning of many of James Connolly's assumptions:

> Investment in Ireland by multinational firms, previously opposed by the party as exploitative of natural resources, was now, if not exactly welcomed, regarded as inevitable and as 'objectively progressive' since it helped to create an industrial proletariat.[177]

Recognition that the industrial working class and not small farmers or businessmen were the social basis of any future electoral support culminated, although not without intense and bitter debate, in the adoption of the name Sinn Fein-the Workers' Party in 1977 and the Workers' Party in 1982. Its emphasis on the failure of the Irish bourgeoisie, criticism of import controls, support for multinationals alongside state-propelled economic growth and job creation, centralised bargaining and equitable taxation was instrumental in shaping debate in the 1970s.[178] The implementation of many of these proposals, however, remains vague and overly technocratic. Moreover, the party has failed to advance any new political or economic analysis since that pioneering work, much of which is rigidly determinist and outdated. The state's fiscal crisis, mass unemployment, spiralling emigration and Labour's coalition experience were electorally unrewarding to the Workers' Party until 1989.

Although considerably smaller, the Workers' Party is often described as an Irish equivalent of a Eurocommunist party.[179] Its profile is high principally because of Labour's abdication of a radical agenda and the absence of a civil libertarian tradition in Ireland. Its TDs and local authority councillors have won support on the basis of hard work in the constituencies, and voter dissatisfaction with the major parties, including Labour; its efforts to combat clientelism, by which the dominant bourgeois parties have maintained and maximised support among the working class, have, however, been less successful.[180] The Workers' Party support base lies principally among the skilled and unskilled urban working class. It has found it difficult to make the leap from those living in publicly owned housing to owner-occupiers (an increasing percentage due to government subsidies and grants[181]), and in this respect its image as the defender of public-sector workers of all grades is not reflected in its campaigning or in votes. The Worker's Party potential base among the inner-city unskilled and unemployed, most of whom are poorly housed in local authority flat complexes, has been successfully challenged by the independent Tony Gregory. Gregory achieved a meteoric rise during the February 1982 election by negotiating a deal for Dublin inner-city development with Charles Haughey, then desperately seeking parliamentary support for his campaign to become Taoiseach. His mixture of radical populism – organised through strong local community associations – and militant nationalism has concentrated on high media issues like drugs and street traders, through which he has formed an informal alliance with Provisional Sinn Fein, whose candidate won a seat on Dublin City Council with Gregory's help.[182]

Sinn Fein's decision in 1986 to abandon the policy of abstentionism, to fight Dail seats and to engage in political activity in the Republic has not been as triumphant as its 1981 election results might have suggested. Held when the IRA campaign for political status for its prisoners in the Northern Ireland Maze Prison was at its height,[183] liberal concern for prisoners' rights combined with nationalist sentiment in electing two IRA prisoners as TDs for Louth and Cavan-Monaghan, both constituencies bordering on Northern Ireland.

> The border republican vote has existed since the 1920s ... and, while durable, is not large enough to elect a deputy except at times of heightened nationalist feeling such as during the campaign in 1957 or the hunger strikes in 1981.[184]

In 1987, it won 2 per cent of the vote, twice as much as in February 1982, but below the 2.5 per cent of 1981.[185] In so far as many of the public and private authorities and institutions have abandoned areas of high-density unemployment, crime, vandalism and poverty, Sinn Fein has adeptly cultivated the image in Dublin of being a radical, militantly anti-establishment party located principally among ghettoised tenants of inner-city flat complexes. Gerry Adams, in an interview in 1986, said that 'Sinn Fein will take an aggressively dogmatic attitude against what we consider to be anti-people policies.'[186] On this basis Sinn Fein enjoys some support from students; the low priority of Northern Ireland and the irrelevance of 'British domination of the economy' for the Republic's electorate ensures that these issues remain geographically specific and largely emotional.[187] Sinn Fein has been reasonably successful in transferring many of its community-based tactics of Northern Ireland to Dublin; in some instances, this has involved vigilante-type action against drug pushers or petty criminals. For the foreseeable future, however, there is little likelihood of Sinn Fein making any impact on the political process in the south.

With the exception of the small Democratic Socialist Party, whose Limerick TD, Jim Kemmy, is its only likely success, and the even more marginal Communist Party of Ireland – which still retains some influence in the trade unions – the Irish Left constitutes the Labour Party and the Workers' Party. There is evidence of some co-operation at parliamentary level between the Labour Party, the Workers' Party, the Democratic Socialist Party, Gregory and a number of independent senators with the publication of a framework for a broad left-wing economic strategy in 1988, but intense rivalry between the Labour Party and the Workers' Party remains, particularly at constituency level. Some Workers' Party seats, at national and local level, have been gained at the expense of Labour, while conversely, Labour deputies have managed to retain seats because of transfers and thereby block Workers' Party candidates.[188] In 1982, taking advantage of public disquiet over successive hung parliaments, Brendan Halligan proposed altering the electoral system from the single-transferable vote form of proportional representation to one which would assure Labour a more reliable outcome, while undermining support for the Workers' Party.[189] The rise of Workers' Party members into prominent positions in the trade unions since the early 1980s has transformed them into a new battle-ground, not least because the younger Workers' Party officials are often more capable and industrially more militant; that the unions used to be virtually the sole preserve of the Labour Party has led to the invocation of restrictions on electoral activity, use of the political fund and promotional outlets.[190]

The level of conflict between the two parties has been in inverse proportion to their electoral results. During the past two-decade period of declining capital investment and employment, the overall left-wing vote has been decreasing; the 10 per cent reached in 1987 was 'lower than at any time since 1957 when Labour, then the left's sole flagbearer, won

9 per cent of the votes'.[191] Labour's Commission on Electoral Strategy explained this phenomenon by acknowledging Ireland's deeply conservative political environment:

> The fact is that the Irish political system is atypical of the European norm. It is unique and the party divisions here have no counterpart in any other European democracy. This situation is not immutable but the society which has produced these political abnormalities is a deeply conservative one, arguably the most conservative amongst the European democracies.[192]

The reason lay in the dominance of traditional nationalist divisions, cultural values and economic backwardness. The attractiveness of the European model lay in the assumption that if Ireland underwent economic and social change comparable with that experienced by other European societies then the patteren of ideological debate and significance of social democratic and socialist parties associated with those societies would come about in Ireland as well.

In the 1970s, the Irish left relied upon modernisation theory's teleological relationship between industrialisation and working-class consciousness to explain the progressive impact that international monopoly capitalism would have on the traditional pattern of clientelist, nationalist and religious behaviour in Ireland. While the Workers' Party and the Democratic Socialist Party's predecessor, the British and Irish Communist Organisation (BICO), were the most strident advocates of this view, Labour was also inclined to the vision that it would naturally reap the benefits of a more 'modern' electorate; its embrace of a 'socialist' strategy in the 1960s was stimulated as much by pragmatic assumptions of the impact of post-Second World War capitalist expansion as by socialist convictions.[193] Consequently part of the mythology surrounding its interminable coalition debate has been the belief among some anti-coalitionists that the working class would vote Labour if only it renounced coalition.[194] One explanation for the present impasse of social democracy must therefore reside in its dogmatic embrace of modernisation theory which has left it theoretically denuded in a situation in which neither economic growth nor crisis has witnessed the working class embrace the socialist agenda. Additionally, like its counterparts in the UK, Labour has no perspective for a gradual socialist transformation. As the crisis in the Irish economy has deepened, it has appealed to the 'power of rational political thought'.[195] Caught within the dynamic and logic of parliamentarianism, the Labour Party has become absorbed with the problems of managing society: Dick Spring's economic proposals – ambiguously placed within the context of a non-coalition strategy – are firmly set within the integrationist mode that has characterised the Labour Party since the 1920s.

> Capitalism was seen not as a mode of production which constantly generates new and old forms of exploitation and inequality on the basis of market relations, but as a static set of arbitrary powers which could be absorbed by nationalisations, administrative controls, or policies of redistribution.[196]

In doing so, Labour has implicitly accepted the notions of class harmony and national interest to the extent that it has acted as a fetter on the development of a socialist critique of the Irish economy and emergence of a class consciousness.

Notes

1. Sean Lemass, *PDDE* (Parliamentary Debates Dail Eireann), Vol.223 cols 2550-1, 8 July 1966.
2. Anthony Gaughan, 'A Scoop that Never Was', *Irish Times*, 12 December 1979; Brendan Halligan, 'The Day Labour Almost Came to Power', *Irish Times*, 6 July 1982.
3. Ken Hannigan, 'British Based Unions in Ireland: Building Workers and the Split in Congress', *Saothar*, No.7, 1981, pp.40-9.
4. Donal Nevin, 'Industry and Labour', in Kevin B. Nowland and I. Desmond Williams (eds), *Ireland in the War Years and After, 1939-51*, Dublin 1969, pp.94-108.
5. Arthur Mitchell, *Labour in Irish Politics*, Dublin 1974, pp.38-9.
6. ILP&TUC. *Report of Special Congress*, Dublin 1930, pp.134-5; see also T. J. O'Connell, ILP, *1st Annual Report*. p.53.
7. Ellen Hazelkorn, 'Why is There no Socialism in Ireland? Theoretical Problems of Irish Marxism', *Science and Society*, Summer 1989.
8. Peter Mair, *The Changing Irish Party System*, Manchester 1987, p.58.

9. Emmet Larkin, 'Socialism and Catholicism in Ireland', *Studies*, Spring 1985, pp.66-91; for influence on trade unionism, see Ellen Hazelkorn, 'The Social and Political Views of Louie Bennett; 1870-1956', *Saothar*, Vol.13, 1988.

10. ILP&TUC, *Annual Report*, 1927 pp.87-88.

11. Charles McCarthy, 'Irish Trade Unions in the Nineteen Thirties (Part One)', *Economic and Social Review*, Vol.5. No.3, 1974, p.358.

12. Leo Panitch, *Social Democracy and Industrial Militancy*, Cambridge 1976, p.1.

13. Brendan Corish, *New Republic* (pamphlet), Dublin 1967; 'Cluskey Says Socialism Won't Be Easily Attained', *Irish Times*, 14 May 1979; Michael D. Higgins quoted in John Horgan, *Labour: The Price of Power*, Dublin 1986, p.147.

14. Charles Haughey, *PDDE*, Vol.292 cols 734-5, 9 September 1976: Michael O'Leary, *Irish Times*, 29 October 1982; Sean Lemass, op.cit.

15. Michael Gallagher. *The Irish Labour Party in Transition, 1957-82*, Dublin and Manchester 1982, pp.67-8.

16. Michael McCann, 'New-Look Labour Gives the Lead', *Labour News*, November 1965.

17. *Irish Times*, 16 October 1967; 'Foreword', *The New Republic*, op.cit.

18. Corish, *The New Republic*, op.cit.

19. Gallagher, op.cit., p.70.

20. Garret FitzGerald, *Planning in Ireland*, Dublin 1968, p.96.

21. Charles McCarthy, *Decade of Upheaval: Irish Trade Unions in the 1960s*, Dublin 1973.

22. Fergal Tobin, *The Best of Decades. Ireland in the 1960s*, Dublin 1984, p.182.

23. Jack Dowling, Lelia Doolin, and Bob Quinn, *Sit Down and Be Counted. The Evolution of a Television Station*, Dublin 1969.

24. Gallagher, op.cit., p.167.

25. Ibid., p.176.

26. M. A. Busteed and Hugh Mason, 'Irish Labour in the 1969 Election', *Political Studies*, Vol.18, September 1970, pp.373-9; for 1967 local government results and comment, see *Labour News*, July-August 1967.

27. Horgan, op.cit., pp.83, 85.

28. Gallagher, op.cit., p.184.

29. Tom Nairn, 'The Left Against Europe', *New Left Review*, No.75, p.43.

30. Michel Peillon, *Contemporary Irish Society*, Dublin 1982, p.118.

31. Horgan, op.cit., p.84.

32. Basil Chubb, *The Government and Politics of Ireland*, London 1982 (2nd edition), Chapter 1.

33. The Labour Party, *Report of the Commission on Electoral Strategy*, September 1986, pp.30-1.

34. Corish, *New Republic*, op.cit.

35. Labour Party, *Electoral Commission*, p.25.

36. Peillon, op.cit., p.119.

37. Labour Party, *Electoral Commission*, pp.30-1.

38. *Sunday Press*, 4 October 1970.
39. Gallagher, op.cit., p.183.
40. Frances O'Rourke, 'The Political Philosophy of Brendan Halligan', *Sunday Press*, 11 April 1976; Brendan Halligan, 'Labour Receives the Kiss of Death', *Irish Times*, 8 July 1982.
41. O'Rourke, op.cit.
42. Horgan, op.cit., p.33.
43. Ibid., p.45.
44. Sam McDonald, 'O'Leary's Unflinching Optimism', *Business and Finance*, 31 October 1974.
45. ICTU, Annual Report, 1976, pp.183-91.
46. Jenny Beale, *Women in Ireland*, Dublin 1986, p.146.
47. John Carroll, 'A Trade Union View of the Economy', *Business and Finance*, 30 January 1975; Matt Merrigan in ICTU, *Annual Report*, 1977 p.400.
48. Basil Chubb, *The Government and Politics of Ireland*, London and Oxford 1974 (1st edition), gives figures for 1970, p.142; by 1979 over 45 per cent of Irish television viewers could and did watch British telelvision, see Chubb, 2nd edition, op.cit., p.73.
49. Horgan, op.cit., p.56.
50. *Irish Times*, 19 October 1976.
51. Donal Musgrave, 'Army is the Muscle of Democracy, Says Donegan', *Irish Times*, 24 June 1976; in 1975. Donegan was quoted as saying: 'In the months ahead, I will have to ask the army to perform things which they will not like, but because of their tremendous loyalty the army will go ahead and perform them.' *Irish Times*, 19 October 1976.
52. 'Dail Report', *Irish Times*, 22 October 1976.
53. *PDDE*, Vol.292 cols 734-5, 9 September 1976.
54. Gallagher, op.cit., p.198.
55. Dick Walsh, 'Kelly Exposes Differences in Coalition', *Irish Times*, 30 March 1976; *Business and Finance*, 11 January 1979.
56. Brendan Walsh, *Population and Employment Projections: 1971-86*, Dublin 1975.
57. 'The Coalition in Government', *Business and Finance*, 9 June 1977.
58. 'The Coalition and Business', *Business and Finance*, 12 May 1977.
59. Donal A. Dineen, 'Anti-Unemployment Policies in Ireland Since 1970' in Jeremy Richardson and Roger Henning (eds), *Unemployment: Policy Responses of Western Democracies*, London 1984, p.249.
60. Full text in Ted Nealon, *Ireland: A Parliamentary Directory, 1973-74*, Dublin 1974, pp.68-9.
61. 'Corish Seeks Economic Plan and More State Enterprise', *Irish Times*, 28 June 1976; 'Brendan Loses Some Friends', *Sunday Press*, 11 April 1976.
62. David Jacobson, 'Theorizing Irish Industrialization: The Case of the Motor Industry', *Science and Society*, Summer 1989.
62. *Economic and Social Development, 1976-1980*, Dublin 1976.
64. Paul Bew and Henry Patterson, *Sean Lemass and the Making of Modern Ireland*, Dublin 1982.

65. Emmett O'Connell, 'Government Policy versus the Central Bank', *Business and Finance*, 11 July 1974.
66. Ian Morrison, speaking on 28 April 1977 and quoted in 'The Coalition and Business', *Business and Finance*, 12 May 1977.
67. Vincent Browne, 'Is There Life After Coalition?', *Magill*, November 1981.
68. Robin Hannon, 'Labour and Coalition', *Watchword* n.d. (1976).
69. Nicos Poulantzas, *State. Power. Socialism*, London 1978, p.186.
70. ICTU, *18th Annual Report*, 1976.
71. ICTU, *17th Annual Report*, 1975, pp.45, 153-5; Dick Walsh, 'Cosgrave Demands Pay Pause to Resist Economic Crisis', *Irish Times*, 11 December 1975.
72. ICTU, *19th Annual Report*, 1977, pp.487-9.
72. ICTU, *13th Annual Report*, 1971, p.177.
74. 'Reminiscence: Socialist Trade Unionist: Matt Merrigan's Political Formation', *Saothar*, Vol.12, 1987, p.98.
75. ICTU, *19th Annual Report*, 1977, p.400.
76. Richard Sinnott, 'Patterns of Party Support: Social Class' in Michael Laver, Peter Mair and Richard Sinnott (eds), *How Ireland Voted: The Irish General Election of 1987*, Dublin 1987, pp.103-5.
77. Ibid., p. 102; Ellen Hazelkorn, 'Class, Clientelism and the Political Progress in the Republic of Ireland' in Patrick Clancy, Sheelagh Drudy, Kathleen Lynch and Liam O'Dowd (eds), *Ireland: A Sociological Profile*, Dublin 1986, pp.335-6.
78. Olivia O'Leary, 'Smile Though Your Party's Breaking', *Irish Times*, 28 October 1982.
79. Sinnott, op.cit.
80. 'Is Sean Lemass a Great Man?', *Business and Finance*, 13 August 1965.
81. Wolfgang Weinz; 'Economic Development and Interest Groups', in Brian Girvin and Rolan Sturm (eds), *Politics and Society in Contemporary Ireland*, Aldershot 1986, p.95.
82. J. Shregele, 'Restructuring the Irish Trade Union Movement', in ICTU, *17th Annual Report*, 1975, pp.345-90.
83. McCarthy, *The Decade of Upheaval*, p.47.
84. ICTU, *16th Annual Report*, 1974, pp.389-90.
85. James Wickham, 'Industrialisation, Work and Unemployment' in Clancy *et al.* (eds), op.cit., pp.70-96.
86. Aidan Kelly and Teresa Brannick, 'Industrial Conflict in the Public Service: An Assessment of the 25 Years, 1960-1984', *Seirbhis Phoibli*, Vol.7. No.3, September 1986.
87. Weinz, op.cit., pp.96-7.
88. 'Trade Unions in the 1980s', *European Industrial Relations Review*, No.176, September 1988, pp.17-20; 'Massive Tumble in ITGWU Surplus', *Business and Finance*, 25 May 1981; Aileen O'Toole, 'The Trade Unions' Finances Revealed', *Business and Finance*, 26 November 1981; Brian Donaghy, 'How the Recession has Taken its Toll on the Trade Unions', *Irish Times*, 3 February 1987: Vivienne Clark, 'Unions Weathering the Unemployment Storm', *Irish Times*, 2 February 1988.

89. W.T. Roche and Joe Larragy, 'The Trend of Unionisation in the Republic of Ireland' in T. Murphy *et al.* (eds), *Recent Trends in Irish Industrial Relations, A Reader*, Dublin 1987, pp.10-1.

90. 'The Facts about Strikes in Ireland', *Business and Finance*, 6 May 1966, pp.14-5.

91. McCarthy, op.cit., p.24.

92. Aidan Kelly and Teresa Brannick, 'The Changing Contours of Irish Strike Patterns, 1960-1984', *IBAR – Irish Business and Administrative Research*, Vol.8, pt. 1, 1986, p.84; 'Difficulties? Yes. Crisis? No', *Business and Finance*, 5 November 1965.

93. ICTU, *Trade Union Information*, No.160, 1970.

94. McCarthy, op.cit., p.26: Anthony Johnson, 'State Plans to Control Unions', *Business and Finance*, 14 January 1966; Bill Roche, 'Social Partnership and Political Control: State Strategy and Industrial Relations in Ireland', in Mary Kelly, Liam O'Dowd and James Wickham (eds), *Power, Conflict and Inequality*, Dublin 1982, p.58-9.

95. Charles McCarthy, *Business and Finance*, 30 July 1965.

96. Martin Morrissey, 'The Politics of Economic Management in Ireland', *Irish Political Studies*, Vol.1, 1986, pp.88-91.

97. ICTU, *12th Annual Report*, 1970. pp.107-17, 137, 227.

98. Roche, op.cit., p.59.

99. Ibid., p.60.

100. Dan Murphy, ICTU, *19th Annual Report*, 1977, p.475.

101. John Carroll, 'Business and Unions: The Friendly Enemies', *Business and Finance*, 19 September 1974, p.40.

102. John Carroll, ICTU, *19th Annual Report*, 1977, p.337.

103. Matt Merrigan, ICTU, *19th Annual Report*, 1977, p.358.

104. Matt Merrigan quoted in 'Unions Keep their Pay Options Open', *Business and Finance*, 7 July 1977.

105. Charles McCarthy, *Trade Unions in Ireland, 1894-1960*, Dublin 1977, p.571.

106. Jim Dunne, 'Peace for the Profligate', *Business and Finance*, 2 October 1980; 'Haughey Crash-Tackles the Unions', *Business and Finance*, 26 August 1982.

107. 'Economic Revival: Haughey Style', *Business and Finance*, 16 April 1981.

108. ICTU, *22nd Annual Report*, 1980, p.126.

109. Jim Dunne, 'Peace for the Profligate', *Business and Finance*, 2 October 1980.

110. Roche and Larragy, op.cit.

111. ICTU, *19th Annual Report*, 1977, pp.377, 380.

112. Seamus Cody, John O'Dowd and Peter Rigney, *The Parliament of Labour – 100 Years of the Dublin Council of Trade Unions*, Dublin 1986, pp.233-4; ICTU, *Annual Report*, 1979, pp.131ff; 'Will PAYE Bring Down the Government?' and 'Divide and Be Conquered', *Business and Finance*, 22 March 1979.

113. ICTU, *21st Annual Report*, 1979, pp.270-3.

114. Weinz, op.cit., p.99.

115. 'Fewer Workers Joining Trade Unions', *Irish Times*, 5 March 1988.

116. 'The FUE's Rescue Net', *Business and Finance*, 5 October 1978; 'Time to Bury the National Understanding', *Business and Finance*, 26 March 1981: 'The Spectre of 69', *Business and Finance*, 12 January 1982.

117. Roche and Larragy, op.cit.

118. Bill Roche, 'State Strategies and Politics', in *Industrial Relations in Ireland. Contemporary Issues and Developments*, Dublin 1987, p.107.

119. ICTU, *23rd Annual Report*, 1981, p.392.

120. Richard Scase, 'Introduction' in Richard Scase (ed.), *The State in Western Europe*, London 1980, p.11.

121. 'Ireland's Attitudes to Trade Unions', *Business and Finance*, 8 December 1977.

122. Stephen Lalor, 'Corporatism in Ireland', *Administration*, 1982, Vol.30. No.4, pp.89-90.

123. John Bruton, 'Politics: Real Issues of Mock Battles?', *Furrow*, April 1986, pp.211-23.

124. Ivor Kenny, *Government and Enterprise in Ireland*, Dublin and San Antonio 1984: Fergus FitzGerald, *Too Much Government, A Bid to Rescue Parliamentary Democracy*, Dublin 1982.

125. Horgan, op.cit., p.136; 'Profile of Michael Mullen, TD', *Labour News*, November 1965.

126. Peter Mair, *The Changing Irish Party Sytem*, pp.101-2; Helen Lucy Burke, 'Links with Labour', *Business and Finance*, 23 June 1967.

127. Horgan, op.cit., pp.172-3.

128. 'Fianna Fail and Unions in Autumn Pay Dialogue', *Business and Finance*, 23 June 1967.

129 'Reminiscence ... Merrigan', loc.cit., p.102; Cody *et al.*, op.cit., pp.233-40; Tim Pat Coogan, *Disillusioned Decades: Ireland, 1966-87*, Dublin 1987, p.68.

130. John Mulhall, ICTU, *Annual Report*, 1977, p.287.

131. 'Fianna Fail and Unions Begin A-Wooing', *Business and Finance*, 23 October 1986; 'It's War – Unions on Govt. 1pc Limit', *Irish Independent*, 7 January 1984; William A. Attley, 'The Role of the Trade Unions', undelivered address prepared for the Irish Management Institute, April 1987, in *Studies*, Vol, 76. No.303, Autumn 1987, pp.294-303.

132. 'Fine Gael Wants to be the Party of the Working Class', *Irish Times*, 5 February 1979.

133. Irish Congress of Trade Unions, *Confronting the Jobs Crisis: Framework for a National Plan*, September 1984, which first proposed the idea of joint government/trade union talks on a national economic programme; 'ESRI Accused of Political Intervention', *Irish Times*, 6 February 1987.

134. Anne Harris, 'Our own Dear Laughing Boy' (profile of Bertie Ahern), *Sunday Independent*, 26 April 1987; 'Ahern choice as Next Party Leader', *Sunday Press*, 10 April 1988.

135. 'Labour–Union Rift is Total After Plan', *Business and Finance*, 15 October 1987: Maev-Ann Wren, 'The Phoney War on Economic Recovery Ends', *Irish Times*, 26 September 1987; Gerald Barry, 'How the

Deal Was Done', *Sunday Tribune*, 11 October 1987; Dick Walsh, 'Carroll Calls for Breaking of Coalition', *Irish Times*, 16 December 1983: 'Spring, Carroll Clash in Dispute over Letter', *Irish Times*, 29 January 1986.

136. Federated Union of Employers (FUE), *Bulletin*, July 1988; Patrick Nolan, 'FUE Calls for More Curbs on Right to Strike', *Irish Times*, 30 June 1988; Dail Questions, 10 March 1988, pp.2466-68.

137. ICTU, *29th Annual Report*, 1987; Joe Larragy and Bill Roche, 'Recent Developments in Union Membership Trends', *Industrial Relations News*, No.36, 24 September 1987. pp.13-15: Niamh Hardiman, 'Trade Union Density in the Republic of Ireland, 1960-1979', *IBAR – Irish Business and Administrative Research*, Vol.5, No.2, October 1983, pp.41-6.

138. Roche and Larragy, 'Trend of Unionisation', op.cit., p.15.

139. Leo Panitch, *Working Class Politics in Crisis*, London 1986, p.204.

140. 'FUE's Hard Sell on Pay Deal', *Business and Finance*, 22 October 1987; 'Unions Face Tough Task on Jobs Boost', *Business and Finance*, 26 November 1987.

141. Goran Therborn, *Why Some People Are More Unemployed Than Others*, London 1986.

142. J.J. O'Molloy, 'Bleeding Hearts, Strokes and Charlie's Carrots', *Sunday Tribune*, 26 July 1987.

143. Patrick Nolan, 'ICTU Must Avoid "British Syndrome" – Quigley', *Irish Times*, 9 July 1988.

144. Ferdinand von Prondzynski, 'Social Partnership in Ireland and Austria' in Alan Matthews and Ede Sagarra (eds), *Economic Performance in Two Small European Economies: Ireland and Austria*, Dublin 1988.

145. Michael Fogarty, Liam Ryan and Joseph Lee (eds), *Irish Values and Attitudes: The Irish Report of the European Values Systems Study*, Dublin 1984.

146. Evelyn Mahon, 'Women's Rights and Catholicism in Ireland', *New Left Review*, November-December 1987, No.166.

147. Noel Browne, *Business and Finance*, 14 June 1968; Noel Browne. *Against the Tide*, Dublin 1986, pp.257-70.

148. Peter Mair, *The Changing Irish Party System*, op.cit., p.104.

149. Dick Walsh, 'Presidency Raises Party Leadership Speculation', *Irish Times*, 30 October 1976.

150. Horgan, op.cit., p.14.

151. Maev Kennedy, 'Leader who Loathed Playboy Image', *Irish Times*, 19 October 1982.

152. Gallagher, *The Irish Labour Party in Transition*, p.226.

153. Frank Cluskey, address to Labour Party conference reprinted in *Irish Times*, 27/28 October 1980.

154. The Labour Party, 'Election Programme '81', in *Annual Report: 1980-82*, Galway 1982.

155. Cluskey, op.cit.

156. Ibid.; Gallagher, op.cit., p.237.

157. The Labour Party, *Report. 1985-1987, Cork*, Dublin 1987, p.35.

158. Patrick Massey, 'A New Approach to Public Sector Pay', *Administration*, Vol.34, No.4, p.460.

159. Brian Girvin, 'Social Change and Moral Politics: The Irish Constitutional Referendum 1983', *Political Studies*, Vol.34 No.1, 1986, pp.61-81; Cornelius O'Leary and Tom Hesketh, 'The Irish Abortion and Divorce Referendum Campaigns', *Irish Political Studies*, Vol.3, 1988, pp.43-62.

160. Gallagher, op.cit., p.248.

161. Mary Holland, 'Dublin's New Dealers', *New Statesman*, 31 December 1982.

162. Sean Kelly and Joe Joyce, 'Garret: Friend or Foe of Business?', *Irish Business*, January 1983, p.14-9.

163. 'Has Cluskey Changed his Spots?' and 'Shaping up for the Budget', *Irish Business*, January 1984, pp.12-5.

164. Geraldine Kennedy, 'How Spring Rates Labour's Role', *Sunday Press*, 27 April 1986; c.f. the Labour Party, *Report, 1985-1987*, Dublin 1987, p.67.

165. 'The Beleaguered Cabinet', *Business and Finance*, 21 April 1983, p.10.

166. Gerald Barry, 'Cluskey Move is Calculated to Alter Nature of Coalition Pact', *Sunday Tribune*, 11 December 1983; 'Labour's Identity Crisis', *Business and Finance*, 19 July 1984.

167. Geraldine Kennedy, 'Why it Was so Tough' (interview with Dick Spring), *Sunday Press*, 13 February 1983.

168. Horgan, op.cit., pp.122-3.

169. Michael Gallagher, 'The Outcome' in Laver *et al.* (eds), op.cit., p.80; the 1985 local elections registered the Labour Party's proportion of the 'left' vote as 65 per cent, see Labour Party, *Report of the Commission on Electoral Strategy*, op.cit., p.39.

170. Richard Sinnot, op.cit., p.102.

171. Joe Joyce, 'Can Dick Spring Ride into a New Red Dawn?', *Irish Times*, 25 September 1987.

172. Labour Party, *Commission*, pp.20, 30-1.

173. Donal Byrne, 'Labour's Coalition Critics Have Their Way', *Sunday Tribune*, 24 August 1986.

174. John Cooney, 'Labour Move to Curb Militant', *Irish Times*. 10 September 1986; Mark Brennock, 'Militant Ousted from Labour's Youth Section', *Irish Times*, 23 March 1988.

175. Dick Spring, *Labour's Alternative. Job Creation and Fair Tax in Tomorrow's Ireland: Proposals for Medium-Term Economic Policy Development Presented to the Economic Policy Committee of the Labour Party*, June 1988; Denis Coughlan, 'Spring Links Industry Policy with Tax System', *Irish Times*, 18 June 1988; Paul Tansey, 'Taking Labour's Economic Policy in from the Cold', *Sunday Tribune*, 19 June 1988; Denis Coughlan, 'Stagg Seeks Labour Youth Support Against Spring Tax Plan', *Irish Times*, 22 July 1988; Mark Brennock, 'Labour Must Restate its Socialist Values – Higgins', *Irish Times*, 15 July 1988; c.f. submission prepared by the Labour Left Co-operative, *Growth, Modernisation and*

Democracy, September 1988 which attempts an analysis of the conservative consensus in Ireland and maintains a commitment to a full employment strategy.

176. Bruce Arnold, 'What is Happening on the Left?', *Irish Independent*, 3 May 1980.

177. Michael Gallagher, *Political Parties in the Republic of Ireland*, Dublin 1985, p.115.

178. Sinn Fein-The Workers' Party, *The Irish Industrial Revolution*, Dublin 1977.

179. Gallagher, *Political Parties*, p.117.

180. Hazelkorn, 'Class, Clientelism and the Political Process'.

181. Paul Sweeney, 'Housing Needs and Costs', unpublished, 1986; T.J. Baker and L.H. O'Brien, *The Irish Housing System. A Critical Overview*, Economic and Social Research Institute, Broadsheet No.17, April 1979.

182. 'The Gregory Interview', *Gralton*, February/March 1983. pp.15-27.

183. Patrick Bishop and Eamonn Mallie, *The Provisional IRA*, London 1987, pp.269-99.

184. Gallagher, 'The Outcome', op.cit., p.81; Jim Cusack, 'Sinn Fein – Back at the Crossroads', *Irish Times*, 30 October 1986.

185. Ibid., p.80.

186. Fergus Pyle, 'What's on the Agenda Now is an End to Partition' (interview with Gerry Adams), *Irish Times*, 10 December 1986.

187. 'Opinion Poll, 1987', *Irish Political Studies*, Vol.3, 1988, p.138; Peter Mair, 'Breaking the Nationalist Mould: The Irish Republic and the Anglo-Irish Agreement', in Paul Teague (ed.), *Beyond the Rhetoric*, London 1987, pp.81-110.

188. Gallagher, 'The Outcome', op.cit., pp.79-80.

189. Brendan Halligan, 'Circumstances Dictate that We Should Look Towards a New Voting System', *Sunday Independent*, 2 February 1982; Horgan, op.cit., pp.166-71; Michael Gallagher, 'Does Ireland Need a New Electoral System?', *Irish Political Studies*, Vol.2, 1987, pp.27-48.

190. 'The Upstaging of Labour', *Business and Finance*, 19 May 1983: Olivia O'Leary, 'TDs' Revolt is Part of a Pattern', *Irish Times*, 22 March 1983; 'The State of the Unions', *New Hibernia*, April 1985.

191. Gallagher, 'The Outcome', p.77; Joseph O'Malley, 'Decline of the Left', *Sunday Independent*, 3 April 1988.

192. Labour Party, *Commission*, p.7.

192. Emmet O'Connor, 'A Fear of the Passions', *Gralton*. October/November 1983.

194. Horgan, op.cit., p.171.

195. Labour Party, *Commission*, p.15.

196. Goran Therborn, *What Does the Ruling Class Do When it Rules?*, London 1980, p. 217.

Conclusion

The rapidity of economic, social and cultural change since the 1950s has not been clearly reflected in the Republic's political system until very recently. As one political scientist commented on these changes:

> The Irish party system has undergone a major shock-wave, confirmed in the February 1987 election ... there are good reasons for supposing that the February 1987 election portends greater Europeanisation and re-alignment.[1]

Central to this claim was the emergence of the Progressive Democrats with 12 per cent of the votes and fourteen seats, replacing the Labour Party as the third largest party in the Dail.[2] The Progressive Democrats put forward a coherent neo-liberal response to the economic crisis – tax cuts to be financed by a comprehensive programme of cuts in public expenditure and privatisation. The party articulates a clear exasperation with the 'over-extension' of the state through clientilism and proposes a strategy of a state 'slimmed down' and less responsive to pressure groups, an aim to be achieved through reforms such as a change in the electoral system, a reduced number of TDs, abolition of the Seanad and of regional and local authorities, like health boards and vocational education committees. A lesser but still significant theme was the reform of church-state relations through a diminution of the confessional nature of the state in the Republic.[3] On Northern Ireland the Progressive Democrats showed signs of being the most advanced of the major parties, with serious discussion of dropping the constitutional claim to Northern Ireland. Its representatives on Foreign Affairs and Northern Ireland told its second national conference:

> We acknowledge that Nationalist Ireland, south of the border, has yet to come fully to terms with the implications of what we all know well for some time: Irish unity, as traditionally conceived in the South is simply not achievable by consent in the short term, politically or economically, and all our policies should reflect this reality.[4]

Brian Lenihan's response to the emergence of the Progressive Democrats demonstrated the clear dangers which Fianna Fail saw in its approach:

> The only end product of right-wing radicalism is destabilisation of the political system leading to class antagonism, which we have never had here. Its based on extreme *laissez-faire*, selfish materialism which takes no cognisance of the weak, deprived and less well-off in our society.[5]

It is true that class antagonism had never threatened fundamentally to disrupt the political system, but this was not because of the non-existence of class antagonisms and conflicts in Irish society. In fact, as we have shown in earlier chapters, a large part of the success of Fianna Fail as a mass party lay in its ability to take up and domesticate demands and grievances which had their roots in the conditions of life of small farmers and urban workers. Fianna Fail's radicalism as it was developed in the inter-war period was dependent on a clearly conservative regime in power and then from a reactionary challenge from the Blueshirts; that is to say it derived more from its conjunctural location than from the substance of its economic and social policies. It also benefited from the role which the Catholic Church played in confining the legitimate scope of ideological debate within narrow limits.

Church and State

Irish Catholicism's deep roots amongst the masses, extending back to the penal period in the eighteenth century, gave it the ability to play a deeply conservative role in the evolution of the new state. Staffed by the sons and daughters of the rural bourgeoisie, it sanctified an economic and social order, the preservation of which depended upon the continuous emigration of those whom an agrarian system dominated by cattle production could not employ or provide holdings for. Hostile to trade unionism and any attempts to introduce socialist ideas, it had bitterly opposed Larkin and Connolly and would subsequently become obsessively anti-communist. It had supported the treaty side in the civil war and the republicans had come in for much clerical condemnation, as well as some actual excommunications. The new leaders of Fianna Fail, while aware that as long as they could demonstrate the support of a substantial section of the electorate the Church would be wary of a confrontationist approach, were concerned to demonstrate their committed Catholicism and, as Inglis puts it, 'seized any chance to appear more zealously Catholic than [their] opponents'.[6] In March 1929 Fianna Fail proposed that the Dail should cease sitting on Catholic days of obligation. In 1930 it defended Mayo County Council's action in refusing to appoint a Protestant librarian, and after taking office in 1932 it sent a message of 'respectful homage and good wishes' to the Pope.[7] The process of incorporating Catholic teaching into Irish legislation reached a peak with the 1937 Constitution; de Valera had extensive consultations with the Catholic Church while framing it and the whole document was shown secretly to the Pope before being published.[8]

The church contributed powerfully to the forces making for a national consensus which lasted into the 1950s and was characterised by a complacent and stagnant conservatism, reinforced by stringent censorship which ensured a stifling cultural isolation.[9] In an important sense, Fianna Fail's radicalism in this period consisted in an avoidance of the excess of a rabid anti-communism indulged in heavily by the Free State government and the Church. While some of its opponents would use anti-communism as a weapon against even the mildest proposals for economic and social reform, Fianna Fail was careful to champion the cause of reform while at the same time distinguishing its legitimate social concerns from attempts to 'import' what were referred to in the Church hierarchy's pastoral letter condemning the socialist republican organisation Saor Eire in 1931 as 'sinful and irreligious' doctrines. In his excellent account of the deportation from Ireland in 1933 of the radical socialist, Jim Gralton, Pat Feeley provides a vignette which captures perfectly Fianna Fail's 'radicalism' – the Minister of Justice who presided over his deportation was Paddy Ruttledge, a man whom Peadar O'Donnell regarded as the most radical member of the government.[10] It was because the populat aspirations for a society which would see an end to emigration and the desolation of rural life, which Fianna Fail had tapped powerfully in the 1920s and early 1930s, would be frustrated that there was a retreat into an increasing reliance on the integrating ideologies of Catholicism and nationalism in the 1940s. It was Lemass who clearly realised that such instrumental use of these ideological resources would, in the continued absence of economic development, ultimately be counter-productive.

Because of the radical shift in economic policy initiated by Lemass the themes of national independence and unity together with commitment to a Gaelic and Catholic culture which remain central to Fianna Fail's image, are increasingly seen to be in some dislocation with the realities of life in the Republic. Catholicism is still a major force in Irish life, but its grip on the masses has weakened substantially. Economic growth created the conditions for a radical shift in demographic patterns, with population growth and a temporary ending of emigration producing a marked alteration in age structure which has given the Republic the youngest population in the European Community.

At the same time the liberalisation of the economy was accompanied by an opening up of an involuted culture with the advent of a national television service in 1962. Unlike the tradition of the national radio station for which most programmes were home-produced and any material which went against Catholic principles was self-censored, from the start Irish television made considerable use of American and British programmes. In addition, it was estimated in 1961 that over 30 per cent of potential television homes in the Republic were already receiving British television, and by

1984 66 per cent of Irish homes were receiving good quality signals from British transmitters; moreover, the 'denationalising' influence of this medium has since been substantially added to by the onset of multi-channel cable television.[11] The practise and discourse of television – the heavy emphasis in many imported programmes and in an increasing number of home-produced ones on the situation and problems of urban individuals instead of portrayals of Catholic ruralism – challenged the dominant cultural forms of de Valera's Ireland. It accompanied a limited growth of a more iconoclastic, critical and investigative type of television as the Republic was influenced by the backwash of 1960s radicalism.[12] Economic growth, urbanisation, a younger population, improvements in the general standard of formal education and the gradual disintegration of an insular culture under the pressure of television all contributed to an attenuation of popular Catholicism. The survey carried out in Ireland for the European Values Study Group in late 1980 showed a country that was still heavily religious in European terms – 82 per cent of the sample claimed to go to church once a week (or more frequently) compared to 52 per cent in Northern Ireland; 14 per cent in Britain and an all-Europe average of 25 per cent.[13] Arguably the continuing significance of experiences and memories of a more disciplined and monolithic Catholicism encouraged a degree of exaggerated religiosity amongst some respondents, and experienced observers tend to believe that the rate of attrition is considerably higher. Even this survey showed that the group with the lowest percentage of weekly attenders was the unemployed, at 65 per cent,[14] and reports from some priests in working-class Dublin parishes estimate that only 10 per cent of their parishioners go to Mass every Sunday.[15] It is also important to note that amongst those who attend church regularly there is an increasing number who do not accept the Church's definition of sin, particularly in that area with which the Church has been most obsessively concerned – sexuality. Thus eight out of ten correspondents in a university survey in 1976 went to Mass once a week, but only two-thirds attended confession as required once a year, and six out of ten did not accept the Church's teaching on contraception.[16]

The growth of a more critical and individualistic type of Catholicism amongst sections of the urban young and middle class was also encouraged by the impact of Vatican II which, as O Tuathaigh notes, 'contributed significantly to the dissolution of the solid consensus of the 1950s'.[17] A key issue here was contraceptives, the import and sale of which were illegal. Debates, prompted by a small but articulate women's movement and by sympathetic media proponents of liberalisation and secularisation went on continuously through the 1970s. The Catholic bishops were relentless in their opposition to legalisation in a series of statements. It was this opposition which ensured that successive governments were unwilling to move on the issue, despite a Supreme Court decision in the Magee case in 1973 that the law violated the constitutional rights of the individual. Opinion polls, however, showed a growing level of public support for legalisation – from 34 per cent (with 63 per cent opposed) in 1971 to 49 per cent (with 40 per cent opposed) in 1977.[18] Differences of age, class and region were clear – it was the young, middle-class and Dublin residents who were most favourable and the old, farmers and those resident in Connaught and Ulster who were still inmajority opposed to contraception.[19] In 1974 an attempt by the coalition to allow for the sale of contraceptives through licensed outlets to married couples only, was defeated in the Dail – not only did Fianna Fail oppose it, but the Taoiseach, Liam Cosgrave and six other Fine Gael TDs voted against it. Desmond O'Malley, who just over ten years later would be expelled from Fianna Fail for not supporting the party's opposition to a more liberal piece of legislation on contraception, in 1974 articulated a traditionalist response: 'Our duty as a legislature is, so far as we can within the confines of our constitution … to deter fornication and promiscuity, to promote public morality.'[20] His movement over the decade that followed towards a more liberal position was a product of several forces.

First was the continuing evidence of popular commitment to the use of contraceptives and the increasing support for the legalisation of their sale. The absurdity of a situation in which condoms could be imported and given away, but not sold, had forced the Fianna Fail government to produce a piece of family-planning legislation in 1979 which the sponsoring minister, Charles Haughey, described as 'an Irish solution to an Irish problem' and legalised the sale of contraceptives to married couples on presentation of a doctor's prescription. It would be for not supporting his party's opposition to the coalition's amendments and liberalisation of this measure in 1985 that O'Malley was expelled. As Inglis points out, this was the first time that the state had passed a piece of legislation in the area of morality without first consulting the Catholic Church and agreeing to make changes.[21]

Secondly, the experience of the women's movement in Britain and the USA and, after 1973, Ireland's membership of the EEC whose Commission urged several significant changes in the latter's labour laws to benefit women, clearly influenced the rebirth and direction of feminism. Predominantly a middle-class movement, its initial publication, *Chains or Change*, included among the 'civil wrongs of Irishwomen' demands for equal pay, equality before the law, equality of education and access to contraception. Despite the persistence of conservative values, feminism has presented the only co-ordinated and sustained challenge to those values – particularly with reference to the position of women and the family which are not just religiously defined but also enshrined within the constitution. In so doing, it successfully exploited the contradictions in the position of the Catholic Church and the nature of democracy in Ireland. Its progress has nevertheless been uneven. There is growing public acceptability of working outside the home with accompanying legislative protection, and in women's determination to fix the terms of their marriages, but the dramatic death of a teenager during the lonely birth of her child, the sacking of a teacher for cohabiting and the results of the two referendums all illustrate the continuing dominance of the Catholic Church.

The other motivating force was the worsening situation in Northern Ireland which encouraged the development of a debate on the need for a more pluralist society in the Republic as a means of trying to help reconcile the

Protestants of Ulster to the idea of eventual unity. As O Tuathaigh puts it,

> Arguments in favour of internal social change have become inextricably bound up with or subsumed in the larger debate on the relations between the two parts of the country, between the different traditions, and on the political structures most likely to lead to peaceful co-existence between the different communites in Ireland.[22]

Garret FitzGerald would be a central figure in this debate. In 1972 he had criticised the policies of previous southern governments, particularly Fianna Fail, for being based on the 'simplistic theory that Ireland is one nation with a single neo-Gaelic, Roman Catholic culture, to which all citizens north and south should conform'.[23] As a move towards pluralism he was prepared to argue for the deletion of the constitutional ban on divorce, although he disputed the need actually to introduce divorce in the Republic – it would be sufficient to allow the North to retain its own divorce legislation in a new federal Ireland. He also proposed a liberalisation of the laws on contraception and censorship, although with the proviso in the former case that any such liberalisation would provide for 'safeguards and limitations on free sales'.[24] This was a cautious liberalism which had nothing to say about such fundamental bastions of the Church's social power as its large degree of control in crucial areas of education, health and welfare. As the decade progressed his timorous liberalism was consolidated and encouraged by evidence of a growing component of public opinion willing to consider changes in the areas of contraception and divorce. As we have argued above, he was also impelled towards the declaration of a 'constitutional crusade' by the increasing difficulties of the social-democratic component of his strategy for resuscitating Fine Gael. His declaration of the need for such a crusade in a radio interview in September 1981 was an honest and self-critical statement for an Irish nationalist to make:

> We have created here something which the northern Protestants find unacceptable. I believe it is my job to try and lead our people to understand how it is that we have divided this

island ... If I was a northern Protestant today, I can't see how I could aspire to getting involved in a state which is itself sectarian in the acutely sectarian way Northern Ireland was in which Catholics were repressed.[25]

Unfortunately for FitzGerald the real, if limited, liberalisation of attitudes on a range of issues which had developed from the 1960s had begun to encourage a traditionalist response. For if the breaking down of an insulated political culture had helped liberalism, international developments were also closely attended to by Catholic fundamentalists. The example of the flowering of new right pressure groups, particularly of a 'pro-life' sort, in both Britain and the USA would be noted in the Republic where fundamentalists feared that the liberalism of the 1960s would lead to secularism and abortion.

FitzGerald's own doubts about the degree to which liberalised attitudes had taken root in Irish society had become clear earlier in the year when, during an election campaign, he was the first party leader to give a pledge to the recently formed Pro-Life Amendment Campaign to introduce an amendment to the constitution against the introduction of abortion, already illegal in the Republic. Although when the amendment was eventually put to the electorate it was drawn up by Fianna Fail and opposed by Fine Gael on a number of obscure technicalities, Fine Gael did not campaign against it and a sizeable section of the party clearly supported it. Two thirds of the 55 per cent of the electorate who voted, i.e. just over a third of those eligible to vote, were in favour of the amendment. The 'yes' vote was highest in rural constituencies in the west and lowest in urban constituencies with a sizeable middle-class population, and five Dublin constituencies rejected the amendment by a small majority. At the time some consoled themselves with the notion that the result was a pyrrhic victory for the Church since, despite mobilising all its resources and having the active support of the dominant party, there was a failure to mobilise a more substantial proportion of the Catholic electorate.[26] It is true that the vote demonstrated the existence of a substantial liberal constituency, but this interpretation would soon clearly be seen to have underestimated the power of traditionalism.[27]

In 1986 FitzGerald's government would suffer a major rebuff in its attempt to amend the constitution to allow for divorce. Although opinion polls had demonstrated clear majorities in favour of removing the ban, the government's proposed amendment would be defeated in a referendum with a result which was almost an exact replica of the abortion vote: 65 per cent rejected the proposal in a turnout substantially higher than in 1983.[28] Again with Fianna Fail and the Church ranged powerfully against, the government's own commitment was seriously undermined by the fact that many Fine Gael TDs were known to be opposed to divorce, and the Fine Gael contribution to the pro-divorce campaign was negligible. Part of the substantial shift to the Progressive Democrats from Fine Gael in the 1987 election may be explained as a protest by sections of the liberal middle class at the débâcle of FitzGerald's 'constitutional crusade'.

Fianna Fail's embrace of traditional values was in part related to certain problems it faced. In an urbanising society the strong traditional affective ties between voters and parties are weakened. Its hold over its voters is greater in the more rural and peripheral areas, and this section of its support is the most conservative on moral issues in the Republic. At the same time this is a shrinking section of the electorate – the proportion of the population living in urban areas increased from 42 per cent in 1961 to 56 per cent in 1986. By 1981 almost one-third of the population of the Republic lived in the greater Dublin area, and the proportion of Dail seats elected from the Dublin area increased from 20 to 29 per cent between 1961 and 1987, while that from Connaught and Ulster fell from 25 to 19 per cent.[29]

It might appear that a Fianna Fail commitment to traditional values would put it dangerously out of touch with long-term social trends, whatever its short-term advantages. However, whilst it may be the case that its position on the referendums may have alienated some of its middle-class support, it is far less obvious that it damaged it amongst the working class. This collaboration with the Church has for

Fianna Fail the added attraction of being an alliance with an institution which, through the health and education apparatuses, is still deeply involved in working-class existence. Moreover, a traditionalism which presents itself as based on profoundly held communal values and concerns, as opposed to those of an unrepresentative 'cosmopolitan' and liberal elite, can also hope to achieve mass appeal. Especially when liberalism is clearly a coherent doctrine for market-led growth and separation of church and state, as to an extent it appeared to be with the Progressive Democrats, it will not have a ready appeal to large sections of the Irish working class. There is no tidal wave of modernisation in the Republic, and Fianna Fail's espousal of traditional values did not put it dangerously out of touch with urban Ireland. In a society so marked by inequality, with a large unemployed and poor element in the working class, as it becomes increasingly difficult for Fianna Fail to use a corporatist strategy towards the working class, the appeal of ideologies of consolation, amongst which traditional nationalism figures as well as religion, should not be underestimated.

The 1987–89 Government

The 1987–89 Fianna Fail minority government forged a historic consensus with Fine Gael and the Progressive Democrats around a neo-liberal economic agenda. Aware that his short-lived 1982 administration had left office discredited by allegations of secret deals, 'cooking the books' and phone-tapping, Haughey's 1987 administration had promised no deals.[30] Instead, jettisoning his 'Keynesian' election rhetoric which had formed the basis of attacks against the 1982–87 coalition's retrenchment policies, Haughey moved swiftly to win support from the middle class through policies of fiscal management and curtailment of unproductive spending, and from the employed working class through an accord on pay and jobs. Fine Gael – which had suffered an electoral defeat and was nurturing a new party leader – underwrote Fianna Fail's budgetary strategy on the grounds of 'putting the nation first', what party leader Alan Dukes termed the 'Tallaght Strategy', with the Progressive Democrats in full agreement. Despite two harsh budgets and a reduction in current expenditure by £900 million in real terms or 8 per cent between 1987 and 1989, 50 per cent of those polled viewed the budgetary strategy as 'good for the country' while acknowledging that their own living standards would fall.[31] A Cabinet memorandum – leaked by the Workers' Party – exposed the extent of Haughey's desire to maintain the newly constructed consensus:

> All options should be considered, including the elimination or reduction of particular schemes and programmes, rooting out overlaps and duplications between organisations, the merger of organisations, the closure of institutions which may have outlived their usefulness, the scaling down of the operations of organisations and institutions and the disposal of physical assets which are no longer productively used. A radical approach should be adopted and no expenditure should be regarded as sacrosanct and immune to elimination or reduction. We do not want a series of justifications of the status quo or special pleadings.[32]

There is little doubt that on an official level the Irish economy under Fianna Fail experienced a dramatic upturn: interest rates fell by 4 per cent between December 1986 and June 1988; inflation at 2.1 per cent in 1988 was the lowest for 25 years and lower than the EC average in the late 1980s; there was a historic trade surplus; the volume of manufacturing production, rising throughout the decade, increased by 12.5 per cent in 1988.[33] That these developments coincided with international factors and did not stem from Fianna Fail policy or any significant industrialisation or restructuring of the domestic economy remained largely ignored by the media which, having lampooned Haughey in 1982 now embraced him as an able convert to responsible debt management. Indeed, the stabilisation of the national debt, which had preoccupied governments since the late 1970s, was due more to the resumption of economic growth in Ireland and internationally, and to the fall in interest rates, than to cut-backs.[34] Similarly, the dominant influence on industrial expansion was the rapid growth in high-technology export-oriented sectors owned by multinationals. The bankruptcy of Fianna Fail industrial policy – *laissez-faire*, costly and ineffective – was sharply evident in the government's continuing efforts to offset unemployment and reduced government spending through £4 billion of EC Regional Fund aid, a large part of which was spent on road-building.

The other side to this story was the alarming growth of poverty – according to a Combat Poverty Report in 1988 one-third of the population was below the poverty line due to unemployment and low pay. By 1989 unemployment had dropped to 245,000 or 18.75 per cent from a height of 254,000 or 19.4 per cent in 1987, but these figures had to be measured against the 40,000 people on varying schemes at any one time, those discouraged from working, eliminated from social welfare or emigrating. The classic Irish 'solution' to the problem of unemployment, emigration, re-emerged in 1984 with over 70,000 leaving the country between 1987 and 1989.[35] Ireland's status as as 'platform economy' with persistent high levels of unemployment, emigration and endemic poverty residing side-by-side with booming economic indicators became more obvious between 1987 and 1989.

A hidden element in Fianna Fail strategy also escalated labour-market restructuring and the shift towards new technological sectors for a developing information economy; the Financial Services Centre located on the Dublin docks – an essential ingredient in Fianna Fail's economic and international marketing approach – extended Ireland's investment attractiveness to telecommunications multinationals.[36] State policy – in line with international developments – sacrificed public sector communications in order to promote and develop private capital exploitation. Rather than adopting a clear-cut privatisation policy as advocated by Fine Gael and the Progressive Democrats, Fianna Fail maintained a commitment to a 'viable and profitable commercial semi-state sector'[37] and presided over a mixed and managed approach to commercialisation and deregulation. The Joint Hospitals Services Board was privatised and the state's share of Tara Mines was sold, but no decision was taken to privatise the profitable Irish Life Insurance Company despite heavy lobbying; at the same time a state forestry company was established. Principally, Fianna Fail policy encouraged private capital investment and the limitation of restrictions on profitability; the independent environmental research agency was absorbed into the Department of the Environment. The government encouraged privatised medicine, trends towards deskilling and the sale of public housing. Tax breaks for capital were extended and the European Community's 'social charter' for workers firmly opposed, while social welfare restrictions and 'job search' schemes enabled the government to increase some payments and redefine 'unemployment' while gaining public approval for attacking 'dole-spongers'. Surprisingly, only cuts in education threatened the consensus. Not until the 1989 election did hospital closures, queues for minor as well as major medical problems and a deterioration in emergency care provide the ultimate stumbling block for Haughey's fourth attempt to win a Fianna Fail majority.

The 1987–89 strategy attempted to reconstruct historic class alliances by engineering public and trade union endorsements of orthodox fiscal measures through the Programme for National Recovery. The unions' support provided the crucial safety valve against public disquiet and industrial militancy, and 1988 registered the lowest number of days lost through strikes since 1960.[38] Indeed, there was a noticeable absence of ICTU statements on the state of the economy, unemployment, the budget or emigration. Not surprisingly, Haughey acknowledged the programme's contribution to the economy's upturn alongside his eagerness to negotiate a new one. The 1989 election, however, signalled the likely collapse of the pact for two reasons. Firstly, key trade union officials, conscious of grass-roots discontent with cut-backs and union endorse- ment of Fianna Fail strategy, have endeavoured to distance themselves by openly criticising the job-creation targets of Fianna Fail and urging a clear alliance with Labour.

Secondly, as both John Carroll of the ITGWU and Billy Attley of the Federated Workers' Union of Ireland acknowledged to their respective annual conferences, it is unlikely that any combination of parties in future government 'would be willing to talk to us as this government has talked to us over the past two years'.[39] To a large extent, this shadow-boxing between the unions, Fianna Fail and the Labour Party is a traditional re-enactment of the contradictory relationship found at election time; in the context of a possible realignment it might signal more significant developments.

Fianna Fail's volte-face in government and its implementation of a relatively serious programme of retrenchment would disorientate both Fine Gael and the Progressive Democrats, who were forced to give effective 'critical support' to the government's economic strategy. One effect was to send erstwhile defectors from Fianna Fail to the Progressive Democrats back to Fianna Fail as it moved clearly to the right. Opinion poll evidence of a slump in support[40] encouraged a blunting of the edge of the Progressive Democrats' radicalism which had its most bathetic expression in an abortive attempt to draw up a constitution with no reference to God in it: as one acerbic secularist put it, by deleting God the Progressive Democrats alienated 70 per cent of the population, by putting God back into the constitution, they alienated the other 30 per cent.

The problem for Fianna Fail was that, while policies of retrenchment may well have brought back middle-class defectors to the Progressive Democrats, there was a real danger of an attrition of working-class support to Labour and the Workers' Party. There was little sign that the government had worked out an economic strategy that could seriously respond to the problems of Irish industry in an unfavourable international environment and at the same time maintain its base in the urban working class.[41]

The Haughey government appears to have calculated that the support of the Progressive Democrats and Fine Gael for the main lines of its economic policy had created such a blanket consensus for 'responsible' policies to deal with the public debt crisis that Fianna Fail's working-class support would be sustained by the widespread acceptance that there was no alternative to such harsh medicine. As we have seen, the government also hoped to benefit from the trade union leadership's continued commitment to corporatism and a resultant muting of criticisms of government policies by the Irish Congress of Trade Unions. The very extensive cuts in public expenditure, however, particularly in the health service, were building up a substantial reservoir of grievance and resentment which was only very partially reflected in opinion polls and hardly received any mention at all in the media. These factors, together with a series of high opinion poll ratings for his own leadership, encouraged Haughey to call a snap General Election to coincide with the European Elections on 15 June 1989.

The 1989 Elections

From an early stage in the campaign it became apparent that Fianna Fail's decision to call on election had been a mistake. Designed to win a majority for Fianna Fail, something the party had failed to achieve in the four elections contested with Haughey as leader, it soon became clear that the government was almost totally failing to set the terms of the campaign agenda. Fianna Fail's manifesto, which stressed that it needed a majority to continue its policies, themselves described as having been an 'outstanding success',[43] was consigned to irrelevance by an upsurge of popular discontent focused on the state of the health service. Even those parties, Fine Gael and the Progressive Democrats, which had given general support to the government's economic policies were now belabouring its 'uncaring' attitudes, with Des O'Malley referring to the 'public's outrage at the cruel and inhuman state of the public health services in this country'.[43] Government disarray was most graphically and damagingly revealed in a comment by Haughey during a radio interview when he claimed that he had not appreciated just how bad the situation was in the health service.

By the end of the campaign Fianna Fail was reduced to

raising the spectre of an increased support for the left, which opinion polls were detecting, as a threat of left-wing parties holding the balance of power in the Dail and allowing the Workers' Party to impose what Haughey referred to as 'the failed economic dogma of socialism on the country'.[44] But as the leaders of both the Labour and Workers' parties had made clear that they would not support any minority Fianna Fail administration they were able effectively to counter the red scare tactic.

The spectre of a major swing to the left leading to governmental instability does appear to have succeeded in winning back to Fianna Fail middle-class support which had recoiled from the decision to have what was seen as an unnecessary election. Early analysis of the election results appeared to demonstrate a swing to Fianna Fail within the middle class. This swing was certainly noted by the Progressive Democrats who blamed it for the radical reduction in support for the party – its vote dropped from 11.8 per cent and fourteen seats in 1987 to 5.5 per cent and six seats in 1989. Fianna Fail's own vote dropped only marginally – from 44.1 to 44 per cent – although its number of seats dropped by three from 80 to 77. But such gross figures disguised a distinct class polarisation. Thus in the four most middle-class constituencies in Dublin Fianna Fail's vote was up from between 2 and 7 per cent while in the remaining constituencies, with one exception, it registered major losses due to a haemorrhage of working-class support. As Richard Sinnott commented, 'The story of this election is undoubtedly the polarisation of voters along class lines.'[45] Fine Gael did improve its position, going from 27.1 to 29.3 per cent of the popular vote (and its Dail seats rising from 50 to 55), but the left's advance was proportionately much greater. The Labour Party increased its support from 6.4 to 9.5 per cent (with its parliamentary representation rising from eleven to fifteen seats) and the Workers' Party from 3.8 to 5 per cent (from four to seven seats). The two parties' 22 seats, together with those of Jim Kemmy, the Democratic Socialist TD from Limerick and Tony Gregory, the independent socialist TD for Dublin Central, represent an historic high for left representation in the Dail in terms of seats, although between them the Labour and Workers' parties still failed to get more first preference votes than the Labour Party had achieved at its high-point in the 1960s. Within the left the most significant development was the radically altered balance between the Labour and Workers' parties in Dublin. In 1987 the Labour Party had 7.1 per cent of the vote and four seats to the Workers' Party's 7.5 per cent and three seats. After the 1989 election the Labour Party vote had increased to 9.5 per cent, although it lost one seat, while the Workers' Party vote rose to 11.4 per cent and it won six seats. The surge to the left in Dublin and the Workers' Party predominance was demonstrated in an amplified form in the European election results in which both parties won seats – the Workers' Party president Proinsias de Rossa with 15.8 per cent of the vote and Labour's Barry Desmond with 12.8 per cent.[46]

Attempts by Sinn Fein to make a breakthrough in the Republic failed miserably, despite the party's decision to drop abstentionism in 1986. Gerry Adams had predicted a gain of two seats based in part on Fianna Fail's 'betrayal' and 'collaborationist' role in relation to Northern Ireland.[47] Fianna Fail had opposed the Anglo-Irish Agreement in 1985 and also the 1986 Extradition Act introduction by the Fine Gael/Labour coalition. In office Haughey had implemented the Anglo-Irish Agreement and operated the Extradition Act, but the very lack of salience of Northern Ireland as an issue in the election – it ranked in importance with the issue of a government attempt to impose a rod license on anglers – ensured that such a volte-face had little significance for the bulk of the electorate. Even if the north had figured higher in national priorities it is doubtful if Adams, with his support for 'armed struggle' and such manifestations of it as the continuous IRA bombing of the Belfast-Dublin railway line, would have been able to win many southern workers from support for Labour and the Workers' Party. In the event Sinn Fein's share of the vote fell from 1.9 to 1.2 per cent in 1989 and no seats were won. Continued modernisation and realignment in the politics of the Republic thus threatens finally to consign militant republicanism to the ghettoes of Northern Ireland.

The Irish left faces a future with some real opportunities. If Catholicism is still a major force, it is no longer the reactionary monolith of the 1940s and 50s – sections of the Church have played an increasingly significant role in highlighting the extent of poverty in the Republic. The dominant bourgeois party faces conditions which clearly undermine its capacity to generate economic growth and sustain all its working-class support. Fianna Fail's previous capacity to resuscitate its 'progressive' image appears to have been exhausted. The emergence of the Progressive Democrats has acted as a catalyst for a clearer demarcation of basic strategic alternatives in the economic and social life of the Republic, even though the new party has not benefited from the realignments to which it contributed. In the aftermath of the election Haughey attempted to win the support of Fine Gael and the Progressive Democrats for a return to the pre-election conditions, but both insisted on a much higher price for their support. Fine Gael demanded half the seats in the cabinet and rotation of the position of Taioseach, while the Progressive Democrats also asked for cabinet representation. Haughey initially ruled out any consideration of coalition as being both anathema to the traditions of Fianna Fail and impractical. The immediate result was his failure to be elected as Taoiseach when the Dail reconvened. Despite this, Haughey continued to reiterate that there could be no compromise on the coalition issue after he had tendered his resignation to the President and become a caretaker Taoiseach. He may have been encouraged in this by memories of how his brief minority government of 1982 had been sustained in power through deals with the Workers' Party and Tony Gregory. This time, however, there was to be no assistance from the left, as the Workers' Party leader, Proinsias de Rossa, put it in the Dail: 'There is no point in waiting to see will the Workers' Party break ranks and offer support for one of the other parties. We do not intend to do so.'[48] The effective closure of this possibility forced Fianna Fail back to the alternative of another election or a deal with the Progressive Democrats. The publication of opinion polls showing a decline in Fianna Fail and Progressive Democrat support,

increases in support for Fine Gael, Labour and the Workers'
Party and massive resistance to the idea of another election
impelled a volte face.[49] On 6 July, three weeks after the
election, Haughey asked the Dail for a further adjournment
to allow him to negotiate the formation of a government
with the Progressive Democrats. A depressed and
demoralised Fianna Fail acquiesced in this historic break
with its role and vocation as the 'natural party of
government'. Haughey had attempted to repudiate the
implication of de Rossa's call for the 'parties to the right' to
form a government –

> he wanted to reject the claim that Fianna Fail was a party of the
> right, or a party in a right-wing consensus. Long before the
> foundation of the Workers' Party, Fianna Fail was in the
> vanguard of the economic and social advances in this country.[50]

Such declarations will be increasingly difficult to square with
reality, especially as the influence the Progressive Democrats have in government will act to kill off whatever residual
populism resides in Fianna Fail. The prospects are therefore
for the effective continuation of right-of-centre policies, and
this will assist in the development of the most serious
movement towards a left-right realignments since the
formation of the state.

The decision to enter negotiations and concede to the
Progressive Democrats' demand for cabinet seats was a
traumatising one for Fianna Fail members at all levels of the
party. Although not as momentous in its implications as an
agreement with Fine Gael, which would have meant a much
more substantial share-out of cabinet seats and a very formal
and institutional end to the historical civil war division, it
still gave the party what a senior Fianna Fail negotiator
referred to as a 'cultural shock'.[51]

Days of prolonged negotiations ended in a deal which
profoundly embittered many Fianna Fail members, particularly those in the constituencies where former Fianna Fail
TDs like Des O'Malley, Bobby Molloy and Mary Harney
had played a prominent role in founding the Progressive
Democrats. Despite the marked reluctance to face another
general election there was strong resistance to giving the

Progressive Democrats more than one cabinet seat. The negotiations ended, however, with the Progressive Democrats obtaining two cabinet seats, with O'Malley as Minister for Industry and Commerce and Molloy as Minister of Energy.[52] Mary Harney also obtained a post as a junior minister.

One long-term implication of the coalition agreement is to threaten the ability of such a small parliamentary group as the Progressive Democrats, with just six TDs, to maintain any distinctive presence in Irish political life, and the great danger facing the party is effective re-absorption into Fianna Fail. Any influence which the Progressive Democrats' ministers can exert will serve to consolidate Fianna Fail's most conservative tendencies in economic policy, although it is clear that Haughey (or any possible successor to him) will exert himself to maintain some vestige of the party's populist and corporatist tradition. Thus the new government's programme for the period from 1989 to 1993 excluded any reference to the Progressive Democrats' privatisation proposals. The programme as a whole was declared to be a development of the Programme for National Recovery and the trade unions were assured that all commitments previously entered into would be honoured.[53] Nevertheless the trade union leadership almost immediately expressed disquiet with the prospect of a continuation of current economic policies, which it claims would still leave over 170,000 without jobs in 1994 and the rate of unemployment in the Republic double that in most other European countries.[54] Rank-and-file frustration with union participation in the existing Programme for National Recovery was demonstrated clearly at the ICTU annual conference on 4 July with the success of a NUJ resolution demanding a special delegate within six months to consider withdrawal from the Programme for National Recovery. Thus the new coalition seems set on a course which, as one knowledgeable commentator noted, 'offers the immediate prospect of a more concentrated left-right division'.[55]

Such governmental developments and continuing (even deepening) economic problems, while they may provide an increase in the left's constituency, will also create major

challenges. Past failures to challenge the clerical and nationalist consensus in the south have contributed to a situation in
which the left vote is a protest vote rather than one for any
coherent vision of a different type of Irish society. Sections of
the left still hanker for a lurch towards an 'anti-imperialist'
strategy aimed at getting Britain out of the north and the
country out of the European Community. Amongst those
more in touch with reality there is no clear consensus on key
issues like Northern Ireland and economic strategy. In the
Republic, as in Britain, there are some who realise the need
for serious strategic thinking but many who still prefer
moralising and posturing. The increasing strength of the
Workers' Party has stimulated a predominantly defensive and
hostile attitude in the leadership of the Irish Labour Party
and, despite continuing discussions, the relations between the
two parties are characterised by friction and competition.
This was reflected most dismally in the decision of the
leadership of the Irish Transport and General Workers'
Union to end the union's traditional policy of allowing its
officials who stand for parliament leave of absence if elected.
Traditionally this had allowed ITGWU officials to sit as
Labour TDs. As the Workers' Party developed both within
the union and electorally, the leadership of the union,
dominated by labour sympathisers, changed the rules. The
result was that when two of its officials were elected as
Workers' Party TDs their employment was terminated.[56]
This petty vindictiveness does not bode well for the future
co-operation on the left. Thus the real evidence of severe
problems for Ireland's ruling class, of a weakening of the hold
of traditional parties and institutions, of dealignment of the
electorate, merely demonstrate an increased 'availability' of
sections of the electorate for alternative policies. The Irish
left has much to do if it wishes to move from the role of protest
to that of posing a real hegemonic alternative.

Notes

1. Brendan O'Leary, 'Towards Europeanisation and Realignment?: The Irish General Election, February 1987', *West European Politics*, Vol.10 No.3, July 1987, p.461.
2. Ibid.
3. See Thomas Lyne, 'The Progressive Democrats', *Irish Political Studies*, Vol.2, 1987.
4. 'Standing by the Republic', speech by Geraldine Kennedy to the second national conference of the Progressive Democrats in the National Stadium, Dublin on 10 October 1987.
5. Quoted in Dick Walsh, *Des O'Malley: A Political Profile*, Dingle 1986, p.92.
6. Tom Inglis, *Moral Monopoly: The Catholic Church in Modern Irish Society*, Dublin and New York 1987, p.76.
7. Michael Gallagher, *Political Parties in the Republic of Ireland*, Dublin 1985, p.. 36.
8. Ibid
9. See Thomas Boylan, 'Versions of Community and Economic Change: Consensus or Conflict?' in M.A.G. O Tuathaigh (ed.), *Community, Culture and Conflict*, Galway 1986, p.34 and Dermot Keogh, *The Vatican, The Bishops and Ireland 1919–39*, Cambridge 1986.
10. Pat Feeley, *The Gralton Affair*, Dublin 1986, p.39.
11. Martin McLoone and John MacMahon, *Television and Irish Society*, Dublin 1984, p.7.
12. Ibid.
13. M. Fogarty, L. Ryan and J. Lee (eds), *Irish Values and Attitudes*, Dublin 1984, Table 1 (ii), p.126.
14. Ibid. Table 4 (ii), p.132.
15. Peadar Kirby, *Is Irish Catholicism Dying?*, Cork and Dublin 1984, p.37.
16. Inglis, op.cit., p.27.
17. M.A.G. O Tuathaigh, 'Religion, Nationality and a Sense of Community in Modern Ireland' in O Tuathaigh (ed), op.cit., p.74.
18. Basil Chubb, *The Government and Politics of Ireland*, 2nd edition, London 1982, p.29.
19. Ibid.
20. Walsh, op.cit., p.47
21. Inglis, op.cit., p.93.
22. O'Tuathaigh, op.cit., p.79.
23. Garret FitzGerald, *Towards a New Ireland*, London 1972, p.175.
24. Ibid., p.152.
25. Quoted in John Cooney, *The Crozier and the Dail: Church and State 1922–1986*, Cork and Dublin 1986, pp. 7 and 8.
26. See Brian Girvin, 'Social Change and Moral Politics: The Irish Constitutional Referendum 1983', *Political Studies*, Vol.34 No.1, p.81.
27. C. O'Leary and T. Hesketh, 'The Irish Abortion and Divorce Referendum Campaigns', *Irish Political Studies*, Vol.3 1988, provides a

useful overview.

28. Inglis, op.cit., p.88.

29. Peter Mair, *The Changing Irish Party System*, Manchester 1987, pp.78 and 79.

30. Denis Coughlan, 'Two Years Spent Turning a Deeply Suspicious Electorate', *Irish Times*, 29 May 1989.

31. MRBI/Irish Times Poll, 2/88 in *Irish Political Studies*, Vol.4 1989, p.156; cf. MRBI/Irish Times Poll4/87 in *Irish Political Studies*, Vol.3 1988, p.140.

32. Quoted in Dick Walsh, 'Solving Inconsistency by Choosing to Ignore it', *Irish Times*, 16 June 1989.

33. Central Bank of Ireland, *Annual Report*, 1989.

34. Paul Tansey, 'Chairman Carlisle must break the political mould', *Sunday Tribune*, 25 June 1989.

35. Ellen Hazelkorn, 'Socio-economic Profile of Contemporary Irish Emigrants and Immigrants in the UK', Irish in Britain Research Forum Paper, Polytechnic of North London, 1989.

36. D. Bell and N. Meehan, 'International Telecommunications Deregulation and Ireland's Domestic Communications Policy', *Journal of Communications*, Vol.38 No.1, Winter.1988, pp.70–84; Bell and Meehan, 'Cable, Satellite and the Emergence of Private TV in Ireland: From Public Service to Managed Monopoly', *Media Culture and Society*, Vol.VII, 1989, pp.89-114.

37. Fianna Fail, *The Next Phase*, 1989.

38. Department of Labour statistics: days lost due to strike action – 1982: 437,000; 1983: 311,000; 1984: 364,000; 1985: 412,000; 1986: 315,000; 1987: 260,000; 1988: 130,000; 1989: projected figures similar to 1988.

39. Patrick Nolan, 'Carroll not Hopeful Other Parties Would Talk to Trade Unions', *Irish Times*, 31 May 1989; Patrick Nolan, 'New National Pact is Unlikely Says Attley', *Irish Times*, 29 May 1989. John Carroll and Billy Attley are leaders of the ITGWU and FWUI respectively – the unions are to merge in 1990 to form the largest union in Ireland with 175,000 members.

40. *Sunday Independent*, 21 August 1988.

41. It needs to be pointed out in this context that in the depressed conditions of the 1980s the sharp rise in unemployment and the weakening of the unions associated with it has enabled Irish industry to record a sharp rise in productivity and profits – profits' share of National Income rose from 25.9 per cent in 1978 to 30.6 per cent in 1986 – Paul Tansey, 'Irish Industry's Profits Boom, and the Rise is Set to Continue', *Sunday Tribune*, 21 August 1988. However a restructured and revived industrial sector shows no sign of resolving the central issues of unemployment and emigration, as Tansey comments: 'Engineering the future growth of industrial employment may prove more difficult than anyone had anticipated, it's proving easy enough to get manufacturing output to grow, much more difficult to get jobs to follow.'

42. Carol Coulter, 'Manifesto Stresses FF Record', *Irish Times*, 7 June 1989.